Development, Security and Unending War

For Bob Drewery
Comrade and friend

Development, Security and Unending War

Governing the World of Peoples

MARK DUFFIELD

polity

First published in 2007 by Polity Press

Reprinted 2008 (three times), 2009, 2010 (twice), 2011, 2012

Polity Press
65 Bridge Street
Cambridge CB2 1UR, UK.

Polity Press
350 Main Street
Malden, MA 02148, USA

ISBN-13: 978-07456-3579-8 (hbk)
ISBN-13: 978-07456-3580-4 (pbk)

A catalogue record for this book is available from the British Library.

Typeset in 11 on 13 pt Scala
by Servis Filmsetting Ltd, Manchester
Printed and bound in Great Britain by the MPG Books Group

The publisher has used its best endeavours to ensure that the URLs for external websites referred to in this book are correct and active at the time of going to press. However, the publisher has no responsibility for the websites and can make no guarantee that a site will remain live or that the content is or will remain appropriate.

For further information on Polity, visit our website: www.politybooks.com

Contents

Preface

For some years I have been aware that development and security inter-connect. It is only now, however, after completing this book, that I fully realize how enduring and essential this relationship is. Usually experi-enced as a benign and practical act of helping others, development is a technology of security that is central to liberal forms of power and gov-ernment. The benevolence with which development cloaks itself – its constant invocation of rights, freedom and the people – conceals a stub-born will to manage and contain disorder rather than resolve it. Development seeks to control and ameliorate the unintended conse-quences of progress such as destitution, environmental collapse or humanitarian disasters. Given the constant making and remaking of societies demanded by progress, development is particularly concerned with those groups and communities that, through the contingencies of poverty, gender or lack of voice, regularly find themselves superfluous, redundant or short of the requirements to live an acceptable life. Development exerts a moral and educative trusteeship over this surplus life. Through coaching in the prudent arts of freedom, it is made com-plete, useful and governable. As a technology of security, development traces its genealogy in the constant need to reconcile the demand for order with the contingencies of progress. As such, it provides a liberal alternative to extermination or eugenics: modernity's other solutions to the problem of surplus population. Development has consequently always existed in relation to a state of emergency or exception. Today, for example, Afghanistan is being pacified militarily so that aid agencies can operate and secure civilian loyalties. This is not a random connection; development has always been linked with what we now understand as counterinsurgency.

The book's most important departure for me relates to the appli-cation of the Foucaldian concept of biopolitics. While the idea of geo-politics is familiar, biopolitics is less so. If geopolitics suggests a combination of states, territories and alliances, territories also come with people or population. Since the nineteenth century effective states have made the support and optimization of the collective life of the nation a central aim of government. While it appears self-evident that development, with its emphasis on promoting life through remedial and educative interventions, is a form of biopolitics, Foucault did not write about development. Using this concept consequently involves extrapolation and extension. Initially I had thought that development involved a universalizing of the technologies that Foucault had outlined in relation to Europe, a sort of internationally scaled-up biopolitics that acts on a 'global' population. The answer, however, now seems as obvious as it is simple; rather than a universalizing biopolitics, development is the opposite. It is a means of dividing humankind against itself in the generic form of developed and underdeveloped species-life. Development is thus central to the new or culturally coded racism that emerged with decolonization. Developed life is supported and compensated through a range of social and private insurance-based benefits and bureaucracies covering birth, sickness, education, employment and pensions. In contrast, the underdeveloped or 'non-insured' life existing beyond these welfare technologies is expected to be self-reliant. Surplus non-insured life is the subject of development, while the stasis of basic needs and self-reliance is its biopolitical object. Rather than development being concerned with reducing the economic gap between rich and poor countries, or extending to the latter the levels of social protection existing in the former, as a technology of security it functions to contain and manage underdevelopment's destabilizing effects, especially its circulatory epiphenomena such as undocumented migrants, asylum seekers, transborder shadow economies or criminal networks. Since decolonization, the biopolitical division of the world of peoples into developed and underdeveloped species-life has been deepening. Today it shapes a terrain of unending war.

The origins of this book lie in a series of postgraduate lectures taught between 2002 and 2005 on 'Development, Security and Conflict', first at the University of Leeds and then at Lancaster. I'd like to thank the students attending these lectures for giving me the opportunity and stimulus to rehearse many of the issues found on the following pages. I also profited from being a member of the research network 'From inequality to insecurity? The place of crime and violence in development thinking and practice', organized by Finn Stepputat and colleagues at the Danish Institute for International Studies, Copenhagen (2003–5). Participation in the network workshops was an enriching experience.

Debts to others are extensive, and I am conscious that in mentioning a few many are missed. For their encouragement and helpful comments on the draft my thanks to David Keen, Vanessa Pupavac, Matt Merefield, Colleen Bell, Vernon Hewitt and Brad Evans. Conversations and exchanges with Mick Dillon, Louis Lobo-Guerrero, Stuart Elden, April Biccum and Nicholas Waddell were invaluable in helping me sort things out or, at least, try to. I'd also like to thank Ray Bush for his comradeship and example. Finally, I must acknowledge the contribution of the Department of Politics at the University of Bristol. Without the time and support that my colleagues have afforded me, this book would never have been finished.

Chapter 5 draws on an ESRC research project completed with Nicholas Waddell in 2004, 'Human Security: The Public Management of Private Agency' (RES-223-25-0035). Chapter 6 utilizes my contribution to a consultancy report written together with Patricia Gossman and Nicholas Leader entitled 'A Review of the Strategic Framework for Afghanistan' (Islamabad: Afghanistan Research and Evaluation Unit, 2003). I'd like to thank all those involved with these projects for their support, inspiration and company.

Mark Duffield
Sedgley

Abbreviations

BDDCA	British Development Division for Central Africa
CAO	Civilian Affairs Officer
CAU	Civilian Affairs Unit
DAC	Development Assistance Committee
DFID	Department for International Development (UK)
DPA	Department of Political Affairs (UN)
EPSAM	Participatory Extension and Household Food Security Project
ERA	Eritrea Relief Association
ERD	Emergency Relief Desk
EU	European Union
FCO	Foreign and Commonwealth Office
ICISS	International Commission on Intervention and State Sovereignty
IFI	International Financial Institutions
IMF	International Monetary Fund
NATO	North Atlantic Treaty Organization
NGO	non-governmental organization
ODA	Overseas Development Administration (UK)
OECD	Organization for Economic Cooperation and Development
OPEC	Organization of the Petroleum Exporting Countries
P.E.A.C.E.	Poverty Eradication and Community Empowerment
RC/HC	Resident Coordinator/Humanitarian Coordinator
REST	Relief Society of Tigray
SCF	Save the Children Fund
SRSG	Special Representative of the Secretary-General
UNAMA	United Nations Assistance Mission in Afghanistan
UNCO	UN Coordination Office
UNDP	UN Development Programme

UNHCR	(Office of the) UN High Commissioner for Refugees
UNHCHR	(Office of the) UN High Commissioner for Human Rights
UNICEF	UN Children's Fund
UNOCHA	UN Office for the Coordination of Humanitarian Affairs
UNOCHAA	UN Office for the Coordination of Humanitarian Assistance to Afghanistan
USAID	United States Agency for International Development
WFP	World Food Programme
ZADP	Zambezia Development Programme

1 Introduction: Development and Surplus Life

Since the end of the Cold War, the claim that development requires security, and without security you cannot have development, has been repeated to the point of monotony in countless government reports, policy statements, UN documents, briefings by non-governmental organizations (NGOs), academic works and so on (DAC 1997; Solana 2003; DFID 2005b). Such has been the widespread acceptance of this circular complementarity that it now qualifies as an accepted truth of our time. Since coming into office in 1997, for example, Britain's New Labour government has consciously placed the mutual conditioning of development and security at the heart of its international development policy (DFID 1997). Reflecting and orchestrating the international policy consensus, numerous speeches and policy documents have argued that globalization, besides bringing great benefits and opportunities, has also brought into existence a shrinking and radically interconnected world in which distant and hence nationally unimportant problems no longer exist (for overview see Abrahamson 2005). The ripple effects of poverty, environmental collapse, civil conflict or health crises require international management, since they do not respect geographical boundaries. Otherwise, they will inundate and destabilize Western society. While building on earlier precepts (OECD 1998; Collier 2000), the moral of al-Qaida in Afghanistan has not been lost on policy makers. That is, ignoring ineffective states and vulnerable peoples opens them to the risk of colonization by criminal interests and groups politically hostile to the democratic world (DAC 2003). Gordon Brown, Britain's Chancellor of the Exchequer at the time of writing, sums up this worldview as follows.

> We understand that it is not just morally and ethically right that develop-
> ing countries move from poverty to prosperity, but that it is a political
> imperative – central to our long-term national security and peace – to
> tackle the poverty that leads to civil wars, failed states and safe havens for
> terrorists. (Quoted in Christian Aid 2004: 2)

While it is accepted that poverty does not cause terrorism, it is argued that it fosters exclusion and alienation, which terrorist organizations can exploit to garner support, if not recruits. The consequent policy demand has been that development interventions should better focus on such risks and, especially, take failed and fragile states more seriously (DFID 2005a). This includes the search for new policy instruments to strengthen state capacity, provide order and, at the same time, deliver basic economic and welfare services to the peoples involved (Leader and Colenso 2005). This book, however, is not so much concerned with development as a series of techniques and interventions for improving or bettering others; it is more interested in examining the role and function of these technologies in securing the Western way of life.

Foregrounding the liberal problematic of security

As reflected in the above quote, guiding current thinking is the assumption that not only is it the moral duty of effective states to protect and better the lives of people living within ineffective ones, but such help also strengthens international security. This enlightened self-interest can also be seen, for example, in the remarks made by Tony Blair, the then UK Prime Minister, on the launch of the Africa Commission's development report in March 2005. British national interest, it is argued, is interconnected with events and conditions in other countries and continents. Famines and instability 'thousands of miles away lead to conflict, despair, mass migration and fanaticism that can affect us all. So for reasons of self-interest as well as morality, we can no longer turn our back on Africa' (Blair 2005). That Africa is currently not high on the list of terrorism-exporting continents does not invalidate this position. Rather, it suggests that the moral logic linking development and security is an expansive and universalizing one. Because development reduces poverty and hence the risk of future instability, *it also improves our own security*. In justifying the post-Cold War phase of renewed Western interventionism, there are many examples of a claimed enlightened complementarity linking development and security (Solana 2003; Bush 2002). Indeed, such claims constitute the ethical canon of today's international activism (Douzinas 2003).

The complementarity between development and security is usually described as signalling a post-Cold War widening of the meaning of security. From a concern with the security of states, international dangers associated with societal breakdown, unsustainable population growth, environmental stress or endemic poverty are seen as widening the scope of security beyond its traditional focus on military threats. Often described as prioritizing the security of people rather than states, the broadening of security to embrace society informs current views on 'human security' (UNDP 1994a). Since the risks to human security are largely associated with underdevelopment, broadening the scope of security to include the protection and betterment of the world's poor and marginalized peoples establishes its complementarity with development. This widening of security is usually seen by politicians, policy makers and academics as a new departure. At the same time, the complementarity between development and security is accepted as unproblematic, indeed, as marking a progressive turn (King and Murray 2001; CHS 2003; HSC 2005). If explained at all, it is presented as reflecting the humanistic advances that international society has made, compared with the restrictions of the Cold War (Mack 2002). According to this position, given a lack of political will regarding underdevelopment, calling for enlightened self-interest staked on the West's own future and security is an important way of mobilizing public interest and commitment.

There are, however, many commentators that are uncomfortable with the increasing invocation of security as the primary means of improving the human condition and strengthening international society. The 'Copenhagen School' of International Relations theory, for example, has drawn attention to the increasing recourse, especially since the end of the Cold War, by politicians, policy makers and security professionals to a process or strategy of 'securitization' (Waever et al. 1993; Buzan et al. 1997; Huysmans 2000). That is, there is a tendency for such groups to describe an ever widening range of social trends, conditions and practices through a lens of security. Security from this perspective is often less an objective condition and more the way in which professional groups compete for visibility, influence and scarce resources. An important question that securitization raises is not that of more or less security, but whether many of the conditions so described should be treated as security issues at all. Securitization draws attention to the dangers and unforeseen political and normative consequences of a too ready willingness on the part of professionals and gatekeepers to invoke security for reasons of institutional or group advantage. In relation to Africa, for example, it has been argued that the securitization of underdevelopment is both undesirable and an inadequate response to the situation (Abrahamson 2005: 61, 70). It not only fosters fear and unease, it tends to divide the continent from the rest of the world, favours policies of containment and is encouraging the militarization of the continent.

While such concerns are of great importance, central to this book is the argument that the relationship between development and security also has a long genealogy. Rather than being a new departure, its current prominence is connected with the return to the political foreground of a liberal problematic of security (Agamben 2005). This foregrounding focuses attention on the existence of a liberal will to power that, in securitizing the present, is also able to vector across time and space, that is, bridge the past and present as well as connecting the national and international. Such an understanding is central to this book. While a liberal problematic of security is well represented in the contemporary idea of human security, since the beginnings of modernity a liberal rationality of government has always been based on the protection and betterment of the essential processes of life associated with population, economy and society. A liberal problematic of security is concerned with people and all the multiform processes, conditions and contingencies that either promote or retard life and well-being. It is concerned with securing these biological and social processes in the name of people, rights and freedom. Although largely 'non-political' in nature, being located within populations, communities and the economy, these processes are nevertheless the foundations of good government. Liberalism embodies the idea of 'government of the population and the imperatives that are derived from such an idea' (Dean 1999: 113). Securitization raises important concerns over the dangers of a too ready willingness by the state and professional groups to invoke the exceptionalism of security in relation to a widening range of life and society processes. This book poses an additional set of questions: why does a liberal problematic of security now dominate the political foreground? and how does it operate within the architecture of post-Cold War humanitarian, development and peace interventionism?

Linking biopolitics, liberalism and development

In addressing these concerns, liberalism is considered as a technology of government involving a specific design or means of strategizing power. A defining characteristic of liberalism is that it takes people and their life and freedom as its essential reference point (Mehta 1999). In understanding liberalism as power, it is useful to introduce Foucault's conception of 'biopolitics' (Foucault [1975–6], [1976], [1978]). While liberalism and biopolitics are not same, as Mitchell Dean argues, biopolitics is 'a necessary condition of liberalism' (Dean 1999: 113). Biopolitics is a form of politics that entails the administration of the processes of life at the aggregate level of population. While the more familiar term 'geopolitics' interconnects and interrogates states, territories and alliances, territories come with populations, livelihood systems and life processes. Besides military readiness and the diplomacy of political alliance, since the nineteenth century effective states have also progressively expanded their knowledge and ability to support life and help populations realize their optimal productive and reproductive potential. The nature and implications of this biopolitical relationship between states, territories and population has been neglected by mainstream international relations and development studies alike (Jahn 2005; Biccum 2005). Yet, as will be argued below, since the beginning of the twentieth century, how groups, communities and peoples are acted upon in order to support and promote collective life has shaped and deepened a biopolitical distinction between 'developed' and 'underdeveloped' species-life – a distinction that is now integral to racial discourse, global insurgency and unending war.

Biopolitics marks the passage from the classical age to the modern one. Compared with the ancient right of the sovereign to take life or let live, biopolitics marks a new power: 'to foster life or disallow it to the point of death' (Foucault [1976]: 138). Beginning in the seventeenth century, this new power over life evolved in two basic forms. The first was a disciplinary and individualizing power, focusing on the *human-as-machine* and associated with the emergence of the great institutions such as medicine, education, punishment or the military (see Foucault [1975]). From the middle of the eighteenth century, however, a complementary but different power over life emerges. This newer form does not discipline the human-as-machine, it is an aggregating or massifying power concerned with regulating the *human-as-species*. It is a regulatory power that operates at the collective level of population (Foucault [1975–6]: 243). This regulatory biopolitics functions differently from the more localized, individualizing and institutionally based disciplinary power. Achieving massified outcomes also requires more complex systems of coordination and centralization associated with the state.

Regulatory biopolitics emerged out of the statistical, demographic, economic and epidemiological knowledge through which life was being discovered in its modern societal form, that is, as a series of interconnected natural, social and economic processes operating in and through population. The multiple factors that are aggregated within a population appear at the level of the individual as chance, unpredictable and contingent events. Rather than acting on the individual per se, a regulatory biopolitics seeks to intervene at the level of the collective, where apparently random events reveal themselves as population trends, social variables and probabilities. The discovery of the dynamics of population 'established the paradoxical position of life both as an autonomous domain and as an object and objective of systems of administration' (Dean 1999: 99). Biopolitics attempts to rationalize the problem of governing groups of humans represented in the form of population. Such problems are manifest in a variety of locations, including the family, health, housing, education and longevity; they connect with rates of economic growth, working conditions, standards of living, nutrition and the environment; they also relate to race, ethnicity, migration and social cohesion; today, problems of population even appear at the level of the genetic make-up of life itself. Biopolitics acts in the interests of collective or aggregate life through knowledge of the 'processes that sustain or retard the optimization of the life of a population' (ibid.: 99).

Liberalism is a technology of government that supports freedom while governing people through the interconnected natural, social and economic processes that together sustain life. Foucault used the emergence of biopolitics as the terrain on which to situate the classical liberal problematic of how much to govern. Too much government – in the form of state planning, for example – and the dynamism and creative potential of the life processes on which freedom depends are destroyed. Governing too little, however, risks failing 'to establish the conditions of civility, order, productivity and national well-being which make limited government possible' (Rose 2000: 70). Since liberalism is not the same as biopolitics it can, importantly, be critical of the excessive disciplining and regulation of population. At the same time, however, it is dependent on such interventions being effective as a condition of order and liberal government. From this perspective, liberalism is not an historical period, the product of specific groups or a substantive doctrine; it is an ethos of government that attempts to govern life through its freedom. At the same time, however, it is conscious of the disorder that excess freedom can bring. As a design of power, there is no essential relationship between liberalism, the rule of law or representative democracy. A democracy is not necessarily liberal, nor is liberalism of itself democratic; liberalism simply embodies a timeless 'search for a liberal technology of government' (Foucault quoted by Dean 1999: 120).

As a technology of governing life through its freedom, the absence of an essential relationship between liberalism and democracy helps to explain the enduring paradox of liberalism. During the nineteenth century, liberalism typically supported the rule of law and democratic reform at home. At the same time, however, it also accepted the necessity of non-representative and despotic forms of imperial rule overseas (Jahn 2005; Pitts 2003). The idea of 'development' is one way of resolving this apparent paradox. Just as biopolitics and liberalism are not the same, development is likewise different. As with liberalism, however, biopolitics is also a necessary condition of development; biopolitics, liberalism and development are different but intimately interconnected. If biopolitics uncovers the dynamics of life at the level of population, and liberalism seeks to govern life through its freedom, then development provides a solution to the problem of governing too much or too little. Since the end of the eighteenth century development has embodied a recurrent deference to the theory and practice of an enlightened, gradualist and educative trusteeship over life (Cowen and Shenton 1996: 27; Mehta 1999: 191–216). The importance of moral trusteeship to liberalism as an art of government explains its frequent criticism of imperial violence and excess. However, it was also able to accept colonial rule when the responsibility of trusteeship was deemed to be humanely and hence effectively discharged (Morel 1920). A developmental trusteeship is a liberal framework of government that allows the powers of freedom to be learned and safely applied.

Once thought to be no longer applicable in a decolonized world, a liberal conception of trusteeship has once again entered the political foreground following the renewed wave of Western humanitarian and peace interventionism in the post-Cold War period. There has been a revival of interest in liberal imperialism – indeed, an attempt to rehabilitate its self-proclaimed role of protecting and bettering the world (Ferguson 2003; Cooper 2002; Coker 2003). With the exception of Iraq, where mismanagement and horrendous violence have damaged hopes of effective trusteeship, liberal opinion has widely supported the West's renewed interventionism (Furedi 1994). Michael Ignatieff's (2003) book *Empire Lite*, for example, captures today's acceptance of the necessity of a period of illiberal rule abroad. Awakened by the threat of world disorder and led by avowed anti-imperialists, today's interventionism constitutes a new form 'of ostensibly humanitarian empire in which Western powers led by the United States band together to rebuild state order and reconstruct war-torn societies for the sake of global stability and security' (ibid.: 19). This new empire is being implemented by novel institutional arrangements and divisions of labour linking donor governments, UN agencies, militaries and NGOs. It promises self-rule, not in some distant future but quickly and within an agreed framework. In dealing with elites, many of whom are the products of modern nationalism, the intention is that they should be empowered to succeed. Today's *Empire Lite* is only legitimate if it results in the betterment of people and their early self-management. It is imperialism 'in a hurry, to spend money, to get results, to turn the place back to locals and get out' (ibid.). For Ignatieff, if there is a problem with this new interventionism, it is that it does not practise the partnership and empowerment that it preaches and is dogged by short-termism and promises betrayed.

There is also another and broader conception of trusteeship. Although connected, it lacks the spectacle and immediacy of Ignatieff's territorial 'laboratories' of post-interventionary society (ibid.: 20). Since it is more pervasive and subtle, however, it is arguably more significant. While also having a liberal genealogy, it is about securing freedom by supporting households and community organizations, based on the small-scale ownership of land or property, in their search for economic autonomy and the possibilities for political existence that this affords. It is a trusteeship that encourages local level self-reliance and self-realization 'both through and against the state' (Cowen and Shenton 1996: 5). Such a trusteeship operates today in the ideas and institutions of sustainable development. It can be seen in the moral, educative and financial tutelage that aid agencies exert over the attitudes and behaviour of those subject to such development (Pupavac 2005). Although a relation of governance, it nonetheless speaks in terms of empowerment and partnership (Cooke and Kothari 2001). While Western politicians currently argue that enlightened self-interest interconnects development and security, for those insecure humans living within ineffective states the reality of this virtuous circle is, once again, an educative trusteeship that aims to change behaviour and social organization according to a curriculum decided elsewhere.

Surplus population and accumulation by dispossession

In examining development as a liberal problematic of security, the way in which political economy has defined the object of development is first considered. Cowen and Shenton (1996) have argued that development doctrine emerged with the turbulent rise and unsettling spread of industrial capitalism. Traced through the work of Malthus, Saint-Simon and Comte, development provides a solution to the disorder that progress unavoidably brings: the disruption and redundancy of established livelihoods and trades, the erosion of traditional rights and responsibilities, unemployment and pauperization. Development, they argue, emerged in the politically seething world of early-nineteenth-century Europe where, to paraphrase the young Marx, everything that was solid dissolved into air. Progress, however, also brought undoubted social benefits and new possibilities; while many positions and trades were certainly ruined, the lives and livelihoods of others were improved. Apart from the constant volatility, from a liberal perspective the problem with capitalism was that the disrupted and marginalized groups were more numerous than those from which capitalism could gain and, in so doing, improve. In other words, there was a problematic and transient 'surplus' population that required remedial attention, not only for themselves but for the stability of society as well.

Anticipated in Malthus, the unending search for progress constantly invokes a surplus population – that is, a population whose skills, status or even existence are in excess of prevailing conditions and requirements. Hannah Arendt has called this by-product, produced at each successive crisis of capitalism, its 'human debris' (Arendt [1951]: 150). This phenomenon was well known and feared during the nineteenth century and fuelled the European settlement of Canada, Australia and the United States. In a contemporary treatment, it is what Zygmunt Bauman (Bauman 2004) has called 'waste-life'. It is a condition of existence that, but for the changes, adaptations or opportunities that progress either demands or presents, would otherwise remain effectively useless, irrelevant or dangerous. Through the practice of trusteeship, development emerged and has remained to this day 'a practice to deal with surplus population' (Cowen and Shenton 1996: xi). Development embodies a trusteeship of surplus life, that is, an external and educative tutelage over an otherwise superfluous and possibly dangerous population that needs help in adapting to the potential that progress brings. In ensuring this transition, development as security is tasked with reconciling 'the moral, intellectual and material qualities of progress with social order' (ibid.: 27). In this respect, development exists as a liberal alternative to modernity's other solutions to the problem of surplus life: extermination or eugenics.

The idea of surplus population is also found in David Harvey's (2003) concept of 'accumulation by dispossession' which is presented as a rectification of Marx's views on primitive accumulation. That is, those varied and often violent pre-modern processes of land privatization, the conversion of collective property rights into private ones, the enclosure of the commons, the monetization of production, consumption and taxation, colonial appropriation, population clearance, the slave trade, and so on, that preceded and then kick-started capitalist accumulation by provided its initiating capital and labour. Whereas Marx saw primitive accumulation as an originatory act, both Rosa Luxemburg (Luxemburg [1913]) and Hannah Arendt ([1951]) have argued the continuing relevance of primitive accumulation and in particular the necessity of capitalism having a non-capitalist exterior if accumulation is to be maintained. This idea has also received support from liberal thinkers such as J. A. Hobson (Hobson [1902]). For these writers the so-called New Imperialism at the end of the nineteenth century was the case in point. This represented the closure of the 'global commons' through the occupation of those territories as yet unclaimed by a European external power. It was a process of fraud, violence and dispossession on an epic scale well reflected, for example, in the genocidal Scramble for Africa (Hochschild 2002). The problem of capitalist over-accumulation, exacerbated by the lack of domestic investment opportunities, is argued to have fuelled this authoritarian imperialist turn.

Accumulation by dispossession embodies the idea that capitalism 'must perpetually have something "outside of [sic] itself" in order to stabilise itself' (Harvey 2003: 140). One example is the continuing relevance of Marx's notion of an industrial reserve army, that is, a floating population of cheap, unskilled labour, lacking protection and entitlements, that can be hired and fired as business expands and contracts. For Harvey, such an 'outside' can be either a pre-existing non-capitalist territory, such as still existed in many regions of the world at the end of the nineteenth century, or a sector or market within capitalism that has not been fully exploited or proletarianized. Additionally and importantly, however, capitalism can 'actually manufacture it' (ibid.: 141). Through a combination of mechanisms, accumulation by dispossession continues to shape the violent geography of continued capitalist accumulation. Periodic crises of over-accumulation lead to recurrent bouts of predation on existing dispensations and accepted entitlements as a necessary requirement for renewed accumulation. Within the underdeveloped world, many forms of primitive accumulation that would be recognizable to Marx are still operating today: the dispossession of peasantries, the displacement of family farming by international agribusiness, forced migration, new waves of proletarianization and re-proletarianization, the wholesale privatization of common property such as water, the suppression of indigenous forms of production and consumption and so on.

At the same time, however, and relating to the mass consumer societies of the developed world, certain aspects of primitive accumulation have been adapted and expanded. The credit system and finance capital, for example, have opened up new zones of predation. Stock promotions, mergers and asset stripping have accompanied the active promotion of high levels of debt peonage. Corporate fraud and dispossession through credit and stock manipulation, including the raiding and decimation of pension funds by stock and corporate collapse 'are all central features of what contemporary capitalism is about' (ibid.: 147). Indeed, the reversion to private hands of public entitlements won through political struggle, such as a state pension, social welfare and national health care 'has been the most egregious of all policies of dispossession pursued in the name of neoliberal orthodoxy' (ibid.: 148). New global mechanisms for dispossession have also opened up, for example regarding intellectual property rights, patenting and the licensing of genetic material such as seed plasma. Biopiracy by international pharmaceutical companies and the pillaging of the world's genetic resources are rampant, creating means of governance that 'can now be used against whole populations whose practices had played a crucial role in the development of those materials' (ibid.). The wholesale commodification of life, including its many natural and cultural forms, histories and intellectual creativity, is currently under way. When coupled with the deepening international privatization of common goods and entitlements such as land, water and public utilities, Harvey has argued that capitalism has launched the world on 'a new wave of "enclosing the commons"' (ibid.).

From political economy one could argue that accumulation by dispossession, in continually evoking a surplus population, not only provides development with an object, it is one that is constantly being renewed. A superfluous and potentially dangerous waste-life is continuously thrown off as markets are relentlessly made and remade in the endless search for progress. This concern arising from political economy is recognized by policy makers. Politicians are fully aware, for example, that while globalization brings many benefits, if badly managed it can exacerbate inequality and instability (Biccum 2005). This contemporary ambivalence towards globalization returns development once more to its founding design of reconciling the need for order with the challenges of progress. Because surplus life is continuously produced, development also periodically reinvents itself. While the context, words and emphasis may change, the central meaning remains the same. In terms of basic tenets this process, since 1949 at least, has been well documented by William Easterly (Easterly 2002). Following decolonization, when it vectored into an interstate relationship, development has regularly reinvented itself within a limited set of axioms. Like penal reform, the endless rediscovery of development has produced a 'a monotonous critique' (Foucault [1975]: 266) which, in this case, invariably calls for an increase in aid spending, a renewed focus on poverty reduction, the delivery of more effective aid, the necessity of better coordination between donors, aid agencies and recipients, the importance of recipients being receptive to policy change and, not least, debt relief. The periodic repackaging of these aims over the past half-century has been helped by development's organizational preference for limited agency competition, low public accountability, institutional amnesia and a willingness to engage in obfuscation and spin control, allowing practitioners always to describe aid efforts 'as "new and improved" ' (Easterly 2002: 228).

Slavery and excess freedom

From the perspective of political economy, the surplus population created through accumulation by dispossession represents life belonging to capitalism. It is a malleable and disposable life that capitalism constantly produces in order to devour it as part of its own unending renewal. However, it is not a life *that necessarily belongs to security*. In order to connect development and security properly the idea of surplus population must also embrace life that is politically superfluous. Although the rise of industrial capitalism is important, so in this respect is the related abolition of slavery (an appreciation of the abolition of slavery is absent from Cowen and Shenton's otherwise path-breaking book (1996)). Emancipation created within modernity the possibility of life with an excess of freedom. Just as an economically surplus life is continually produced and consumed in the maintenance of capitalism, so a politically surplus life is produced and consumed as a necessary adjunct of political order (Agamben 1998: 27–8). At the same time emancipation allows the liberal problematic of security to be understood as an essentially expansive and globalizing will to power. Surplus life can be both economically and politically charged, the one superfluous to requirements, the other a threat to order. These forms of exception easily move in and out of each other, sometimes one displacing the other, sometimes merging. During times of emergency, however, all surplus life can become the 'bare life' of security existing beyond morality, religion and the law. It is a life that can be killed without murder being committed (ibid.: 10–11).

The abolition of slavery was an essential part of the founding and international expansion of industrial capitalism. The abolitionists not only argued against the horrors of a morally corrupt and non-sustainable economy, they supported their case with enthusiastic descriptions of Africa's vast potential for legitimate trade and business (Hochschild 2006: 146; 154–5). This vision went beyond the slavers' preoccupation with sugar to embrace the many legitimate products, services and riches that such a great continent possessed. Moreover, it was argued that this abundance could only be effectively realized by free people living under God and the rule of law. In many respects the abolition of slavery set the world on its modern trajectory through helping to initiate the still ongoing process of accumulation by dispossession. Freedom through emancipation, however, was never unconditional; it was always uncertain and once attained could be taken away. The struggle to outlaw slavery in the British Empire took fifty years, spanning the eighteenth and nineteenth centuries. From the beginning, freed slaves began to appear within the contradictions and lacunae that the struggle exposed. An early development, for example, was the discovery that under English law slavery within England itself was illegal. Slaves availing themselves of this dispensation, however, constantly ran the risk of abduction and return to the slave colonies. Pockets of freed slaves also emerged in the interstices of the American and French revolutions, where they also existed as precarious anomalies. Although the French Revolution initially abolished slavery in French territories, this was quickly rescinded. As slave revolts spread and intensified, Haiti gained its independence from France in 1804. It was the second country after the United States to free itself from colonial rule; it remained, however, a country of free blacks in a world of slaves. While the trade was abolished by Britain in 1807, slavery in its colonies was not outlawed until over thirty years later. One can draw from this hesitant process a distinction between abolition and emancipation; while the trade in slaves might be abolished, actual emancipation was a gradual process in which widening privileges, keeping pace with a deepening Christian enlightenment, were to be earned rather than granted outright (ibid.: 227, 232). Even after the outlawing of slavery by the major European powers, it remained common in much of the world well into the twentieth century.

In conditions where slavery was the norm, freed slaves had an excess of freedom; they were effectively politically superfluous. The abolitionists were confronted by an originatory problem: when such an ambivalent freedom had been won, what do you do with such 'free' men and women? From the beginning the answer was development, an institution of trusteeship holding their freedom in trust until it could be prudently and safely exercised. The idea of development, for example, leaps out of the abolitionist's extensive and idealized 1780s' plans for the communal self-reliance and self-government of Sierra Leone's founding colony of freed slaves (ibid.: 146–7, 175, 202). Development trusteeship is also unmistakable in the Baptist missionary endeavours in the post-abolition Jamaica of the 1830s to create free villages (Hall 2002: 120–39). By means of the ownership of land, spiritual guidance and careful instruction in farming, civic responsibly, hygiene and domestic economy, the missionary vision was of a reborn Jamaica based on a new relationship between men and women, the former self-reliant and able to discharge their social responsibilities, the latter dependent and respectful within the bounds of home, marriage and church. In both Sierra Leone and Jamaica, the abolitionist aim was to prove to a sceptical audience that the fruits of freedom, through proper education and guidance, could be enjoyed by all, black as well as white.

Life that is politically surplus raises the issue of the relationship between emergency and the law. As a political phenomenon, emergency has been gaining ground as an object of critical study (Waever 1995). With the advent of an indefinite war on terrorism, however, it is now a pressing issue for us all (Agamben 2005). An emergency is a situation of danger threatening the state which allows it to suspend the normative rule of law. The notion of exceptional powers is well established in the history of the law. What constitutes an emergency is elastic and can range from riots, invasions and constitutional crises to natural disasters, economic slump and terrorist threats. However, in all these situations, the law 'knows that it will not be sufficient, that something else will be required' (Hussain 2003: 19). Since it is the sovereign power that decides between the normal and the abnormal, emergency can be understood 'as a constitutive relation between modern law and sovereignty' (ibid.: 17). This constitutive relationship, moreover, appears in a dramatic form in the instance of colonization. After losing its first empire in the West, based on America, by the late eighteenth century the British Empire passed largely from communities of free people of British origin tied by trade and naval power to an empire in the East of more numerous peoples 'who were not British in origin and who had been incorporated into the Empire by conquest and who were ruled without representation' (ibid.: 25). This empire was tied together not just by the Royal Navy but by the deployment of troops as well. By the nineteenth century, in the empire of India and later Africa and the Middle East, people were not slaves, 'but, because deemed utterly incapable of participating in their rule, were not quite free subjects either. *This Empire required a new conception of sovereignty, one that was neither despotic nor democratic*' (ibid.: 25 (emphasis in original)).

In the colonies, law in general, and the juxtaposition of the rule of law with emergency powers that could override it, historically assumed greater weight than in the domestic sphere. Impelled by emergency measures introduced during the first and second world wars, however, Georgio Agamben has argued that the state of exception or emergency, has progressively become 'the dominant paradigm of government in contemporary politics' (Agamben 2005: 2). It is the juxtaposition of law and emergency, and the ability of a sovereign power to decide what threatens security and what does not, that has a special significance for the dangerous life that is politically surplus. Nasser Hussain suggests a bracketing together or 'basic coincidence between colonial expansion and domestic and constitutional change' (Hussain 2003: 23). In this respect, in offering a liberal solution to the problem of surplus population, development embodies a will to power that also interconnects the borderland and the homeland. Development is simultaneously a technology of international betterment *and* security. While the connection between an internal development regime, based around culture, equal opportunity and social cohesion, and external or international development is examined in chapter 8, this book is mainly concerned with development and surplus life in today's former protectorates and colonies. Central to this analysis is that the biopower outlined by Foucault in relation to Europe and the nation-state is different from development as an international biopolitical regime. Drawing out this distinction is necessary, moreover, to establish the organic connection between development and emergency.

Separating development and underdevelopment biopolitically

The idea of biopolitics has so far been discussed in general terms – that is, as regulatory power that seeks to support life by intervening in the biological, social and economic processes that constitute a human population. Foucault's observations, however, constitute a seminal discussion of the emergence of a European biopolitics or, to put it another way, a biopolitics of 'developed' society (for an exposition see Dean 1999). Foucault did not directly consider biopolitics in relation to colonialism or development. Moreover, a number of writers have invoked his work in this context without using the concept (e.g. Said 1995; Escobar 1995; Crush 1995). Where biopolitics has been employed in relation to colonialism the authoritarian and exterminatory face of empire has been emphasized (Brigg 2002; Patel and McMichael 2004). While this is important, it tends to underplay the associated liberal strategies of governance, including development, thus highlighting only half of the equation. Where biopolitics has been used regarding the contemporary international context, it addresses those technologies of security acting at a universal or global level (Dillon and Reid 2000; Dillon 2004; Patel and McMichael 2004). Although Ferguson (1990) makes a number of useful observations in relation to biopolitics and development, he does not elaborate them. Such work has been instrumental in establishing an emerging field of analysis and extending Foucault's insights to the international level. The view adopted here, however, is that development is a regime of biopolitics that generically divides humankind into developed and underdeveloped species-life. As such, it is intrinsic to racial discourse (see Stoler 1995).

In distinguishing a biopolitics of development and underdevelopment, the great Asian tsunami emergency of December 2004 is instructive. Despite the destruction being of a different order of magnitude, within twenty-four hours of the great wave, the world's leading reinsurance companies had estimated their losses as half the £14 billion incurred when Hurricane Charlie devastated Florida in the summer of the same year (Harding and Wray 2004). Whereas the hurricane claimed twenty-five lives, the tsunami killed over 200,000. At the same time the great wave devastated whole communities, local industries and livelihoods around the Indian Ocean rim. At the time of writing, many of these communities are still rebuilding their lives. For the reinsurers, the reason for their limited financial exposure in the tsunami disaster was clear: 'fewer people in the areas affected by the huge sea surges are insured' (ibid.). This distinction between life that is 'insured' as opposed to 'non-insured' provides a fertile metaphor for distinguishing the different but connected biopolitical strategies that constitute 'developed' and 'underdeveloped' populations respectively.

For insured life, as a general responsibility of government, an important factor in ameliorating the contingencies of existence is a social insurance regime offering a range of compensatory benefits supported from contributory payments and taxation (McKinnon 2004). Together with private insurance and personal savings, as well as support from voluntary agencies, 'developed' life is promoted through a range of public welfare bureaucracies, benefits and safety nets covering maternity, health, family support, education, housing, employment injury, unemployment protection and pensions (Wood and Gough 2006). A system of public infrastructure involving massified energy, transport, nutritional, retailing and environmental systems also underpins these bureaucracies and safety nets. While plagued by issues of access and availability in the past, the idea of the welfare state and what Nikolas Rose (2000) has called the 'the social' captured the spirit if not the extent of this complex biopolitical architecture. At the moment, a neoliberal reworking of the social is well under way. In particular, a shift of ethos has taken place from the collective to the individual, based on the encouragement of active and informed citizens who take more responsibility for their own welfare choices (ibid.: 87–8, 159–60). The point being made here, however, is that the expansion of publicly administered or regulated insurance-based welfare technologies is of great significance. In terms of a comparative biopower, 'underdevelopment' is the fate of life existing beyond or outside these insurance-based welfare systems.

Estimates suggest that within industrialized countries, on average 80 per cent of the workforce is included within a contributory social insurance regime. In Africa or Asia, however, only a small minority are involved. Usually less than 10 per cent of the population is covered and for a more restricted range of contingencies; globally, as little as 20 per cent of the world's population is regarded as having adequate social insurance (McKinnon 2004: 9–10). Conventional contributory approaches fall far short of a universal reach 'especially in developing countries' (ibid.: 10). The non-insured life exposed by the tsunami was similar to that regularly revealed in other humanitarian emergencies. That is, it existed in largely self-reliant communities, predominantly organized around family and kinship and dependent on the small-scale ownership of land or property. In the absence of insurance, resilience hinges on how adept and entrepreneurial such communities are in maintaining their self-reliance and coping with the contingencies of their exposed existence (Twigg 2004). In the global South 'experience . . . reminds us of the central contribution of personal and family resources to the universal need for security' (Wood and Gough 2006: 1697). Within development policy, as will be discussed further below, there is a longstanding, indeed, unconscious acceptance that non-Western populations, except for basic needs and essential public goods, are essentially self-reliant in terms of their general economic, social and welfare requirements, and, moreover, that development is essentially about improving self-reliance through helping to meet basic needs. As a corollary, it is widely assumed that people in under-developed countries do not need the sort of welfare safety-nets on which the more atomised populace of mass consumer society is dependent. In relation to this set of developmental practices and assumptions, when self-reliance breaks down humanitarian assistance functions as *a regime of international social protection of last resort*. As such, it comes complete with its own small print, inefficiencies and exclusion clauses (Forman and Steward 2000; Marriage 2006). As a biopolitical regime, international development combines the protection of humanitarian assistance with betterment through self-reliance.

To present development and underdevelopment biopolitically illustrates the systemic gulf in life chances that separates insured and non-insured life. Compared with the compensated life styles of the West, international statistics on the distribution of poverty, longevity and social exclusion (CPRC 2005), together with the rising volume of humanitarian expenditure (Development Initiatives 2003), suggest that the developmental assumption that a large part of humanity is capable of self-reliance makes for a cruel taskmaster. Indeed, a state of emergency among self-reliant populations is now a permanent condition. Rather than questioning the biopolitics involved, however, aid agencies usually infer that the emergency exists because communities and peoples are not self-reliant enough. Consequently, each disaster initiates a fresh developmental attempt to return the population concerned to a new and more resilient condition of homeostatic self-reliance. This constant reproduction of the global life-chance divide cautions against naively assuming that development is about narrowing this gulf, for example by extending to Africa levels of social protection similar to those in Europe. The reality of development is, and always has been, very different.

The enlightened self-interest that connects the security of mass consumer society with bringing the world's non-insured life within an effective developmental trusteeship is based on improving the self-reliance of those involved. Since decolonization, the dangers of not doing this have been regularly cast as increasing the risk of international disorder. In particular, underdevelopment has the ability to foment all manner of destabilizing and illicit forms of global circulation. Cumulative restrictions on international immigration, for example, have for decades been justified as resolving the problem of the asymmetric demands made by non-insured migrants on European insurance-based welfare systems (Duffield 2006). Rather than narrowing the life-chance gulf, development is better understood as attempting to contain the circulatory and destabilizing effects of underdevelopment's non-insured surplus life.

The divergence of insured and non-insured life

Regarding how the biopolitical divergence between development and underdevelopment emerged, Cowen and Shenton (1996) have argued that until the end of the nineteenth century, as a technology of trusteeship, development was usually regarded as a solution to the social problems associated with the underdevelopment of capitalism *within* Europe (ibid.: 5). Apart from experiments involving former slaves, it was not until the early part of the twentieth century and, especially, following decolonization, that development took on its present geographical and human focus, that is, as means of protection and betterment associated with former protectorates and colonies (see Escobar 1995). Having origins as a remedy for the problem of surplus population within Europe, development has now assumed a similar role in relation to an international surplus population.

During the nineteenth century development within Britain emerged from a number of abolitionist, free-market radical, liberal and socialist strands. It combined, for example, Saint-Simonian and Comtian concerns with social breakdown and trusteeship, radical antipathy to landed interests and liberal anxieties over the negative consequences of industrial capitalism. Cowen and Shenton (1996) have argued that concerns over the surplus population, presented at the time as the 'agricultural question', were prominent between the

1870s and the First World War. Due to the increasing use of mechanization and growing livestock production, rural migrants were swelling the ranks of the urban unemployed, exacerbating unstable labour markets and exposing the limited amenities of the towns. With radicals well represented in Parliament, the developmental approach to this problem took the form of an attack on landed interests and large-scale land ownership. Not only was it inefficient, it degraded the agricultural labour force. Both liberals and radicals advocated land reform and its redistribution as a way of reabsorbing the surplus population. Land societies, for example, were formed for the purchase and redistribution of land in order to turn the surplus population into rentiers able to provide for their own welfare independently of the state. Liberal and Chartist land societies, for example, fed into the early-twentieth-century campaigns for smallholdings (ibid.: 258). The small-scale ownership of land and property was argued to encourage community cohesion, local enterprise and, through the freedoms and responsibilities of self-reliance, political citizenship. At the same time, the induced labour shortage within the industrial areas would increase average wage rates, generating benefits for all workers. As Cowen and Shenton cogently argue, it was a palliative doctrine of development that promoted rural colonization as a way of connecting surplus land with surplus population 'and so eliminate the urban decay and destitution of British underdevelopment' (ibid.: 260).

Such pressures exerted through Parliament eventually resulted in the 1909 Development Act. It proposed help and financial assistance to agriculture, rural industries, land reclamation, forestry, roads, inland navigation, harbours and fisheries *within* Britain. With a rural bias, and not wishing to alarm industrial interests, the Act called for special attention to those sectors 'which had little expectation of profit' (ibid.: 285). The 1909 Act eventually petered out, being overtaken by other and more effective liberal solutions to the problem of surplus population. As community-based development was moving overseas, in Britain it took a back seat. As argued in chapter 8, it would not come to the fore again until the 1960s. When it did so, this 'internal' development regime was concerned with integrating communities of immigrant origin within British society. A number of factors help to explain development's geographical relocation at the beginning of the twentieth century.

Mike Davis argues that the international 'development gap' first emerged in the closing decades of the nineteenth century, 'when the great non-European peasantries were initially integrated within the world economy' (Davis 2001: 1) Using the electric telegraph, railways, steamships and photography, and taking in the Americas, Africa and the East, this economy now interconnected the prairies of America with the steppes of Russia. In placing the acquired territory under the control of competing colonial powers, the New Imperialism tended to restrict this market. At the same time, from annexation flowed the responsibility of government. This responsibility gave the liberal problematic of security a new concern. As Hobson argued, almost the whole of the regions appropriated by the New Imperialism consisted of tropical or sub-tropical territories 'with large populations of savages or "lower races"; little of it is likely, even in the distant future, to increase the area of sound colonial life' (Hobson [1902]: 124). At the same time, by its acts and deeds the British Empire had already shown itself to represent the very antithesis of the art of free government. As a consequence, imperial expansion 'has increased the area of British despotism, far outbalancing the progress in population and in practical freedom attained in our few democratic colonies' (ibid.). The surplus population, initially internationalized in the scattered territories of freed slaves, and until now usually thought to be a problem of European underdevelopment, had been glimpsed as a global danger. In the wake of two world wars, liberal opinion nurtured this global vision, first in the League of Nations and then in the United Nations.

Arising from a critique of the barbarity of the New Imperialism, Hobson's remedy for the 'lower races' (which he always places within inverted commas) was that of educative trusteeship. In the years leading to the First World War, development found its way into a complex of Fabian, liberal, idealist and radical opinion that, from different perspectives, arrived at 'a common presumption that there was a natural African community of persons and producers, who had to be protected from the historical degradation of industrial capital' (Cowen and Shenton 1996: 292). This 'Fabian nexus' would grow to include liberal activists, Colonial Office officials, colonial governors and missionaries, and would eventually mature into the doctrine of Dual Mandate associated with indirect rule or, as Lord Lugard calls it, Native Administration. In discharging the responsibilities of the 'superior races' to the 'backward races', indirect trusteeship favoured existing or natural rulers. It was based on the delegation of appropriate authority and administrative tasks to such leaders, including the establishment of free courts, the provision of appropriate education 'which will assist progress without creating false ideals; the institution of free labour and a just system of taxation; the protection of the peasantry from apprehension, and the preservation of their rights to land, etc.' (Lugard [1922] 1965: 58). Based on self-reliance, indirect rule was a developmental trusteeship (Cooke 2003). Through sympathetic and paternalistic guidance, together with local trial and error, it provided a framework through which, in the fullness of time, the subject races could grow in social and political maturity (MacMichael 1934: 233–42). Chapter 7 returns to Native Administration when current policy on failed and fragile states is discussed.

Concerning the abandonment of development as a solution for Britain's surplus population, it is relevant that Fabianism also contained another strand: a remedy whereby the state acted as the trustee of capitalism as a system, taking on 'in the name of humanity' the responsibility for the orderly redistribution of profit in excess of that required for economic reproduction (Cowen and Shenton 1996: 270). Since state officials could be non-sectarian, and their advancement ideally rested on the ability to increase social productivity in general, they had the potential of becoming the trustees of society as a whole. Mixed with liberal and radical concerns, from the 1880s there were growing political demands for more selective and less punitive poor law assistance and, especially, the extension of such measures beyond relief to encompass the deserving poor: the sick, unemployed and aged, that is, those destitute through no fault of their own. Demands were made for local and central government to improve the housing, sanitation and nutrition of this group (Foucault [1975–6]). By the turn of the century many municipalities had begun to monopolize urban gas and water supply. During the 1900s, for certain categories of the population, free school meals, old-age pensions, measures against child abuse, legislation on the minimum wage, and housing and town planning acts limiting the spread of slums began to make an appearance (Thane 1989).

In Britain the 1911 National Insurance Act introduced social insurance for the regularly employed, giving the worker entitlement to health and unemployment benefit in exchange for compulsory weekly payments. Social insurance was intended to build strong collaborative values within a state venture that mediated capital and labour. The regular payments reminded workers of their obligation to save and exercise self-help, while at the same time granting them 'a contractual right to benefit' (ibid.: 150). As Mitchell Dean has argued, social insurance is not the only technology of social government, yet it is a particularly fecund one that encounters risk at the level of population in a way that 'both optimized solidarity and left the individual free. To the extent to which it avoids the eugenic approach to social problems . . . it is a decisive and exemplary illustration of the potential of liberal techniques of government' (Dean 1999: 188). A regulatory biopolitics continued to expand as a result of the social requirements and expectations generated by the First World War and then, especially, by the Second World War. Britain's 1944 Education Act provided general education, in 1945 family allowances appeared and the National Health Service was formed in 1948. Such measures reflected a commitment to extend the benefits of education, health and social insurance, previously reserved for the regularly employed, to the whole community. At the same time, it reinforced the biopolitical tendency to foster the centralization of state power, in this case the growing control over local government. This centralizing tendency is intrinsic to 'the long-run liberal idea of equalizing opportunity' (Thane 1989: 153). This also serves as a reminder that the growth of the social was not always welcomed by those whose autonomy and independence were being curtailed.

While addressing the international situation President Truman of the United States announced a developmental Point Four Programme in his 1949 inaugural address. His address signalled that the problem of surplus population was now international in scope and, in so doing, he relaunched development and its security role in its contemporary interstate form. With half the world's population living in 'conditions approaching misery', for the first time in history 'humanity possesses the knowledge and skills' to do the right thing and better this situation; moreover, the urgency of this moral obligation was underscored by their poverty being a handicap 'and a threat to both them and to more prosperous areas' (quoted in Escobar 1995: 3). While today's politicians are still periodically rejuvenating this basic formula of enlightened self-interest in 'new and improved' ways, the inauguration of interstate development concealed the contrast between the biopolitics of developed and underdeveloped populations. The welfare state ameliorated the problem of surplus life through social insurance and, in so doing, assisted the emergence of mass consumer society. For populations in the former protectorates and colonies, however, as will be seen in the following chapter, ideas of people-centred development continued to be framed in relation to self-reliance based on small-scale land and property ownership operating at the level of community. The continuing and widespread assumption of a self-reliant, natural economy is illustrated, for example, in the International Monetary Fund's post-Cold War futurology of global welfare regimes. In the former Soviet Union, where modernization has already atomized households, it is felt that extended welfare safety nets are required. In less developed countries, however, the extended family and community 'operates relatively well as an informal social security scheme obviating the need for the urgent introduction of large-scale public pensions' (Kopits quoted by Deacon et al. 1997: 64). In other words, it avoids the need for centralized social protection based on insurance or other guarantees.

From internal war to global instability

The biopolitics of insured and non-insured life are different but interconnected. They both act to address the contingencies of life and so maintain population equilibrium. However, one supports the dependent consumers of mass society through public/private technologies of insurance while the other attends to populations deemed to be self-reliant. Although different, to borrow a phrase from Nasser Hussain, they are also temporally bracketed together. Rather than extending the level of social protection enjoyed by insured life to its non-insured counterpart, development is better understood as a liberal technology of security for containing and managing the effects of underdevelopment. Since decolonization, the security of the West has been increasingly predicated on establishing an effective developmental trusteeship over the surplus population of the developing world. In addressing the present conjuncture, this book offers a reflection on the significance of decolonization for the security of the West and its relationship to the advent of unending war. While decolonization provided an opportunity for the expansion of developmental technologies among an emergent world of peoples, it also constituted a threat in terms of the new possibilities for global circulation that it made possible.

In situating these possibilities and threats, the fact that the number of ongoing internal or civil wars has noticeably declined since the early 1990s is of fundamental importance (HSC 2005). Perhaps counterintuitively, while the Cold War decades of rising internal war offered an opportunity to expand developmental technologies, it is the decline in the level of open conflict that is more clearly associated with the appearance of underdevelopment as dangerous within policy discourse. From the 1950s to the end of the Cold War there was a steady and unbroken increase in the number of wars in the Third World. The overwhelming majority of these were civil in nature (Gantzel 1997). This trend was encouraged by superpower rivalry and the competitive sponsorship of states and internal oppositions groups (van Creveld

1991). As examined in chapter 2, on the basis of emergency and the politics of exception, these decades of conflict, humanitarian disaster and increasing refugee flows provided an opportunity for international NGOs to expand within an emergent world of peoples.

NGOs are the direct heirs of nineteenth-century and colonial technologies of development based on community, the small-scale ownership of property and self-reliance. In their championing of 'bottom-up' populism they also provided a liberal critique of the independent state at a time when nationalist elites were pursuing modernization strategies based on 'top-down' industrialization and the expansion of public infrastructure. Expanding and deepening through the permanent emergency of self-reliance, by the 1980s the NGO movement had reached the zenith of its 'non-governmental' trajectory. Having expanded through emergency and the ability to decide between the life to be supported and that which can be disallowed, the NGO movement had established itself as a non-state or petty sovereign power among the world of peoples. Through an examination of the natural economy of sustainable development in rural Mozambique, chapter 4 examines the nature of this power. Sustainable development is opposed to ideas of modernization based on material advancement and closing the economic gap between rich and poor countries. It is more concerned with introducing new forms of social organization that encourage homeostatic conditions of self-reliance. Chapter 4 also considers how the petty sovereignty of NGOs was governmentalized during the 1990s – that is, how it was drawn into, and orchestrated as, a self-managing component of, the strategic designs and interests of donor states, and how such petty sovereignty would become a normal administrative attribute of post-interventionary society.

According to the Human Security Centre, in the early 1990s, just as the West was worrying about a global epidemic of ethnic violence, 'the numbers of armed conflicts began to drop rapidly' (HSC 2005: 22). While there are concerns regarding the interpretation of these figures (ibid.: 18–20), according to several independent data-sets, from around fifty largely internal wars in 1992 the number of major conflicts had almost halved by 2003 – a much steeper decline than the earlier upward trend. For a time, Africa was thought to be an exception to this downward movement. Even here, however, the overall picture is of a marked decrease in open civil war (Marshall 2005). The explanation given by the Human Security Centre involves a combination of factors. For example, colonial wars of liberation had practically died out by the beginning of the 1980s. The end of the Cold War was another important consideration. Estimates suggest that one-third of post-Second World War conflicts were driven to varying degrees 'by the geopolitics of the Cold War' (HSC 2005: 148). While there has also been an increase in the number of democracies, in economic interdependence and in the importance of international institutions, of prime importance for the Centre has been the post-Cold War explosion of international humanitarian development and peace interventionism.

This has been particularly, but not exclusively, associated with the reinvigoration of UN internationalism during the 1990s. The number of UN peacekeeping operations, for example, increased from four in 1990 to fifteen in 2002. A similar step change has occurred in relation to the growth of international support for peacekeeping, the number of negotiated settlements, and the increase in the number of post-conflict peace operations. Moreover, compared with the Cold War, such operations are not only more numerous, they are larger and more ambitious; from monitoring ceasefires the UN has graduated to nation-building.

This activity, moreover, goes beyond the UN, since it also involves the active participation of such bodies as the World Bank, donor governments, regional organizations and literally tens of thousands of NGOs that 'have both complemented the UN activities and played independent prevention and peace-building roles of their own' (ibid.: 152). The international community has now accommodated the use of sanctions regimes, the questioning of the culture of impunity, an increase in the number of international tribunals and states prosecuting war criminals, stronger emphasis on reconciliation and, importantly, a greater willingness to use force in the interests of international stability. The argument made by the Human Security Centre is that while individually such initiatives have a limited impact, when drawn together they become significant. Indeed, the 'main driver for change has been the extra-ordinary [sic] upsurge of activism by the international community that has been directed towards conflict prevention, peacemaking and peacebuilding' (ibid.: 155).

The Centre takes a rather sanguine view of the marked decline in open civil war. It is seen as auguring well for international peace and stability. As the opening remarks in this introduction suggest, however, other commentators view the future in more uncertain terms. Indeed, while 'conflict' was a defining motif of the 1990s (Kaldor 1999), it is now being replaced by 'instability' as the main threat to global security. In Britain, the Prime Minister's Strategy Unit report *Investing in Prevention* is a sign of this important shift in security discourse. While acknowledging the role of interventionism in reducing the level of open warfare, it argues that this 'is due to its suppression or containment rather than its resolution' (Strategy Unit 2005: 22). If a wider view of human security – beyond deaths resulting directly from conflict – is adopted, and the high levels of sporadic violence, criminality, economic collapse, displacement, chronic poverty and the absence of public infrastructure are taken into account, it is felt that although open war and its direct effects have declined, the number of people dying through generalized instability is actually increasing (ibid.). Furthermore, despite countervailing trends that favour stability, if the possible impacts of climate change, HIV/AIDs, the strategic competition for oil and resources and the further isolation of non-integrating countries is taken into account, it is likely that political instability *will be an enduring characteristic of the strategic landscape rather than a temporary phenomenon*' (ibid.: 24 (emphasis in original)).

Occupation and contingent sovereignty

One could be forgiven for thinking that a decline in open warfare would lead to a lessening of interventionism and, so to speak, a return of the troops. It is coterminous, however, with a waxing rather than a waning liberal urge to deepen the West's external sovereign frontier. The steady reduction in civil war following the end of the Cold War signals an ongoing process of pacification resulting from the step-change in Western interventionism within crisis states. International humanitarian development and peace activism, while not resolving the problem of political instability, have succeeded in reducing the number of open wars. Because of the persistence or threat of instability, however, intervention and pacification has blurred into a new and enduring political relationship: *a post-interventionary terrain of international occupation.* In policy terms, it signals a shift from humanitarian assistance in ongoing wars to social reconstruction and the transition from war to peace. However, if there is a single lesson from the past decade it is that ending wars within ineffective states is relatively easy; as Iraq and Afghanistan suggest, winning the peace among the world of peoples is much more difficult. All of those interconnecting UN, donor, military and NGO endeavours that mobilized to intervene, save lives and end conflict now increasingly appear as assemblages of occupation defining a new post-interventionary society. That is, they constitute the enduring multi-agency apparatus of *Empire Lite.*

The conceptual shift from internal war to a future world of generalized instability and insurgency announces the onset of unending war. As part of the enduring relationship between development and security, it signals the conscious repositioning of development as a component of counter-insurgency within a post-interventionary environment (OECD 1998; DAC 2003). With the notable exceptions of Iraq and Afghanistan, the security role of development is largely institutional and civilian rather than constituting an occupation in a military or legal sense. During the Cold War, the political architecture of the international system combined respect for territorial integrity with sovereign competence or non-interference in domestic affairs. Post-Cold War interventionism has significantly altered this architecture. While respect for territorial integrity remains, sovereignty over life within ineffective states has become internationalized, negotiable and contingent (Elden 2006). Contingent sovereignty constitutes a zone or frontier that is shaped by the interactions between national and international actors and institutions (Harrison 2004). It constitutes a contested post-interventionary political terrain. In consolidating this frontier the state has reoccupied the centre ground of Western development discourse. As discussed in chapter 5, this is not the modernizing state that took the stage at the time of independence, it is a 'human security' state in which the core economic and welfare functions of population are now designed and managed by international actors and agencies. Contingent sovereignty is a zone of donor and NGO experimentation in the biopolitics of state reconstruction, basic needs and self-reliance.

As a hallmark of their legitimacy, pacification and occupation have necessarily involved multiple international agencies. Because of the competing agendas and visions among these agencies – state/non-state, public/private, military/civilian and so on – the development environment along the West's external frontier is intrinsically anarchic. The struggle to bring order to chaos involves attempts to orchestrate and centralize the numerous independent loci of agency authority. For the NGO movement, the shift from intervention to post-intervention is synonymous with the governmentalization of its activities (see Foucault [1984]). That is, while ostensibly being 'non-governmental', it has been absorbed into a web of mutual interests and overlapping objectives that entrepreneurially connect it with donor states, recipient governments, UN agencies and militaries. Since the mid-1990s the liberal urge to govern has expressed itself in a search for greater 'coherence' between aid and politics (Macrae and Leader

2000). Reflecting the governmentalization of petty sovereignty in Mozambique discussed in chapter 4, the emergence of human security suggests that the NGO movement is no longer outside the state; it has reinvented itself as intrinsic to its reconstruction and power projection. In order to illustrate the inherent difficulties in the search for coherence, chapter 6 includes an examination of the critical tension between the UN's development and political wings in their engagement with the Taliban regime in Afghanistan. More widely, however, as open war has declined, the search for coherence has involved more coercive and politically directed programming. Symptomatic of this change has been the shift toward the UN integrated mission (Eide et al. 2005). At the beginning of the 1990s the preferred form of UN intervention was negotiated access which, indirectly, recognized political opposition. Since the close of the decade, in supporting the transition from intervention to post-intervention through state reconstruction, the UN has defined its mission in terms of isolating and, if necessary, taking on, political spoilers; the political terrain of post-intervention is one of narrowing and closure.

Disturbing the boundaries of time and space

Through a critical examination of fragile state discourse, chapter 7 explores the post-interventionary institutions of contingent sovereignty. Since the 9/11 terrorist attacks on the United States, in terms of the risk to global stability the problem of ungoverned space has risen up the international political agenda. The idea of the fragile state encompasses a range of thinking and experimental technologies currently active in, for example, Afghanistan, the Democratic Republic of the Congo, East Timor, Haiti, Ivory Coast, Liberia, Sierra Leone and Sudan. In seeking a prognosis for fragile states, their opposite is consulted. That is, the donor declared 'good performers', such as Mozambique, Tanzania or Uganda. Graham Harrison (2004) has called these countries 'governance states'. They are examples of contingent sovereignty where the international community, rather than being external to the state, is an integral part of it. Through new development technologies such as funding through the budget and a system of shadow committees monitoring performance, governance states provide a model for a stable donor–government post-interventionary relationship in aid-dependent societies. In terms of the degree of international penetration and control involved, the preferred future of ungoverned space is the governance state. While fragile state policy is at the forefront of development thinking, as a technology of governance it resonates strongly with the earlier liberal colonial practice of indirect rule or Native Administration. As an evolutionary stepping stone to greater political maturity, for example, practitioners are urged to adjust the mechanisms of government to the realities of existing social and political conditions. In a striking restatement of the liberal paradox, such an adjustment unavoidably means having to accept 'good enough governance', provided that the resulting educative trusteeship allows for a progressive increase in capacity (DFID 2005a).

A liberal problematic of security now operates unconnected with actual trends in refugee flows, asylum seekers or internal wars (Hörnqvist 2004). It has instead focused on containing and reducing the limitless risks of global instability (Strategy Unit 2005). In fighting this unending war, invoking a state of emergency by politicians and policy makers has now become a normal part of government (Waever 1995; Agamben 2005; Blumenthal 2006). Given the movement of the 'state' to the centre of development policy, it is ironic that at 'the very moment when it would like to give lessons in democracy to different traditions and cultures, the political culture of the West does not realize that it has entirely lost its canon' (Agamben 2005: 18). A liberal problematic of security, in defending freedom and rights, acts on the genuine fears of ordinary people and the possibility of multiplying risks. It is concerned with pre-emption and, if necessary, it acts beyond morality and the law. While decolonization proved an opportunity for technologies of development to penetrate the world of peoples, it also affected a world-historic reversal in global migratory dynamics (Balibar 1991) – that is, from a previous North-to-South flow to the present broad South-to-North orientation. In a globalizing world, decolonization introduced a need to police international circulation, that is, to separate 'good' circulation – such as finance, investment, trade, information, skilled labour and tourism – from the 'bad' circulation associated with underdevelopment: refugees, asylum seekers, unskilled migrants, shadow economies, trafficking, drugs and terrorism.

Chapter 8 is concerned with the contemporary bracketing of the biopolitics of developed and underdeveloped life. As such, it explores the interconnection between racism, migration and development. A liberal problematic of security now interconnects these different sites. In the case of Britain, due to growing concerns over the asymmetric demands of non-insured migrants on the welfare state and their negative impact on social cohesion, in the mid-1960s a political consensus emerged on the need to control immigration. This took immigration, and hence the immigrant, out of politics, creating a politically surplus population. In order to compensate for this exceptional measure – a manoeuvre that now informs an EU immigration and asylum regime – measures were taken to integrate those immigrants already settled. At the same time, international development was given its modern state-based institutional form. The control of immigration called forth both an internal development regime, in the shape of the race relations industry, as well as an external aid industry. This security architecture is essentially globalizing, having the collapse of the traditional national/international dichotomy predicated within it. Within its episodic logic, periodic crises of circulation have bracketed together changes within the internal and external sovereign frontiers. The move towards external occupation and the post-interventionary terrain of contingent sovereignty, for example, interconnects with an internal shift from multiculturalism to promoting a shared sense of identity and Britishness in the interests of social cohesion (Burnett 2004; Fekete 2004). They are the effects of a security technology that, in seeking to make non-integrating enemies more visible, now operates across the national/international divide. It is a liberal architecture of unending war that has planetary ambitions.

In writing this book many of the key historical departures and contemporary refinements in the emergence and deepening of the biopolitics of development and underdevelopment have been authored by liberals, Fabians, socialists, social democrats and NGOs. Progressive liberal-left institutions and actors appear to have a longstanding affinity with the synergy between biopolitics, development and security. Drawing out this connection was not the intention of this book; at the same time, coming to this conclusion is unavoidable. While speaking on behalf of people, freedom and rights, it would seem that all liberal empires emerge 'in a fit of absence of mind' (Sir John Steely quoted by Hobson [1902]: viii). Issues relating to pacification, international occupation and resistance will shape the history of our times. Is the West capable of ameliorating this situation by working to reduce the root causes of instability? Or, in attempting to control better and to manage instability through the continued invocation of security, will it further encourage global insurgency? To a large extent, answering such questions will depend whether liberalism itself, rather than being seen as a solution, is counted as one of the problems. With its focus on humanitarian relief and development, this book is a modest contribution to this debate.

2 NGOs, Permanent Emergency and Decolonization

Speaking in the name of people, freedom and rights, non-governmental organizations (NGOs) embody a liberal problematic of power. The modern NGO movement can trace its history from the philanthropic organizations and missionary societies that populated the civic landscape of late-eighteenth- and nineteenth-century Europe. For our purposes, however, international NGOs are the natural heirs of the people-centred, community-based and self-reliant model of development that, apart from the experiments among former slaves, was exported from Europe to the colonies at the beginning of the twentieth century. NGOs inherited the urge to protect and better that vectored through the liberal colonial practice of indirect rule to the rural cooperative and community development movement that gathered pace during the 1930s and 1940s as part of the prelude to independence (Kelemen 2006). Drawing on these strands, today's international NGO movement emerged in response to two interconnected episodes that globalized a liberal problematic of security during the twentieth century: the humanitarian consequences of the two world wars and, especially, the unlimited opportunity for expansion within the world of poverty that decolonization revealed.

It is common to regard humanitarian emergencies, such as those resulting from wars, famines and natural disasters, as a temporary breakdown of an otherwise normal condition of relative stability. Reflecting this assumption, most aid agencies regard humanitarian assistance and immediate life-saving relief as essentially different from development (Buchanan-Smith and Maxwell 1994). Although they can interconnect, separate approaches and priorities are involved (Macrae 1998). Some NGOs are dedicated to either relief or development work, while many others, such as Oxfam, Save the Children Fund (SCF) and CARE, have separate emergency departments within organizations that primarily define themselves in development terms. Humanitarian relief is usually described as denoting impartial, externally directed, short-term emergency measures geared to saving life. Development, however, as already discussed, is regarded as longer-term help to improve social resilience through strengthening community organization and self-reliance. During the 1990s there was much debate over the need to sequence better and to interlink relief and development – here also called protection and betterment – to ensure that humanitarian assistance did not contradict or undermine the wider aims of development (DAC 1997). Of particular concern was the claim that poorly managed humanitarian assistance, because it is a free handout in conditions of scarcity, can encourage dependency among beneficiaries, distort local markets and, not least, prolong wars and political instability (Anderson and Woodrow 1989; Anderson 1996).

Rather than a temporary breakdown or deviation from the norm, however, states of emergency are essential for the existence of liberal governance, including development. Like the reproduction of capitalism through the constant production and consumption of an economically surplus population, the liberal problematic of security – indeed the political order itself – is produced through the recurrent exclusion and inclusion of life that is otherwise politically surplus (Agamben 1998: 9). While the ability to decide the exception, or that which can be excluded, defines sovereign power, as a liberal alternative to the extermination of surplus life, relief and development effect the *re*inclusion of excluded populations. This *re*inclusion through the redemption of development is constitutive of international liberal political order. Humanitarian emergency, moreover, is the site of this manoeuvre. While protection and betterment are different, they are intrinsically interconnected and mutually conditioning. Humanitarian relief and development are expressions of the intersecting axes of 'emergency' and 'emergence' respectively that constitute liberal global governance (Dillon and Reid 2000). In so far as the NGO movement embodies a liberal problematic of security, it has internationalized and deepened its institutional reach through the expediency of permanent emergency. Like all states of exception, humanitarian emergencies challenge existing laws, override social constraints and question political limits. Since decolonization, the need to protect the non-insured peoples exposed by the permanent emergency of self-reliance has been intrinsic to the globalization of liberal governance. In separating life from politics – by holding it above the fray of battle in the name of neutrality – humanitarian emergency strips away the history, culture and identity of the peoples concerned. On ground so prepared, the foot-soldiers of development follow behind, rebuilding communities and promoting the small-scale ownership of property in the interests of improved self-reliance.

This chapter addresses the paradox of the necessity of emergency for a movement that defines itself in terms of development. In this respect the growth of the NGO movement exemplifies the interconnection between protection and betterment within a liberal problematic of governance. Since the 1920s, development actors have regularly criticized the short-termism, excessive discipline and programmatic narrowness of humanitarian action. Yet, at the same time, without permanent emergency NGOs would lack the public profile, funding base, media access, civic constituencies and international infrastructure on which their development work depends.

Total war and the paradox of biopolitics

So far, biopolitics has been examined in relation to supporting and promoting the life of population. Foucault has pointed out, however, that biopolitics contains a fateful paradox. At the same time as fostering life, biopolitics also has the ability to disallow life 'to the point of death' (Foucault [1976]: 138). Death in this sense can be both literal and, importantly, indirect and metaphorical. As well as forms of social death through marginalization and exclusion, this can include, for example, the regular exposure to risk associated with the way of life within mass consumer society (Foucault [1975–6]: 256; Beck 1992). While Western states support and promote life to the full, through mass transport systems, centralized food chains, agribusiness, manufactured vulnerabilities, carbon emissions or pollution, people are also directly or indirectly exposed to unprecedented risk and violence 'in the most profane and banal ways. Our age is the one in which a holiday weekend produces more victims on Europe's highways than a war campaign' (Agamben 1998: 114). In decoding life itself, biogenetics is creating the potential for new and far-reaching forms of social exclusion that can as yet only be glimpsed. As Harvey, Bauman and Agamben would no doubt agree, this is possible because we are now all potentially surplus to requirements.

The paradox of biopolitics is graphically expressed in the emergence of total war in Europe at the same time as the appearance of social insurance and the welfare state. During the nineteenth century, as the state began to consolidate its ability to promote and support life at the level of population, the simultaneous modernization of warfare was exposing that same population to death on a widening scale. The great world wars of the twentieth century not only established the paradigm of total war, they were formative events in the spread of social insurance and the emergence of a centralizing welfare state (Thane 1989). The biopolitical tension between the state's increasing power to optimize collective life and its ability to wage war at the level of entire societies is expressed in Foucault's often quoted argument that wars are no longer waged in the name of a sovereign who must be defended, 'they are waged on behalf of the existence of everyone; entire populations are mobilized for the purpose of wholesale slaughter in the name of life necessity: massacres have become vital' (Foucault [1976]: 137).

Since they have become managers of life, modern regimes have been able to wage wars of incredible destructiveness. Martin van Creveld has given an account of the emergence of total war in relation to the dissolution of the laws and customs of eighteenth-century European interstate warfare and the rise of industrialized forms of procurement, logistics and munitions (van Creveld 1991; see also Kaldor 1999; Smith 2006). Legal or contained 'trinitarian war' first emerged with the birth of the European nation-state in the mid-seventeenth century. It involved the slow development of codes of conduct and legal instruments that distinguished and separated the *people*, the *army* and the *government* for the purposes of war (van Creveld 1991: 39–42). During the course of the eighteenth century, trinitarian distinctions were progressively refined. As the state asserted its legal monopoly over the use of armed force, ordinary people were prohibited from taking part in wars. These became affairs of state, and governments used war as an instrument of politics. To distinguish it from crime, war was defined as something waged by sovereign states alone. People should show loyalty, pay their taxes and generally keep out of the way of armies. During the nineteenth century the legal separation of people, army and government would be converted into positive law, giving rise to modern ideas of the 'civilian' and the disparagement of 'civil' war. Conventions stipulated that hostilities could not commence without previous and explicit declarations of war and they were to be ended by formal peace treaties negotiated between the belligerent states. Soldiers were those licensed to bear arms and engage in conflict on behalf of the state. Civilians were not to be abused, but, in exchange, they must not become involved and must accept the political outcome

of contained battles. To reinforce this point, private or partisan warfare together with its encouragement was made illegal.

This model of contained interstate warfare, however, was seldom applied outside Europe. Wars of colonial conquest and pacification, especially against non-European peoples, have traditionally been waged with little restraint against non-combatants (Schmitt [1963]). The hapless 'lower races' entered history, as it were, as a politically surplus population or what Agamben would call bare-life, with the trinitarian distinction between peoples, armies and governments already blurred and obscured. In this respect, the genocidal closure of the global commons effected by the late nineteenth century's New Imperialism, in terms of its pioneering methods of cowing, dispossessing and destroying on a societal scale (Hochschild 2002), was a rehearsal for the great wars and totalitarianisms to come (Arendt [1951]). Within Europe total war has been described as the blurring of the boundaries between established trinitarian divisions and the weakening of the restraints on violence (van Creveld 1991: 42–9; Schmitt [1963]: 6–8). From the mid-nineteenth century innovations in communications, such as the railways, steamships and the telegraph, together with advances in the mass production and destructiveness of armaments, not only supported the New Imperialism, their implications began to question and push against the laws and conventions of war that separated state and society. During the world wars of the twentieth century, through declaring states of emergency, whole societies were mobilized for the purpose of war (ibid.: 14). At the same time, national populations were exposed to death in new ways, not only directly through mass conscription, but since society was now the human and industrial embodiment of the war effort itself, civilians also became targets. To paraphrase Agamben, like the surplus life of the colonies, the 'civilian' in Europe and Asia entered a zone of non-differentiation where it was possible to kill without committing murder. Although seemingly protected by laws and conventions, through the licence that emergency provides, civilians routinely became the targets of indiscriminate military intimidation, blockade and destruction. Total war made the twentieth century the most calamitous and bloody in human history (Hobsbawm 1994).

NGOs and total war

In the state of exception prevailing during the two world wars, civilians in Europe frequently found themselves outside the normal restraints of law and morality. The naval blockage proved itself to be a powerful biopolitical weapon; with trade and essential supplies cut, whole populations suffered as industries and livelihoods were pressured. The Second World War would bring to this strategic bombing and the destruction of public infrastructure, including housing, transport and factories. The movements and clashes of vast armies added to the millions of refugees, destitute and orphaned thrown off by total war on a continental scale. It is in relation to this politically surplus population that the modern NGO movement emerged. The ending of the First World War in 1918, for example, revealed a devastated Europe, with starvation reported in parts of Germany itself. While initially threatened with infringing the emergency Defence of the Realm Act, in May that year, the Save the Children Fund (SCF) was publicly launched during a meeting in the Royal Albert Hall, London (SCF 2006).

Through pioneering the use of newspaper appeals and filming its famine and disaster work as a way of raising public awareness, SCF grew by raising money to support charities working with children in Germany, Austria, France, Belgium, the Balkans and Turkey. In these early years SCF found itself dealing with 'emergency after emergency' resulting from the effects of war, including famine in Russia in 1921 (ibid.: 4). The American Friends Service Committee (AFSC) and the International Federation of the Red Cross and Red Crescent Societies (IFRC) were also established at this time. Besides SCF expanding its work within Britain, initially with the families of redundant miners, its leading light, Eglantyne Jebb, also framed a Declaration of the Rights of the Child that was taken up by the League of Nations and subsequently formed the basis of the UN declaration of the same name. To support its nascent international work, a Child Protection Committee was established to lobby for the rights of children across Britain's African and Asian colonies. In 1936, as an offshoot of this work, a nursery school was founded in Addis Ababa in the then independent Abyssinia (now Ethiopia). Much of SCF's early work in Europe and beyond was rolled back, however, by the renewed outbreak of world war.

The second time round, the catastrophic humanitarian effects of total war within Europe were much greater. By 1942 some liberal critics, for example the bishop of Chichester, Dr George Bill, 'had come to feel that the pursuit of total war had taken dangerous and unworthy forms' (Jones 1965: 26). Especially within occupied territories such as Greece and Belgium, it was felt that the bombing of civilian areas and the food blockade were producing no significant

hardship for German forces but great suffering and misery for millions of civilians. In October that year, in the Old Library of the
University Church of St Mary the Virgin, Oxford, the Oxford
Committee for Famine Relief was formed. The minutes of this
meeting record the aim of the Committee, which would become
widely known during the 1950s by its telegram abbreviation Oxfam,
as being 'the relief, to the extent that the law for the time being per-
mitted, of famine and sickness arising from the result of war'
(Whitaker 1983: 14). Most of the founding members of Oxfam had
Quaker backgrounds and included a future mayor of Oxford, a vicar,
a retired Indian Civil Service administrator and a businessman. Like
the founders of SCF, they were part of the liberal establishment.

The government dismissed Oxfam's initial appeals on the grounds
that food shortages within the occupied territories were forcing the
German command to transfer labour from the factories to the farms,
thus helping the Allies. Regardless of official opposition, however, in
March 1943 Oxfam was registered as a charity and launched its first
public appeal. Encouraged by public sympathy, by May the following
year its Greek initiative was under way. Irrespective of the British concerns, the Canadian government had already sent two shiploads of
wheat. Oxfam contributed a cargo of dried milk from South Africa for
distribution by the Greek Red Cross to needy women and children.
This founding humanitarian endeavour drew support from the Vice-
Chancellor of Oxford University, the mayor and bishop, and both of
Oxford's MPs (ibid.: 15). The eventual liberation of Europe in 1945
revealed a continent in hunger and disarray. Humanitarian appeals
for France, Belgium, Holland and especially Germany quickly became
the order of the day. Just as the effects of the First World War prompted
the founding of a number of organizations that would become international NGOs, the Second World War had the same effect. Apart
from Oxfam, for example Christian Aid, the Cooperative for
Assistance and Relief Everywhere (CARE), Catholic Relief Services
(CRS), the International Rescue Committee (IRC) and World Vision
International were also formed. Oxfam expanded through raising
public funds and material to support the soup kitchens and second-
hand clothing distributions already being run by other organizations
that, apart from local charities, included SCF, the Society of Friends,
the IFRC and the Salvation Army.

By the end of the 1940s the worst of the human dislocation within
Europe had been addressed and the US Marshall Plan for economic
recovery was taking effect. Many of Britain's town-based relief

committees, like Oxfam established towards the end of the war, decided to close. The founding members of Oxfam, however, elected to continue and began to look beyond Europe to 'where hunger was the normal condition' (Jones 1965: 32). In 1948 Oxfam opened its first permanent shop in the centre of Oxford and, at the same time, its members formally agreed on 'widening and extending the work' (ibid.). In the same year, the British mandate in Palestine collapsed and, as a result of Arab and Israeli fighting, three-quarters of a million Palestinians were made refugees. In responding to this non-European emergency, Oxfam realized that it was 'committed to help in any future situations, whether the result of war, natural calamity, or simply basic poverty' (ibid.). Over the next couple of decades the process of decolonization would produce a new world of independent territorial nation-states. President Truman's 1949 inaugural address is widely credited with launching development as an interstate relationship (Easterly 2002). In describing half the earth's population as living in 'conditions approaching misery', Truman conjured up an ambivalent 'world of peoples' within the new interstate system, a world that qualified for help in its own right but, if that help was not given, was capable of menacing global order. With Europe's emergency drawing to a close and the welfare state about to expand, this was the world that the NGO movement would claim as its own.

The colonial inheritance

Decolonization was an often violent and contested process that spanned several decades. While the NGO movement originated in relation to the humanitarian consequences of European total war, its expansion within the world of peoples interconnected with colonialism in many ways. It should be emphasized that it is an overlap with *colonialism* as opposed to the nationalist-led struggles for independence. It is noticeable, for example, that all Oxfam's official historians – Mervyn Jones (1965), Ben Whitaker (1983) and Maggie Black (1992) – make no mention of any active support within the organization or noticeable stance on independence as these events were unfolding. What is more to the fore is the NGOs' inheritance of the official attempts to modernize colonialism in what proved to be a last-ditch effort to weaken the nationalist case and prolong the colonial relationship – that is, the reform of local government during the 1940s and, especially, the pioneering of community development as an alternative to the then perceived failure of indirect rule to halt the nationalist advance. Second, there was an overlap in terms of the personnel and activists who would staff the expanding overseas voluntary sector. Decolonization demobilized an army of colonial officials, employees, military personnel and business-men who had worked within the parameters of Empire. As nationalist leaders pursued state-led strategies of modernization well into the 1970s, those now surplus to Empire but anxious to 'give something back' kept alive a critical flame of non-state development based on self-reliance through community-level organization.

By the end of the First World War the idea of development, origi-nating as a nineteenth-century solution to Europe's surplus popula-tion, had found its way into a 'Fabian nexus' linking socialist, liberal and, increasingly, enlightened colonial opinion. This liberal colonial-ism supported indirect rule through native authorities as the best way of protecting 'natural' African communities from the degradation of capitalism (Cowen and Shenton 1996: 292). In 1926, for example, the British Labour Party issued a statement on the colonies in which a favoured 'Africa policy' was counterposed to a 'Capitalist policy'. That is, it supported the defence of individual producers on communal land as opposed to the forcing of the native population into wage labour and thereby dissolving traditional community bonds (see also Hobson [1902]: 230). In this interpretation of imperial trusteeship, responsi-bility lay in protecting traditional African society from capitalist exploitation and restoring the organic cohesion presumed to be its natural condition (Kelemen 2006: 229). By the early 1930s, however, doubts were growing among colonial officials and political activists over the ability of indirect rule to secure a future for Empire and reverse Britain's declining international influence. Whereas a decade earlier, Lord Lugard's *Dual Mandate in Tropical Africa* had formalized indirect rule through native authorities, Lord Hailey's *Africa Survey*, completed in 1935–6, would significantly reorder the priorities of liberal trusteeship (Hewitt 2006).

The *Africa Survey* was instigated by Joseph H. Oldham, the founder of the International Institute for African Languages and Cultures and secretary to the British Missionary Society and World Council of Churches. Oldham had been active in, for example, supporting native interests in their struggle against dispossession by white settlers in Kenya. The gist of his case was that since indirect rule had evidently failed to protect native peoples from these depredations, the colonial administration was now duty bound to prepare them for modernity. Reflecting such sentiments, Hailey's subsequent report argued that 'indirect rule was ideologically incompatible with indigenous interests and British economic needs' (ibid.: 6). It attracted support from a range of non-state actors, including activists working for the Fabian Colonial Bureau, the Empire Marketing Boards, the Royal Africa Society and a number of missionary organizations. Encouraged by the rising tide of nationalism and its rejection of indirect rule ('Abd al-Rahim 1969), the ensuing debate began to realign colonial policy in the direction of transforming native authorities into British-style local government institutions and the expansion of tertiary education, together with support for trade unions, producer cooperatives and community development.

During the 1930s the Labour Party had advocated the introduction of trade unions to represent workers' interests and, in rural areas, the formation of producer cooperatives. The latter were seen as an antidote to the detribalization that capitalism had induced (Kelemen 2006: 235). The Fabian Colonial Bureau was an important focal point for the discussion of such reforms during the 1940s. Buoyed by the change of public opinion towards the colonies during the Second World War in favour of development, cooperatives were regarded as having the potential to increase productivity and 'provide administrative experience for Africans, by bringing together small peasant producers in mutual support and preserve the communitarian basis of traditional Africa' (ibid.: 12). Conscious of the link between development and security, cooperatives also linked a 'concern for political stability with the desire to increase colonial production' (ibid.). While such measures were seen as an alternative to indirect rule or Native Administration, it should be pointed out that the essence of both was similar: *the preservation of an authentic African community through the devolution of self-management responsibilities judged appropriate to local capacity and conditions.* While different in nature, they had similar ends; moreover, it is a basic formula that, as we shall see, is repeated in 'sustainable development'. Like indirect rule and the tribe, the cooperative was seen as a community-based foundation for developing appropriate traits of character, skill and capacity. The Atlee government's first secretary of state for the colonies, George Hall, hailed cooperatives not just for their economic benefit but also their educative value in encouraging thrift, 'self-help, fair dealing and above all practical training in the working of the democratic processes' (quoted in ibid.: 13).

By the late 1940s the Labour administration in Britain had initiated the switch from Native Administration to the expansion of local government. This was introduced on the grounds of improving welfare and 'to help build community organisations' (ibid.). Such reforms also attempted to weaken the growing nationalist agitation for complete independence. The resulting Colonial Development and Welfare Acts sought to address both the disintegration of traditional institutions and, at the same time, to satisfy the demands of educated Africans to be able to decide their own destiny. The Earl of Listow, a junior minister in the Colonial Office, advocated fostering 'local patriotism' that could reverse community disintegration and satisfy nationalist aspirations. Central to this was the promotion of community development as a way of forming new, energized and collegiate citizens, 'propelled by their own enthusiasm, sustained and carried forward by their own effort and industry . . . they would sally forth as a team to build for themselves, from local materials, the schools and dispensaries they urgently need' (quoted in ibid.: 14). During the 1940s and 1950s, community development was codified in a number of books and journal articles typically written by former colonial officials and consultants. Having served for twenty years in west and east Africa before joining London University's Institute for Education in 1949, T. R. Batten is a leading example. Works like his *Communities and Their Development* (1957) and I. C. Jackson's *Advance in Africa: A Study of Community Development in Eastern Nigeria* (1956) were not only influential at the time, they resonate and overlap with current approaches to sustainable development. Paradoxically, the essential elements of an empowering, people-centred development, pioneered by liberal colonialism as a means of weakening the nationalist case, have periodically been reinvented as the best way to emancipate the postcolonial world (Chambers 1983; Booth 1993; Pronk 2001). As Bill Cooke (2003) has argued, there is a close affinity between liberal forms of colonial administration and contemporary development management.

Expansion without imperial reconciliation

As the 1945–51 Labour government was laying the foundations of the welfare state in Britain, it was also modernizing colonial rule abroad. Regarding colonialism, however, it is important to emphasize that the energy invested in the reform of local government, expansion of education, cooperatives and community development was *not* in support of independence but embodied a vision that 'foresaw an eventual self-government *within the Empire*' (Hewitt 2006: 6 (emphasis in original)). As Paul Kelemen argues, while the pressure for these reforms arose from a combination of Fabian, liberal and socialist tendencies, the contribution of the Labour government, while not wishing to specifically block an increase in independence, was to seek instruments that channelled nationalist aspirations 'into institutions which would make them operate within the framework of colonialism' (Kelemen 2006: 240; see also Davies 1963). As democracies are not necessarily liberal and liberalism is not necessarily democratic (Dean 1999: 120), so development is also politically permissive. Development embodies a timeless search for a liberal technology of governance that does not necessarily have any affinity with either colonialism or independence. Kenya, for example, did not gain independence until 1963. The African District Councils Ordinance of 1950, however, as an attempt to introduce the reforms discussed above, gave the colonial administration extensive power to intervene in agriculture in support of desired methods of farming and animal husbandry. It initiated a 'second colonial occupation' by introducing to the Kenyan countryside 'several thousand technical advisers, specialists in various fields of rural development' (Kelemen 2006: 239). Regarding the NGO movement, for example Oxfam's first grant to Africa was made in 1953. At this stage, apart from Liberia (1847) and Egypt (1951), most of the continent still lay under colonial rule. Consequently, until the mid-1960s Oxfam mainly worked with colonial administrations, in particular the British High Commission territories of what was then Basutoland, Bechuanaland and Swaziland (Black 1992: 76–7).

> In this instance, it is the official department that gets the grant and acts as Oxfam's agent . . . When the development project gets under way, the Government allots experts or administrators to it and pays their salaries . . . Oxfam finances the project itself and gives the tractors or Land Rovers or the fishing boats . . . In this way, a great deal of development work has been carried through which the authorities would never have undertaken without Oxfam's offer of help, but which Oxfam also could not have managed alone (Jones 1965: 41).

Today, a number of NGOs are concerned that, following the renewed post-Cold War interventionism by the West, they have been absorbed within a series of internationally sponsored nation-building projects (Donini et al. 2004). The overlap with colonialism, however, even to the basic mechanics of such state-partnered projects, gives this claim a certain déjà vu. While charity law restrictions on political campaigning could be cited as a reason for development's general inability to distinguish occupation from independence, one can also detect a functional dimension to this oversight. Mervyn Jones, for example, tells a symptomatic story of a white South African farmer who, in 1962, began selling cheap milk on a nearby native reserve. Forced by apartheid to live on poor, overcrowded land, its inhabitants, especially children, were suffering from malnutrition and its resultant ailments. In contrast, neighbouring white farmers were pouring milk away in the absence of a market. Through buying surplus milk at bulk prices and selling cheaply, a 'self-betterment' project was instigated in the reserve. In exchange for organizing its distribution and collection of payment, the surplus population of the reserve gained access to surplus milk. The Zulu term for self-betterment – *kapugani* – was chosen as the project name. The idea caught on and, with the help of Oxfam bridging grants, the scheme soon became national in scope. During this period, the apartheid regime was busy zoning and forcibly moving populations. While Jones acknowledged that due to the political situation, the Kapugani project could not end poverty, he nonetheless justified support. Poverty's political causes were clear 'and the political obstacles are unhappily just as clear. But if you have seen the skinny limbs of a child in the Reserves, you cannot simply wait for *apartheid* to come to an end. People are hungry. Kupugani feeds them' (Jones 1965: 54).

The sentiment expressed here is important. Reflecting the liberal reference point of people, rights and freedom, development argues that the alleviation of poverty must come before politics; people must be taken out of politics, reduced to a life of exception, if they are to be helped. This manoeuvre has been used repeatedly by NGOs to justify interventions in countries where an agency has no previous history or, as in the above South Africa example, as a means of justifying working within illiberal regimes. Variants of the South Africa argument have been used on many occasions by NGOs to defend not speaking out or continuing to operate in repressive environments. More recent examples include Ethiopia, Sudan, Sierra Leone and Liberia. The argument has usually been that public condemnation of the regime would invite expulsion and hence penalize the poor and disadvantaged who were being helped. When examined on an individual basis, such an argument gives pause for thought. When viewed as a monotonous refrain spanning several decades and continents, however, the liberal paradox once again emerges. In relation to non-Europeans, in a way similar to nineteenth-century liberalism, NGOs have shown a tenacious ability to accommodate despotic rule as a necessary price of betterment.

Development addresses the problem of surplus population through a liberal, educative trusteeship. It has no necessary association with either democracy or despotic rule and can be found in both. As a result, while decolonization provided an important opportunity for the internationalization of a liberal problematic of governance, development itself did not furnish a critical break with imperialism. Similarly, Britain's Labour Party never came to terms with the nationalist rejection of Empire or the role of liberalism in authoring a moral trusteeship over others (Davies 1963). Following the lead of President Truman, in place of critique one finds the sidelining of the struggle against colonialism and its political implications *by the endless and threatening world of poverty that the West experiences the struggle for independence as revealing.* This experience disarms any critique of the liberal urge to better others; indeed, the urgency of the situation was such that even before decolonization was complete, the need for developmental stewardship had reasserted itself. In 1953, for example, the future Labour leader, Harold Wilson, argued that the most urgent problem facing the planet was now poverty and hunger.

> Over 1,500,000,000 people or something like two-thirds of the world's population, are living in conditions of acute hunger, defined in terms of identifiable nutritional disease. This hunger is at the same time the effect and the cause of the poverty, squalor, and misery in which they live. (Wilson 1953: 11)

For Wilson, the struggle against imperial domination arose from two main factors: first, the poverty and hunger exacerbated by European colonial mismanagement as reflected in economic chauvinism, the plantation system and commercial mono-crop agriculture; second, the awakening effect of the Second World War resulting from, for example, the unprecedented movement of colonial troops, the mobilization of the export economy and the construction of new roads and port facilities. All these developments were understood to 'have widened the horizons of colonial peoples' (ibid.: 98). In other words, the basis of nationalist revolt was, essentially, a combination of poverty through colonial mismanagement and, within an interconnected world, the widening horizons of a hitherto ignorant population. As colonial peoples were awakening to a world of independent states, global poverty presented a new risk – *would the normally ignorant be able to manage their own freedom effectively?* During the 1950s the spread of communism in the Third World was understood in

relation to the risks posed by poverty and ignorance. This fateful interconnection explained

> the success of the Kremlin in the backward areas of the world. The twen-
> tieth century has stood Marxism on its head: its successes have been not
> among the urban proletariat to whom Marx appealed, but among landless
> peasants and starving families in under-industrialised areas. (ibid.: 14)

Apart from the practicalities of a reluctant and often violent han-
dover, by the beginning of the 1950s the Empire had already been
pronounced dead as a public issue (Howe 1993). As soon as liberal
opinion realized that a reform of colonialism was not acceptable to
its nationalist critics, it embraced poverty as both an explanation of
the past and the driving concern of future development. Wilson, for
example, was instrumental in the founding in 1953 of the campaigning non-governmental organization War on Want (Luetchford
and Burns 2003). Rather than the global anti-colonial struggle
prompting a critique of the basic assumptions of liberal tutelage,
even before the majority of protectorates and colonies had achieved
independence a new form of developmental trusteeship stood
waiting. By the early 1950s all but extreme conservatives 'accepted
the prospect of independence for British colonies, and saw too that
the new nations would have a difficult row to hoe. *The economic and
social conditions were ready for Oxfam to expand*' (Jones 1965: 36
(emphasis added)).

Emergency and the dilemma of development

The NGO movement did not expand politically within the world of
peoples. That is, through supporting struggles against imperial domination or racial oppression *it expanded on the basis of emergency*.
Although the UN had designated the 1960s as the World Development
Decade, in seeking to draw attention to the continuation of chronic
poverty, in 1960 it also launched the Freedom from Hunger Campaign.
On the basis of the recurrent humanitarian disasters that kept it in the
headlines, Oxfam's annual public funding broke the £1 million mark
in 1960, with its cash income exceeding in-kind donations for the first
time (Whitaker 1983: 19). By 1964 the cash receipts of SCF also broke
this barrier (SCF 2006). Most of this income was also now going to
Africa and Asia rather than Europe. Regarding War on Want, although
its income would temporarily fall back, it similarly exceeded the £1
million threshold in 1968 (Luetchford and Burns 2003: 61). In 1980 the

name 'Oxfam' entered the *Oxford English Dictionary*. It was then Britain's largest charity, its annual income of £16 million for the first time exceeding all other voluntary organizations including the National Trust, Dr Barnardo's and the major cancer charities (Whitaker 1983: 40). This growth was not confined to Oxfam. All the international NGOs that had emerged in response to the humanitarian consequences of total war expanded in the world of poverty revealed by decolonization. By the early 1980s UNDP estimated that international NGOs were reaching about 100 million people (Demirovic 1996: 2–3). It was around this time that donor governments also came to appreciate the scope and growing professionalism of the NGO movement (Kent 1987: 85).

This level of penetration and visibility had been achieved on the back of the permanent emergency existing among the world's non-insured peoples. In the case of Oxfam, for example, between the end of the 1940s and 1980 major public appeals included Palestinian refugees (1949), war in Korea (1950), famine in Bihar (1951), Ionian Islands earthquake (1953), the Hungarian uprising (1956), the Algerian war of independence (1957), World Refugee Year (1959), civil war in the Congo (1960), civil war in Nigeria (1967), earthquake in Peru and cyclone in East Pakistan (1970), the independence struggle of Bangladesh (1971), earthquake in Guatemala (1976), cyclone in India (1977) and the devastation of Cambodia (1979). It was a roll-call of emergencies 'which echoes the campaign honours of a venerated regiment' (ibid.: 19). A similar story of growth through permanent emergency in these early decades could also be told about SCF (SCF 2006). Moreover, like the world wars, these humanitarian emergencies prompted the formation of new international charities such as War on Want, Médecins sans Frontières (MSF), Action contre la Faim (ACF) and, in the 1980s, ActionAid and GOAL.

At the time of writing, the UN's World Food Programme (WFP) had recently announced that 20 million Africans are in danger of starvation due to a persistent and region-wide drought. NGOs, moreover, have already been making public appeals in newspapers on behalf of the victims. Within the public domain, this emergency has followed on quickly from the Pakistan/India earthquake (2005) and the great tsunami disaster of December 2004. Reflecting preceding decades, however, the whole of the post-Cold War period has continued to be a succession of formative emergencies. With the Ethiopian and Sudan famines of the mid-1980s as a prelude, this includes the first Gulf War (1990–1), famine and conflict in Somalia (1992), the break-up of the former Yugoslavia (1993), genocide in Rwanda (1994), region-wide war in central Africa (1997), the Kosovo conflict (1999) and the military intervention in Afghanistan (2001) to name but a few headline events. In response to these 'complex emergencies' (Edkins 2000), new NGOs such as International Alert, Saferworld and War Child have continued to form. At the same time there has been a new organizational phenomenon; encouraged by the international response to such emergencies, tens of thousands of local NGOs have also emerged in the territories concerned. By the early 1990s, UNDP estimated that, at 250 million, NGOs had more than doubled the number of people they were reaching compared with a decade earlier (Demirovic 1996: 2–3). Reflecting this picture of continued growth, in 2004 Oxfam's annual budget stood at around £120 million, a seven-fold increase in twenty years.

The point under discussion here is not so much the spectacular growth of the international NGO movement since the 1950s as interpreting this growth as the internationalization of a liberal trusteeship that takes people, rights and freedom as its reference point. For NGOs this power design has been, and remains, premised on the state of exception among non-insured peoples popularly known as humanitarian emergency. Emergency has provided a means of penetrating the world of peoples, ignoring existing laws, conventions or restraints; it has allowed the colonization of new countries or increasing a presence where a foothold already exists. At the same time emergencies readily engage public opinion and generosity. As a way of internationalizing a liberal problematic of government, humanitarian emergencies contain a powerful globalizing impulse as well as countervailing tendencies to centralize and governmentalize power. By the early 1960s, for example, commercial airlines had already reduced the flying time from Britain to India to thirteen hours, shrinking the 'distance' between an emerging mass consumer society and an opening world of poverty.

> The bustee-dweller is no more likely to see London than to explore the moon. But the English boy or girl who has just left grammar school and signed on for a year's voluntary service overseas may well be locked in the sedate traffic of West Cromwell Road one afternoon, and gazing at Dum Dum Road next morning. (Jones 1965: 12)

At the same time, however, the globalizing humanitarian urge to protect exists in constant and formative tension with a remedial logic of betterment and development. While in practice the outcome remains equivocal and unresolved, emergencies continually invoke development as a 'once and for all' means of eradicating the crisis of poverty among the non-insured through new or better forms of self-reliance. Consider, for example, the plea made by Eglantyne Jebb in 1927 when contemplating the future of SCF:

> It must not be content to save children from the hardships of life – it must abolish these hardships; nor think it suffices to save them from immediate menace – it must place in their hands the means of saving themselves and the world. (Quoted in SCF 2006: 1930s, 2)

The same sentiment is found, for example, in the famous slogan of the UN's Freedom from Hunger Campaign launched in 1960: 'Give a man a fish and feed him for a day; teach him to fish and you feed him for a lifetime.' Not only are charity's material limitations being flagged given the millions living in abject poverty, so too is the moral undesirability of helping in this way. Importantly, this manoeuvre deftly places self-reliance over the space occupied by social insurance in the developed world. Humanitarian assistance is both finite and different from social insurance. Having made no prior contributions, the victims of humanitarian emergency have no contractual right to assistance. Hence the dilemmas, inefficiencies and lack of accountably that surround humanitarian aid (Marriage 2006). Whereas social insurance stems from the acceptance that such contingencies as ill-health, unemployment or old age touch everyone at some stage (Dean 1999: 188), humanitarian assistance is a discretionary international protection of last resort that comes into play when an otherwise self-contained and homeostatic condition of self-reliance breaks down. As a solution, the sporadic and selective nature of humanitarian assistance constantly invokes a more thoroughgoing self-reliance as the best way to proof non-insured peoples against disaster. While the dismal and entrenched global statistics on poverty, health and mortality would suggest that self-reliance is impossible, the typical aid agency response to recurrent emergency is that the population concerned *is not self-reliant enough*. Each crisis of self-reliance is used to restate self-reliance as the only possible future for non-insured surplus life. In the mid-1970s Oxfam's Council members reconfirmed the organization's development objectives in terms of being a small-scale catalyst 'helping and encouraging people to realise their full potential; helping small groups to become self-reliant and to combat the oppressive factors of their environment' (Whitaker 1983: 30). This core mission has remained unchanged.

The tension between protection and betterment is ever present;

while they are different, each is the necessary condition of the other. While NGOs have expanded through emergency, as a movement they define themselves in terms of development; this points to a recurrent dilemma at the heart of development as a liberal problematic of government. Writing in 1973, an Oxfam worker records this persistent and unresolved quandary in the following way:

> The man you feed this year will starve next [...] unless he has been taught to irrigate, till, sow or somehow produce food for himself. Symptomatic relief may only postpone a cure; and yet on the other hand emergencies are emergencies, famine is famine, and we can hardly allow people to starve because of dogmatic anxieties about their future. It is a desperate dilemma, and most major foreign aid charities have come to accept a double responsibility as inevitable. (Benedict Nightingale, quoted in ibid.: 22)

While relief and development are acknowledged as a double responsibility, deciding between them is never resolved one way or another. Having to choose presents itself afresh with every new emergency of self-reliance. When looking back at the international expansion of Oxfam during the 1950s, Mervyn Jones expressed the ever-present dilemma of choosing between protection and betterment by using the iconic figure of the vulnerable child; an image which has long been associated with expressing the immorality of famine (Campbell et al. 2005). While Jones accepts that humanitarian assistance is vital, it nonetheless tends to treat poverty 'as an immutable fact' and does little to improve the long-term conditions of the impoverished majority (Jones 1965: 36).

> To decide between present need and future hope, between the child that will die next week unless he is fed and the child who will live a hungry life unless his conditions are bettered: this is the most painful of tasks. (Ibid.: 43–4)

By the 1990s the debate over the relationship between humanitarian relief and development had become a monotonous critique, constantly rehashing this basic dilemma and reproducing its lyrical dispositions. Hugo Slim, for example, redefined the moral dilemma linking protection and betterment in terms of the differences between *deontological* or duty-based ethics and *teleological* or goal-based, consequentialist ethics. Protection belongs to a moral universe of duty where actions are right in themselves. Betterment, however, demands that good must be seen to come out of actions. Consequentialism involves 'the complicated and uncertain process of anticipating wider outcomes and holding oneself responsible for events well beyond the present time' (Slim 1997: 8). The relationship between relief and development is similar to that between duty and consequentialism; it is the difference between being right in itself rather than being tasked with securing the future by deciding between multiple options. The recurrent need to choose between protection and betterment allows development continually to reinvent and present itself as 'new and improved'. In this respect, they are not exclusive opposites but mutually conditioning categories that constantly move in and out of each other, development holding out a solution to the permanent emergency of self-reliance while humanitarian assistance attends the impossibility of this formula.

Cold War liminality and non-state sovereignty

There is a paradox at the heart of biopolitics: the ability to value and promote life while also disallowing it to the point of death. This has already been mentioned in relation to the contrast between the welfare state and total war, institutions conjoined in the development of industrial society. The distinction between supporting life and allowing death is also contained, however, in the tension between relief and development. It inhabits the developmental trusteeship asserted over non-insured peoples. To choose between the starving child and the poor child is to decide between life to be valued or disallowed. While premised on emergency, the expansion of the modern NGO movement has involved a constant act of separating these two possibilities of human existence: that is, of deciding the point of exception. In the case of Oxfam, for example, when it began to redefine itself as a development agency during the 1950s, this involved separating its founding surplus population, for example blockaded civilians, refugees and the victims of earthquakes or famine, from the majority of the world's inhabitants, that is, 'people for whom poverty was the lifelong environment' (Jones 1965: 35).

Drawing on Georgio Agamben (1998 and 2005) in deciding the point of exception – that is, when NGOs choose between saving the starving child or helping the poor child – whatever the final choice, a sovereign power over life is being exercised. In its approach to humanitarian emergency, mainstream international relations theory ignores such a pervasive, everyday non-state sovereignty. Since its focus is on the state, it understands humanitarian intervention primarily in terms of *military* intervention (Wheeler 2000;

Chesterman 2001). Such work tends to overlook the relentless expansion of the NGO movement as an independent sovereign power among the world of peoples. It is a banal sovereignty that is enacted in the daily routine of relief and development programmes, project encounters and advocacy campaigns (Mitchell 2002). In relation to aid agencies in the Balkans, Mariella Pandolfi (2002) has dubbed this routinized administrative authority 'mobile sovereignty' and, in a non-aid context, it is what Judith Butler has called 'petty sovereignty' (Butler 2004: 56). The sovereignty of the NGO movement lies in the endless decision making concerning whom to help and champion and, consequently, who can be left behind – *is it all poor farmers or just the chronically poor?* Which groups have priority, and which do not – *is it women generally or just female-headed households?* What issues have priority and what can be ignored – *is it debt relief or human rights abuse?* Whether teaching poor peasants how to farm better, organizing micro-credit schemes or giving women a voice, based on the finite availability of resources, a petty sovereign power has expanded through colonizing that species-life judged to have the best potential for achieving self-reliance while excluding that which does not. During the 1990s, in relation to conflict-related emergencies, this administrative sovereignty was theorized, for example, in terms of designing aid projects that rewarded authentic and unifying community interests while excluding the false and destabilizing (Anderson 1996).

Reflecting the permissiveness of liberalism, depending on circumstances, the NGO movement has been able to define itself as both with and against the state. During the Cold War, it actively colonized the world of peoples by ignoring, outwitting or working around the state (Slim 2004a). NGOs expanded as a non-state or petty sovereign power within the liminal space between the West, the Soviet bloc and independent Third World states emerging from colonization. The world of peoples within this liminal space was experienced as endless and multiform poverty. In Mervyn Jones's *Two Ears of Corn* (1965), for example, the people who are the object of Oxfam's assistance occupy a vividly drawn picture of unending need; from refugees unable to survive, or peasant farmers working exhausted land, to the teaming slums and chronic destitution of Asia, it is a vista of generalized but ethnically modulated want. While gender and the state are largely absent, when the latter does make an appearance in this panorama of peoples, ethnic groups and minorities, *it features as a problem*: the author of refugee flight, the site of indifferent or corrupt officials, or the absence of skills or capacity. Reflecting liberalism's distrust of the state, by the 1970s, with decolonization all but complete, Third World governments were firmly associated with corruption and inefficiency. In his Foreword to Whitaker's history of Oxfam (Whitaker 1983), the journalist Conor Cruise O'Brien was of the opinion that many, possibly most, Third World governments 'are corrupt, incompetent, and – in every sense of the word – irresponsible' (ibid.: x).

Faced with bad governance in the Third World, many NGOs were concerned that official donor assistance was liable to be stolen, wasted 'or actually used – in a variety of ways – against the poor, whom it is supposed to help' (ibid.). There were grounds therefore to be sceptical about the effectiveness of international aid, especially when, as during most of the Cold War, official aid was mainly disbursed through the governments concerned. Consequently Western donors, UN organizations and the World Bank typically stood accused by the NGO movement of complicity with corrupt Third World states 'which themselves may be contributing to the causes of underdevelopment' (ibid.: 50 (emphasis in original)). In contrast,

> The voluntary agency can free itself from local red tape and from the politics of the receiving country more easily than a donor government can. An Oxfam Field Director can give help to local labour to build a brace of wells while the visiting dignitaries from the World Bank and the local politicians are still being photographed at the airport . . . (Andrew Smith, quoted in ibid.: 42).

Until well into the 1970s a reciprocal disdain of NGOs was often expressed by donor governments. In emergencies, for example, voluntary agencies would sometimes be derided as 'as bleeding hearts where each [NGO] wanted to be the first and where problems arise with coordinating the junk that the public immediately unleashes from its medicine cabinets and closets' (USAID official in 1980, quoted in Kent 1987: 85). Despite such views the NGO movement enjoyed a moral superiority with regard to 'top down' official aid. It saw itself as working with communities from the 'bottom up', employing highly motivated staff and, due to lack of bureaucracy, able to innovate. NGOs were 'unfettered by high administrative costs; they were dealing directly with the afflicted; and they were not so ostensibly embroiled in the political machinations of recipient governments' (ibid.). They were 'freer from political bias and distortion than official government programmes' (Whitaker 1983: 49).

The international political architecture of the Cold War combined respect for territorial integrity with non-interference in domestic affairs. From the 'non-governmental' perspective of the NGO movement, the liminal space in which it expanded was bound on one side by corrupt, ineffective and often violent Third World states and on the other by complicit, bureaucratic and hidebound Western governments and multilateral aid organizations. At this time the interconnection between development and security was largely geopolitical in nature. Official aid was used to cement international political alliances favouring the West and against the Soviet Union and the spread of communism. Compared with today, the liminality of the NGO movement gave it room for manoeuvre in relation to Western foreign policy. At this time it was acknowledged that 'NGOs can operate in countries their governments do not favour' (ibid.: 50). Examples during the 1970s included Cambodia, Vietnam, Ethiopia and Nicaragua. Western foreign policy generally favoured the isolation of such regimes. Brandishing their neutrality, NGOs were able to work in these countries because unlike *some governments with their aid NGOs do not seek to turn recipient countries into political colonies*. And unlike the IMF and World Bank, NGOs do not dictate internal economic and social policies' (ibid. (emphasis in original)).

Based on the permanent emergency of self-reliance, an NGO petty sovereignty over international surplus life expanded within the liminal space between Third World corruption and Western complicity. This room for manoeuvre significantly narrowed with the ending of the Cold War. As will be discussed in chapters 3 and 4, NGOs were not simply taken over by donor governments or just turned into auxiliaries of Western foreign policy; rather the independent sovereign power they already enjoyed in the world of peoples was orchestrated, pulled together and given a new strategic direction by changes in the funding, direction and management of international aid. In short, the petty sovereignty of NGOs was governmentalized. An increasing security-related need by Western states to fund aid programmes acting directly at the level of population would encourage a new bout of NGO expansion and, as self-acting loci of power and authority, provide fresh designs and possibilities for liberal governance. The remainder of this chapter will examine sustainable development, that is, the community-level technology of security developed by NGOs among the world of peoples. Comments will also be made on issues of agency and comportment within the NGO movement.

Sustainable development: knowledge makes free

While facing great resistance, the nationalist project brought the contemporary world of independent territorial nation-states into being. Importantly, however, the doctrine of social advancement pursued by nationalist elites was not development in the sense discussed so far, that is, community-based self-reliance based around the small-scale ownership of land or property: it was state-led modernization. It involved what Cowen and Shenton (1996) have called constructivist policies that aimed to reduce the economic gap between the developed and the underdeveloped worlds. In this respect, newly independent states inherited much of the earlier attempts to reform the colonial system, including the marketing boards and producer cooperatives mentioned above. The emphasis, however, was on state-led modernization. This involved expanding public health and education bureaucracies, and, in order to catch up with the West, support for industrialization through import substitution and the protection of infant industries (Nassau Adams 1993). The construction of transport and energy infrastructures was also prioritized. During the 1950s and 1960s such policies found widespread support in the West. Economists such as Tinbergen (1954) and Myrdal (1957), for example, were concerned with the growing income gap between rich and poor countries and saw official overseas aid working in concert with local industrialization as a means of reducing it. Walt Rostow's well-known *Stages of Economic Growth: A Non-Communist Manifesto* (1960), apart from the subtitle capturing the way in which development and security were then connected, contains a similar vision. That is, how state-led industrialization supported by science and a modern public infrastructure would eventually allow the underdeveloped world to enjoy a standard of living similar to that of the developed. Rostow does not regard the emergence of the welfare state and social insurance in the West as integral to the development of consumer capitalism. Instead, through delineating various stages of growth, he offers a theory of modernization the aim of which is to achieve a condition of mass consumption. For Rostow, welfare equates with economic security and the diffusion of consumer durables and services. The welfare state figures only in passing as a spin-off or secondary effect of mass consumption and economic security.

At a time when international communism was competing with Western influence, Rostow's vision no doubt attracted many Third World elites. While the threat of communism has now passed, the idea of development as a process of modernization, whereby underdeveloped countries eventually come to resemble developed ones, still influences popular ideas of what international development is or, at least, should be. As Vanessa Pupavac (2005) has argued, however, despite having supporters in the West, from the outset state-led modernization was also accompanied by a rival liberal counter-critique framed by social psychology and emanating from the security concerns associated with social breakdown. These worries aptly reflect development's nineteenth-century origins as a means of reconciling the need for order with the unintended consequences of progress. This recurrent crisis of modernity (see Bauman 2001) contains a fear that modernization – with its associated redundancy of livelihoods, enforced change, unchecked urbanization and population growth – inevitably leads to social breakdown, anomie and insecurity. Speaking in the name of people, freedom and rights, the NGO movement was instrumental in articulating a liberal critique of state-led modernization in the Third World.

During the 1960s and 1970s, as mass society came into being, concerns grew in the West about the negative effects of consumerism, especially the creation of endless needs and, as a consequence, endless frustrations. Such views resonated with the bucolic anti-capitalism inherent within development thinking. In this outing, development began to embrace the prospect of moderating Third World expectations and wants 'for the sake of international peace and security' (ibid.: 169). Just as modernization had its supporters in the West, this moderating position was reflected by such prominent economic theorists as Kenneth Galbraith and Amartya Sen (see Pupavac 2005). The work of Ernst Schumacher, represented in his influential *Small is Beautiful: A Study of Economics as if People Mattered* (1974), is particularly important. It represents a contemporary capture of the nineteenth-century development doctrine of community-based self-reliance and its updating as sustainable development. At the same time it provided an intellectual rationale for the expansion of the NGO movement and the power over life it exercises.

Schumacher provides an anti-industrial explanation for the widely perceived failure of the first World Development Decade of the 1960s. At this time official aid was dispensed on a government-to-government basis and, reflecting its modernizing bias, what benefits it imparted were largely concentrated within urban areas and their associated classes. The conventional wisdom debated problems of modernization in terms of whether aid should be dispensed bilaterally or multilaterally, the effect of terms of trade, trade barriers, private investment guaran-tees, birth control and so on, as if these 'were the only things that really mattered' (ibid.: 161). For Schumacher, the problem was that state-led modernization only benefited the cities, bypassing people living in the countryside and small towns – that is, the majority of the population. The result was the so-called dual society, divided between an urbanized and progressive 'modern' sector and a rural and conservative 'trad-itional' sector. Rather than being transitional, however, Schumacher argues that the modern sector can never be expanded enough to include the whole of the traditional sector. Instead their relationship was one of 'mutual poisoning' (ibid.: 138), in which industrialization and urban-ization erode the social fabric of the countryside. In its turn, the result-ing surplus population takes its revenge through uncontrolled migration and non-sustainable urbanization.

Sharing concerns similar to those that gave rise to the colonial prac-tices of indirect rule and community development, that is, the threat to order posed by societal breakdown, a familiar developmental anti-dote was suggested: to extend an educative trusteeship over the surplus life of the countryside in order to support, energize and vali-date its existence in order to resist the anomie induced by progress. Schumacher having formed his ideas during the 1960s, the object of development was again reconfirmed as the poor, under-employed and resourceless. Schumacher's aim was to get this semi-indolent surplus population active and working. In this respect, the causes of chronic poverty were not material, 'they lie in certain deficiencies in educa-tion, organization, and discipline' (ibid.: 140). In rectifying these defi-ciencies, developmental trusteeship was again restated as a gradual process of evolution rather than a single heroic act of creation. Development had to penetrate the surplus population of the country-side. For this to happen, rather than the latest scientific advances, the fabrication of an 'intermediate technology' of cheap, robust practical tools and implements adapted to local conditions and capacities was required.[1] Apart from wishing to separate the Third World from tech-nological advancement, thus reflecting development's anti-capitalist tendencies, in order to absorb the surplus population Schumacher held that it was unnecessary for projects to be economically efficient

[1] A 1965 conference on technology and development organized by UNESCO formed the basis for the Intermediate Technology Development Group founded by Schumacher in London the following year. It is now called Practical Action (http://practicalaction.smartchange.org/).

or even, as a last resort, to be of great practical use. More important was that everyone should be active and produce something, rather than 'a few people should each produce a great deal'(ibid.: 145).

Compared with the economic concerns of modernization, what was being suggested was, in effect, a therapeutic 'non-material' development (Pupavac 2005). The practical implications of this form of development, which entered the policy foreground during the 1980s, are examined in chapter 4 in relation to Mozambique. For Schumacher the best aid is intellectual rather than material. Whereas material assistance can create dependency, a gift of knowledge is different: knowledge has to be worked at and acquired. Without a 'genuine effort of appropriation on the part of the recipient there is no gift' (Schumacher 1974: 165). Not only can material aid foster passivity and corruption, one can test that knowledge has been effectively grasped and comprehended. In this respect development as trusteeship has since the nineteenth century habitually favoured educational measures; not only do they lend themselves to an evolutionary framework, they allow for the monitoring and testing of progress. The active acquisition of knowledge in preference to material aid is for Schumacher so important that it matters little what is actually being done. It is knowledge, acquired through the discipline of organized activity, that 'makes them free' (ibid.: 165).

In removing the deficiencies in education, organization and discipline, Schumacher argued that the poor have simple needs. In satisfying these basic needs, however, their own methods are primitive and inefficient. They consequently required 'upgrading by the input of new knowledge' (ibid.: 167). Based on small catalytic inputs of self-help guidance and support, this non-material development 'also has the advantage of being relatively cheap, that is to say, making money go a very long way' (ibid.: 165). Taking advantage of this required the formation of international action groups that 'should ideally be outside the government machine, in other words they should be non-governmental voluntary agencies' (ibid.: 169). As Schumacher notes, by the mid-1960s many such groups were already involved in development. Operating at the level of people from the outset, many NGOs had been practising 'intermediate technology' for some time in their project-based work. Functioning as a practical framework for the biopolitics of self-reliance, projects can be seen as offering multiple sites for social experimentation. They can be used to test the ability and willingness of an emergent developmental life to change and strengthen its self-reliance through the acquisition of knowledge.

In terms of the flow of knowledge, projects are a two-way process. Not only do they impart knowledge to the beneficiary, but in exchange the NGO also gains knowledge about the development process. It follows that to be knowledgeable about development requires the experience derived from many projects. In this respect, however, the work of NGOs comes to little unless there is an 'an equally systematic organization of communications – in other words, unless there is something that might be called an "intellectual infrastructure" ' (ibid.: 169). Through the mobilization of administrators, businessmen and communicators, Schumacher envisaged an international matrix of projects interconnecting countries, regions and continents. With NGOs at the nodal points of such a knowledge enterprise, the matrix would operate as a transmission belt of information, directing those encountering problems in the field to places where there was a solution. It was a system of information that would not hold information in one centre and that was geared 'to hold "information on information" or "know-how on know-how"' (ibid.: 170).

While writing about NGO-supported international development, in some respects Schumacher anticipated Manual Castells's (1996) views on the 'network enterprise'. At the same time, however, making development more effective through harnessing the two-way flow of knowledge was based on a fear similar to that which drove the expansion of colonial indirect rule half a century earlier. That is, to stem the disintegration of rural life, for, should that disintegration continue, 'there is no way out – no matter how much money is being spent' (Schumacher 1974: 171). At the same time, however, if the poor are helped to help themselves, a genuine development is possible, a development without slums and misery belts around every big city, 'and without cruel frustrations of bloody revolution' (ibid.: 171). Unlike the surplus population faced by indirect rule, however, Schumacher's surplus life was now global in scope. It was a dilemma 'of two million villages, and thus a problem of two thousand million villagers' (ibid.: 161).

The question of agency: being the right type

During the 1950s and 1960s the expanding overseas voluntary sector, in terms of staffing both its home offices and the numerous charitable organizations working within the colonies and former colonies, would depend on people who, through colonial administration, military service, missionary societies or the business world, had come of age within the Empire. Oxfam's first Field Director for Africa (and its first permanent representative abroad), for example, was appointed in 1961 (Whitaker 1983: 22). He was Tristan 'Jimmy' Betts, the brother of the celebrated Labour politician Barbara Castle. For twenty-four years he had been a forestry officer in the Nigerian colonial adminis-tration. After Nigeria's independence in 1960, he worked for a while as a researcher for the Fabian Colonial Bureau. Following Betts's appointment, Oxfam's first African field office was in what was then Basutoland, a British High Commission Territory (Black 1992: 76–7), which became Lesotho five years later on independence in 1966. While there was an overlap in terms of personnel between the Empire and the expansion of the NGO movement, there was also an impor-tant and formative break. The men and women involved were of a special type; they were the sort who wanted to use their experience, skills and relative good fortune in 'giving something back' (Jones 1965: 208). Rather than a coming to terms politically with liberalism as a design of power, however, this was more a private distancing from the formal trappings and signs of Empire at the level of emotions and personal comportment. Like many in this heroic age of NGO devel-opment, Betts was 'a larger-than-life personality, given to extravagant behaviour which could estrange as well as endear' (Black 1992: 77).

Together with a mixing of irreverence, the main organizing princi-ples of 'giving something back' were those of self-sacrifice, modesty and service to others. In surveying the charitable works of such bodies as the Society of Friends, the Red Cross, Salvation Army, missionary soci-eties, together with the numerous expatriate-run local self-help groups which Oxfam was funding in the early 1960s, Jones (1965) describes a gallery of self-effacing volunteers – nurses, missionaries, ex-service-men, settler farmers and so on, all giving something back, usually living modest lives, and hoping for little in return except a greater awareness and support for the work they were doing. Jones's description of Dudley Gardiner is worth quoting at length. Gardiner had spent thirty-two years in the British army, mostly in India, and had risen from the ranks to become an officer. When Jones met him in the mid-1960s, he was working for the Salvation Army in Calcutta, running a soup-kitchen for the destitute. He lived in the Salvation Army Centre and, like the slum-dwellers he helped, had few material possessions.

> He works from dawn to dusk helping the poor and takes no salary. Most of his pension goes on maintaining eight bustee orphans at boarding schools. He is tall, broad, and upright, with an enormous untrimmed beard: he wears a loose shirt outside his trousers, and sandals. Thus he

looks so remarkably like Tolstoy that, if you met him in Hampstead, you would at once dismiss him as an ageing poseur trying to look like Tolstoy. Three things have to be realised: he wears a loose shirt because it is the habitual Indian dress; he wears sandals because the Japanese beat his feet so badly while he was a prisoner that he cannot wear shoes; and he resembles Tolstoy because he is the same sort of man. (Ibid.: 9)

In expanding the NGO movement, the right type was the person prepared to give something back, be it knowledge, patience, skill or time, while expecting little in return. Although there was an overlap with colonialism in life histories, in terms of subjectivity there was a contrast with the colonial administrator. The aid worker appeared as the alter ego or conscience of colonialism. Importantly, it established the basis for the move away from the masculinity of colonialism to the more feminine subjectivity of aid. It denoted a shift from ruling to helping and advising, from being an integral part of the system to being outside it, from being rewarded by the fruits of office to being satisfied that a debt has been repaid. This relational change not only defines the ethos of voluntarism; in shaping personal comportment it also indicates how aid workers would act on themselves to change their own behaviour and expectations – at the same time as changing the behaviour and reducing the expectations of others. By the early 1960s younger people, in their twenties and thirties, were joining Oxfam to help expand fundraising or publicity. One encountered journalists, photographers and advertisers 'who had abandoned without regret what used to be called the glittering prizes' (ibid.: 209). In attempting to define the 'Oxfam type' at this time, Jones makes the following social observation.

The regular Colonel started helping refugees in his spare time in Germany; the District Commissioner got unconventional ideas in Kenya; the research worker in anthropology began to sympathise as well as observe in Tanganyika. There is a strong representation of that particularly English type, the Establishment figure whose unorthodoxy is in the mind and not on the surface. He keeps going for years – maybe in the Army or the Foreign Office, maybe Shell or Unilever – effortlessly conforming to the uniform standard in speech and manners, but all the time thinking his own thoughts; then, when he judges the time ripe, he goes to Oxfam, able to unite his idealism and his habits of system and precision. (Ibid.: 209)

During the 1960s and 1970s, as the theory and practice of sustainable development were consolidated as the NGO alternative to permanent emergency, the ethos of a self-effacing, voluntaristic agency began to merge with this non-material vision of world development. Personal comportment became inseparable from the experience of development itself. It even impacted on the architectural design and spatial location of offices. Like the people in them, they have to send the right message. The building of Oxfam's new headquarters in Summertown, Oxford, in 1963, for example, involved a fraught question of design, with much debate on the best location, neither too remote or too close to the centre, as well as the appropriate building specification to reflect the values of an international charity. In the view of one observer, Oxfam House was about right. It was 'neither luxurious nor scruffy, neither ample in space – there is certainly no lounging room in the corridors or landings – nor cramped' (Jones 1965: 200). The building not only reflected the values of its occupants, it also projected a non-material, collective and homeostatic view of development based on basic needs and self-reliance.

While dependent on permanent emergency, the consolidation of sustainable development as the ethos of the NGO movement – indeed, as the only viable future for the world's surplus population – meant that it was necessary to explain the shift from relief to development to its public contingencies. At a time when official overseas aid still focused on state-led modernization through industrialization, buoyed by emergency-fuelled growth, NGOs became the ambassadors of people-centred, community-level development that emphasized self-reliance. In justifying its approach to the public, Oxfam's early educational activities, for example, targeted schools and universities. Thousands of primary schools were taking its materials in the early 1960s; these included project folders that related 'an Asian or an African child to British children, showing in what ways his life is similar and in what ways it is different' (ibid.: 217). Apart from maintaining public support, what was at stake in this relational exercise was stimulating a 'new way of thinking' about the world (ibid.: 213).

The two-way flow of knowledge between overseas development projects and Western public opinion, suggested by Schumacher, complemented the liminal space between Third World corruption and Western complicity. This was the space that allowed the linking of corporate identity to the experience of what development is. After more than two decades of uninterrupted growth, by the end of the 1960s Oxfam was feeling the strains. It was concerned with its ability to sustain expansion and, especially, to continue to attract young and committed professional people into its ranks. This gave rise to several years of internal debate, including the employment of management consultants, leading to a renewed focus on its public identity, advocacy and educational work. A sovereign power is that which is able to make the developmental distinction between the life to be supported and that which can be disallowed. Public education about people-centred development, its nature, challenges and dilemmas, becomes vital to explaining the agency's expertise and competence, thus legitimizing such a power and its self-appointed global mandate.

The OPEC-inspired oil crisis of 1972 brought to an end the long post-Second World War wave of Western economic expansion (Wallerstein 1996). At the same time, the interdependence of the world economy entered public view and debate. So, too, did concerns over the social and ecological limits to continued commercial growth. In 1974 a radical among Oxfam's middle-level management issued a memorandum arguing for a new partnership between the world's rich and poor. Rather than modernization or industrialization – approaches which were now in terminal crisis – the aim was to strive for justice and freedom through an 'equitable sharing of resources' in pursuit of 'basic human rights of food, shelter, education and reasonable conditions of life' (Richard Sharp, quoted in Whitaker 1983: 29). In this endeavour Oxfam's practical, people-centred knowledge, obtained through its direct support of community projects, was paramount. Projects alone, however, were no longer sufficient. Oxfam must also work to change attitudes between rich and poor, to shape public opinion and inform policy makers. Given the emerging environmental concerns and doubts over increasing consumerism, possibly using Oxfam staff as an example, Sharp advocated research on 'ways in which the people in the advanced countries can reduce their consumption to levels required for a more equitable distribution of the world's finite resources' (ibid.: 30). With the creation of a Public Affairs Unit in 1974 the broad thrust of this argument, while not without doubters, shaped Oxfam's organizational development well into the 1980s.

Whereas 'being the right type' was largely seen as an individual trait during the first decades after the Second World War, by the 1970s it became an expected part of NGO corporate identity. In particular, the interpretation of development as a more equitable sharing of the world's resources between rich and poor offered an important site of identity formation for institutions as well as individuals. In 1975, for example, Oxfam's governing council confirmed the objectives of the organization as relieving poverty and suffering in any part of the world. While this provided the basic ethos, it was not the only interpretation, however. Oxfam supported the essential dignity of people and their ability to overcome problems. Anticipating what would be understood as a 'complex emergency' in the mid-1990s, these problems were defined as multiform and variously 'rooted in climate or geography, or in the complex areas of economics, politics and social conditions' (Oxfam Council quoted in ibid.: 30). The generic solution to such complex problems was to advocate using modest inputs of knowledge and assistance as a catalyst in helping small groups to become self-reliant, at the same time as working for the equitable sharing of the world's material resources such that those non-insured, self-reliant groups would be able to exercise their rights to having basic needs satisfied and hence 'reasonable conditions of life' (ibid.).

While sharing the world's material resources equitably is, at best, a distant possibility, people within mass consumer societies can act on themselves now; they can reduce personal consumption and make lifestyles more sustainable. In this respect, the restrained personal comportment of NGO staff and volunteers can be partnered with the message of self-reliance through basic needs being promoted among the world's poor as a solution to their superfluousness. In this respect, Oxfam's 'patterns of consumption both personal and corporate should reflect the same values we work towards in our overseas development programme. The lessons learnt there should help shape our public opinion forming work, and our educational work' (ibid.: 31). It was expected, for example, that staff would give up threshold payments and regularly undertake unpaid work. In addition, new recruits joined on the understanding that salaries were 10–15 per cent below market rates; in the case of senior managers this dropped to 50–60 per cent. In a letter to all staff in February 1975, Oxfam's new Director summed up the purpose of this secular evangelism: 'what right have we to urge the poor to change, or the rich to alter their lifestyle, if we ourselves are disinclined to experiment and adapt?' (ibid.: 32).

Postscript

Until well into the 1980s the NGO movement was able to recruit most of its fieldworkers and senior headquarters staff from people who had already had previous overseas experience, through either volunteering, employment or academic research (Pratt 2003). Through the availability of such people, getting the right type was largely a process of self-selection.[2] Since the 1990s, however, with the continued expansion of

---

[2] The author, for example, joined Oxfam in 1985 as its Country Representative for Sudan, having completed Ph.D. fieldwork there as well as working at the University of Khartoum during the 1970s.

the NGO sector, new staff have tended to be university graduates lacking direct experience but having degrees in development studies (Jones 2003). One reflection of this change has been a growing technocratic culture within the NGO movement. At the same time, getting the right type is increasingly dependent on internal managerial techniques, especially staff training and identity awareness programmes. Rather than comportment being externally formed, it is now shaped internally. Compared with the stand-off a generation ago between donors and NGOs, and despite an increased emphasis on NGO identity and 'value-added', NGO and donor aid personnel are now generally regarded as interchangeable (Bookstein 2004). Indeed, successful career paths in the aid world regularly interconnect the two.

3 The Emergence of Contingent Sovereignty

This chapter takes a broad look at the transition from the Cold War to the post-Cold War period. In particular, it provides a background to the governmentalization of the non-state or petty sovereign power that NGOs had asserted among the world of peoples – that is, the absorption of this pre-existing, people-centred technology of governance and its redeployment as part of the strategic designs and policy preferences of effective Western states. Since decolonization, the international NGO movement has grown on the basis of the permanent emergency of self-reliance. The governmentalization of the aid industry and the post-Cold War re-expansion of the West's external sovereign frontier have also depended on emergency, in this case relating to the increased involvement of leading states in the funding and direction of humanitarian interventions associated with the internal wars and regional instabilities encouraged by the Cold War. Prior to the mid-1980s, Western involvement in humanitarian emergencies had largely fallen to independent NGOs. The step change in funding and political access, together with the collapse of the nationalist project of modernization in much of the Third World, encouraged a reworking of the relationship between development and security in the new and emerging zones of crisis and state failure.

Whereas NGOs had used the existence of permanent emergency as a means of expanding within the world of peoples, the involvement of Western governments in the 'humanitarian wars' of the early 1990s significantly reconfigured the international political system. It initiated a shift from the formal or *de jure* state equality of the Cold War to today's situation of actual or *de facto* inequality (Tamás 2000). This reordering is reflected in the pacification and reduction in the number of open civil wars within the global borderland as a result of increased multi-agency humanitarian and peace interventionism (HSC 2005; Strategy Unit 2005). Within a liberal problematic of security, the urge to protect life invariably gives way to a post-interventionary need to better it through proofing it against future emergency. Pacification has consequently yielded to a new and enduring phase of occupation or liberal trusteeship concerned with developing and remaking societies anew. The political architecture of the Cold War was based on a respect for territorial integrity and non-interference. While territorial integrity remains central, sovereignty over life within ineffective states has now become internationalized, negotiable and contingent (Elden 2006). Although pioneered as a liberal means of allowing people to exist independently of states, in seeking to secure surplus life development now acts to deepen governance by states within post-interventionary societies. In charting the emergence of contingent sovereignty, the mainstreaming of sustainable development is first outlined.

From modernization to sustainable development

While drawing on colonial precedents, the NGO movement consolidated the theory and practice of sustainable development during the 1960s and 1970s. At this time, sustainable development was a community-based technology of self-reliance that defined itself in opposition to states and the strategies of modernization then being pursued. With the rise of neoliberalism and the demise of state-led models of advancement, however, the idea of sustainability through self-reliance increasingly came to define official development policy. With its promise of accommodating concerns over the environmental limits to growth, sustainable development grew to become the developmental leitmotif of the 1980s. Its most common definition is that of the 1987 World Commission on Environment and Development. It is 'development that meets the needs of the present without compromising the ability of future generations to meet their own needs' (quoted in Bill Adams 1993: 208). While quickly entering official policy discourse, the conceptual rigour of sustainable development has been widely criticized as ill-defined. As Adams has argued, however, this lack of clarity was the reason for its success. It embraces 'diverse and highly complex ideas, yet manages to seem both unifying and simple'. It provides a mediating term between developmental and environmental specialists, not because of its analytical power but because 'of its tradeability, and the facility with which it could be used to package diverse and sometimes radically opposing concepts' (ibid.). In other words, like the more recent but related concept of human security, sustainable development 'is less an analytical concept than a signifier of shared political and moral values' (Mack 2002: 3). It is a mobilizing concept of governance that, in relation to the emergence of an international biopolitics of self-reliance, encouraged different and largely unconnected actors to interact and forge new, overlapping and hybridized assemblages of knowledge and power.

The entry of sustainable development into mainstream debate reflected the new acceptance and respectability of the NGO movement at the donor court. At the same time, it signalled that participative community-level self-reliance pioneered in the nineteenth century was formally adopted by multilateral aid organizations as the welfare policy of choice for the world's non-insured peoples. It represented a deepening of the biopolitical division in global population established during the period of decolonization. In the 1970s, for example, the International Labour Organization (ILO) supported a shift in emphasis away from industrialization and towards human capital, rural development and the promotion of Schumachian labour-intensive activities. At the time, it was evident that the thrust of international development thinking 'was turning against transforming the means of production and re-orienting around securing the basic needs of populations, primarily through policies of maintaining labour-intensive production' (Pupavac 2005: 171).

The acceptance of sustainable development marked a victory for the liberal counter-critique of nationalist modernization that had attended the process of decolonization and independence. It marked an end to earlier assumptions that, through state-led industrialization, the underdeveloped world would pass through various stages before coming to resemble the developed. Demanding a more equitable sharing of the world's resources in order to maintain the self-reliance of global surplus population, sustainable development breaks this aspirational goal. Its effect is to confirm a biopolitical distinction between insured and non-insured peoples. Rather than reducing the life-chance gap between the developed and underdeveloped worlds, sustainable development is better understood as a means of containing the latter. Poor and non-insured communities are expected to live within the limits of their own powers of self-reliance. Fuelled by environmental concerns and the need to stabilize migration flows, the acceptance of sustainable development by Western governments signals the emergence of a disciplinary and regulatory approach to underdevelopment now conceived as a homeostatic condition. When not overwhelmed by contingency and emergency, self-reliance is a system of dynamic adjustment, adaptability and risk management that, in effect, simply maintains the status quo. With its concern to reduce poverty by changing behaviour and attitudes as opposed to economic advancement, sustainable development is the coming of age of Schumacher's vision of non-material development.

Sustainable development rests on a relativist view of underdevelopment based on ideas of basic needs. During the 1980s, for example, comparative statistical evidence from China, Sri Lanka, Cuba and Costa Rica indicated that longevity was not confined to countries with high per capita income levels. While economic growth remains important, overall quality of life is not directly related to it. Indeed, the single-minded pursuit of economic growth can have detrimental social effects (Cornia 1987). A more nuanced approach to development was emerging that, while still encouraging economic growth, recommended acting on unsecured populations more widely and inclusively to improve health, education and economic activity. The importance of dedicated poverty-reduction measures, as opposed to simply relying on the trickle-down effect of economic growth, were encouraged (World Bank 1990). Capturing this trend, the United Nations Development Programme (UNDP) launched its annual *Human Development Report* in 1990 by dedicating it to 'ending the mismeasure of human progress by economic growth alone' (UNDP 1996: iii). Rather than growth per se, in terms of sustainable development social well-being is 'the result of complex interactions between individuals and groups endowed with different and changing amounts of knowledge and power' (Booth 1993: 56). Development became those practical interventions that act on these endowments in favour of 'expanding people's choices in almost any relevant way' (King and Murray 2001: 587). 'People' in this holistic and people-centred development are valued in terms of their ability to embrace risk and effectively manage life's contingencies.

Sustainable development reflects a neoliberal political agenda that shifts the burden of supporting life from states to people. It is a population, however, reconfigured in risk-management terms as social entrepreneurs or active citizens, in this case operating at the level of the household, community and basic needs. Development interventions create enabling choices and opportunities for such entrepreneurs to prove themselves by bettering their individual and collective self-reliance. Sustainable development is a security technology that attempts to contain the circulatory effects of non-insured surplus life by putting the onus on potential migrants to adjust their expectations while improving their resilience through self-reliance *in situ*.

Sustainability involves a developmental formula that aspires to an equitable and renewable sharing of the earth's resources. At its most basic level, however, the policy is seriously challenged. Rather than moving towards global equity, for decades Western politicians have proved to be either unable or unwilling to moderate mass society's hedonistic thirst for unlimited consumption. The inability to formulate a coherent response to global warming is but one reflection of this. At the same time, the expectation that those excluded from the feast – the international surplus population thrown off by a globalizing search for progress – will be satisfied with basic needs and homeostasis is, at best, unrealistic and, at worst, racist in its implications. The continuing toll of malnutrition, preventable disease and illiteracy, together with a rising flow of people looking for a better life or fleeing a bad one, graphically illustrates *the impossibility of self-reliance*. Faced with this global crisis, however, development as trusteeship simply reinvents itself as a technology of containment. Since the end of the Cold War, Western sovereign power has expanded through trying to control and manage this crisis rather than resolving it. Instead of permanent emergency standing as a damming indictment of the way we live, it is more likely to be experienced as an entrepreneurial opportunity to innovate in the face of a new and challenging threat (Strategy Unit 2005).

Emergency and contingent sovereignty

By the mid-1980s, the political architecture of the Cold War had already begun to come apart in Africa (Clough 1992). Drawn deeper into the quagmire of Afghanistan, the Soviet Union was a declining influence. Until this time, the respect for non-interference in domestic affairs contained in the UN charter had encouraged a restricted engagement by UN agencies and Western governments with humanitarian emergencies. In contrast, however, since the 1950s the NGO movement had expanded on the basis of recurrent emergency. It was not until the end of the bitter Nigerian civil war (Biafran war) in 1970 that a formal international relief system, involving states and intergovernmental organizations, began properly to emerge (Kent 1987: 52–3). Spurred on by the growing international refugee crisis during the 1970s (Suhrke 1993), specialist relief units began to appear within established government aid departments and UN agencies. While then only around 2 or 3 per cent of total Overseas Development Assistance, humanitarian aid was disbursed both bilaterally and through the UN system (Development Initiatives 2003: 14–15). In practice, non-interference meant that the main recipient of Western humanitarian assistance was the relevant ministry or department of the independent Third World state. Importantly, diplomatic etiquette demanded that such help was dependent on a formal request first being made. Since emergency appeals could be politically sensitive, sometimes heightening internal tensions through accusations of incompetence or complicity, 'the importance of this principle to recipient governments cannot be overestimated' (Kent 1987: 74). By the nature of their mandates, UN agencies only worked with internationally recognized governments. In comparison, NGOs had more room for manoeuvre.

Institutional distinctions between so-called natural disasters, such as floods, earthquakes and drought, and man-made emergencies, especially those relating to war and civil conflict, were well established in the Cold War period. Initially, the former were dealt with by government aid departments while the latter usually fell under the remit of foreign ministries. However, given that even natural disasters can expose political fault lines within weak states, 'there is a general tendency to clear more and more relief decisions with foreign policy counterparts' (ibid.: 80). At the same time, Western governments frequently alluded to the difference between development assistance and humanitarian relief in terms of the former being part of the politics of favour while the latter aspires to be *above* politics. Like development aid, however, Cold War humanitarian assistance tended in practice to reflect the process of geopolitical alliance-building. In the early 1970s, for example, Henry Kissinger held that US disaster relief was useful in cementing ties with friendly governments (ibid.: 55). Humanitarian emergencies, however, periodically broke into the public arena, not least because of the well-practised fundraising activities of NGOs and, by the late 1970s, the advent of video-based television reporting. Despite the diplomatic niceties of non-interference or the need to service political allies, emergencies often resulted in public pressure being placed on Western governments to act, or be seen to be acting. This was particularly problematic in relation to civil wars, which, since the 1950s, had been the most commonly occurring form of conflict (HSC 2005). In Biafra, for example, the British and US governments refrained in the late 1960s from helping civilians suffering under a Nigerian government blockade 'because their paramount interest was to preserve the territorial integrity of Nigeria' (Kent 1987: 81). Some NGOs ignored this official restraint (Black 1992: 118–31).

However, in war-related emergencies in pro-Soviet Ethiopia, Mozambique and Angola the United States was able to maintain its anti-Soviet stance while placating public opinion by channelling humanitarian assistance through UN agencies (Kent 1987: 83). While respecting the rules of the Cold War, some Western governments also used NGOs in a similar arm's-length way.

In the early 1980s the volume of international humanitarian assistance was less than a quarter of what it is today (Development Initiatives 2003: 5). At the same time, it was mainly directed through the relevant departments of the recipient state. Western governments, however, were coming to appreciate that in politically sensitive situations channelling humanitarian aid in a low-key way through ostensibly neutral NGOs could both satisfy public concerns and maintain the appearance of domestic sovereign competence. Indeed, few NGOs were unaware 'that non-governmental organisations do indeed serve a useful purpose for governmental donors' (Kent 1987: 84–5). At the same time, due to their growing capacity, effectiveness and quality of reporting, NGOs had begun to be compared favourably as implementing partners with more bureaucratic and diplomatically enmeshed UN agencies. Importantly, however, while Western states were becoming familiar with the informal role NGOs could play in difficult political environments, it was in relation to *maintaining* a creaking Cold War architecture rather than replacing it, in particular by respecting sovereign competence while 'reconciling the domestic pressures that governments face' (ibid.: 86). In the mid-1980s, this political architecture began to break down, not least because NGOs, embodying a liberal critique of the state, were pressing to expand beyond its constraints and limiting conventions.

The organizational neutrality staked out by NGOs in the liminal space between Third World corruption and Western complicity allowed them on occasion to take a humanitarian stance at odds with Western foreign policy. Apart from contesting the effects of total war, this has already been mentioned in relation to Biafra. It was also evident in Cambodia at the end of the 1970s (Black 1992: 281–3). Many Western governments chose to regard Vietnam's invasion of Cambodia and toppling of the genocidal Pol Pot regime as an act of external aggression. An official ban on international recognition and assistance, including humanitarian aid, was pursued. A number of NGOs, however, including Oxfam, publicly disregarded this boycott. This solidarist trend within the NGO movement also saw some organizations developing direct humanitarian links with political movements engaged in wars of liberation and self-determination. During the 1980s, for example, some two hundred international NGOs were involved in a discrete cross-border relief operation from Pakistan into war-torn Afghanistan, on this occasion having the tacit support of Western governments. Many of these worked with the different Muhajideen groups fighting to expel the Soviet Union (Baitenmann 1990). In terms of the emergence of contingent sovereignty, the low-profile NGO cross-border relief operation that ran from Sudan into Eritrea and Ethiopia's northern province of Tigray during the 1980s is particularly instructive (Duffield and Prendergast 1994).

Based in Khartoum, the Emergency Relief Desk (ERD) was established in 1981 as an initially Scandinavian ecumenical NGO consortium to channel publicly low-key humanitarian assistance into the rebel areas of Eritrea and Tigray. According to Duffield and Prendergast (1994: 65–74), ERD worked directly with the relief wings of the Eritrean and Tigrayan liberation fronts, that is, the Eritrea Relief Association (ERA) and the Relief Society of Tigray (REST) respectively. Typically, ERD trucked donated food aid to the Sudanese border, where ERA and REST officials took charge of its onward movement and local distribution. The involvement of indigenous organizations in this way was unusual in an NGO operation and attests to the political organization of ERA and REST. Although the Ethiopian military regime was classed as a Soviet ally, Western states frowned on aiding civilians in rebel areas other than through government institutions or officially sanctioned initiatives. During the early part of the 1980s, while ERA discreetly moved NGO-donated humanitarian supplies across Ethiopia's northern borders, official humanitarian assistance was confined to government-controlled areas and was channelled directly either through the Ethiopian government or approved UN agencies.

By 1984 the war and the drought-related famine had deepened significantly. In October that year, the BBC correspondent Michael Buerk made his famous televised broadcast from the refugee camp at Korem, shocking public opinion and initiating the Band Aid phenomenon. Some NGOs, such as War on Want, had been campaigning for several years regarding the Ethiopian government's repression and its manipulation of Western humanitarian assistance as a means of furthering its war aims (see Firebrace 1982 and 1984; Galloway 1984). Such agitation typically contrasted the illegitimate practices of the military regime with the accountability of NGOs and the efficiency of liberation fronts. Public pressure, together with the lobbying of USAID and the European Community by ERD consortium members, saw a significant shift in Western humanitarian policy that would have major implications for the emergence of contingent sovereignty more generally. During the mid-1980s major donors moved away from the government as their principal agent in Ethiopia and began to direct humanitarian aid through NGOs and NGO consortia. More importantly, for the first time the same donors also started to channel assistance through the discrete ERD conduit into rebel-controlled areas.

Several US NGOs, including Lutheran World Relief (LWR), had been lobbying USAID on behalf of the ERD consortium since 1983. In April 1984 USAID donated 5,000 metric tonnes of food aid to LWR in the knowledge that it would be used in the ERD cross-border operation. Later that year, following the international outcry over the famine, a further 23,000 metric tonnes were passed through the same channel. In 1985, despite their dual-use capability in a war situation, USAID also donated 150 trucks. Thereafter it quickly established itself as ERD's main supplier of food aid. As a means of balancing what was a major departure from political convention, within Ethiopia USAID agreed to a government-supported Food for the North (FFN) programme to feed civilians in contested areas from the government side. Rather than the government or the UN, however, USAID used NGOs – in this case the Catholic Relief Service (CRS) and World Vision – as its main agents. While the FFN initiative would do little more than feed government-held towns, NGOs henceforth became USAID's principal interlocutors within Ethiopia, including, in a low-key and indirect manner, rebel areas as well.

Regarding the European Community, ERD's initial contact was with what was then the EC's Emergency Division. This department, however, was governed by the Lomé Conventions governing the cooperation between the EC and developing countries and which, following Cold War conventions, ruled that humanitarian assistance could be given only to recognized governments. This excluded civilians in rebel areas and led Dutch Interchurch Aid (DIA), a leading ERD member, to begin discussions with the EC's Food Aid Division, which was not covered by the Conventions. Following the lead of USAID, in 1985 the EC also became a significant donor to ERD. At this time, however, such a policy change, even for major donors, was still politically sensitive. Not only did USAID and the EC use NGOs as a buffer between themselves and ERD (itself a cover for the liberation fronts), they both cloaked their support in the folds of their respective Sudan country programmes. For its part, the UN would not be drawn into any negotiations or actions regarding aid to rebel-controlled areas until 1990. By this time, the collapse of the Ethiopian regime was imminent. While the precise motives of those involved in the shift of humanitarian assistance away from states and towards NGOs can be questioned, it had historic implications for sovereign competence.

At a time when donor governments were adopting the precepts of sustainable development, through a growing familiarity with the sovereignty utility of the NGO movement, they were also learning how to use humanitarian emergency to govern in new ways. Compared with Biafra or Cambodia, where NGOs found themselves occupying the humanitarian vacuum created by Western geopolitics, Afghanistan and especially Ethiopia in the mid-1980s signalled an important sea-change. Ethiopian sovereignty had been effectively downgraded on two interconnected accounts: first, foreign non-state aid organizations were used in place of government ministries, and, second, through the legitimizing effect of aid transfer, domestic non-state opposition movements gained implicit recognition. Rather than prioritizing the Third World state, which had been the custom and practice of the Cold War, humanitarian emergency demanded of Western politicians new ways to act directly in support of civilians, irrespective of their location or side in a civil war. Humanitarian assistance, backed by the material, moral and political resources of donor states, could now penetrate the affected population more effectively and, through NGO outreach, could routinely operate at the level of the household and community. The political space of contingent sovereignty that had opened in Ethiopia would spread and deepen with the ending of the Cold War. In this respect it represented 'the first international humanitarian intervention of the modern, post-Cold War era. The West had begun its hesitant and confused journey to Kurdistan and Somalia' (Duffield and Prendergast 1994: 74). New post-interventionary possibilities for using this power over life, and the petty sovereignty of aid agencies that administered it, would begin to emerge. Contingent sovereignty is now synonymous with an array of liberal technologies of security that, together with their associated state/non-state coordination mechanisms and implementation arrangements, are variously acting on populations to alter anew the balance of power between social groups, resolve conflicts, support peace processes or reconstruct societies.

Negotiated access and the humanitarian boom

By the end of the 1980s the NGO-encouraged shift in Western humanitarian policy in Ethiopia had gathered a life of its own and had begun to replicate itself beyond the Horn of Africa. In relation to the newly exposed threat of civil wars, through official demands for UN involvement, contingent sovereignty initially took the form of what has been called 'negotiated access' (Duffield 1994). Until around the mid-1990s, when the setbacks in Somalia, Bosnia and Herzegovina, and Rwanda initiated a rethink and a turn to more coercive forms of international engagement (Eide et al. 2005), negotiated access was an important and innovative organizational tool of Western humanitarian intervention. It usually involved a UN specialist agency playing a lead role in securing an agreement between warring parties, including recognized governments and rebel movements alike, to allow UN agencies and accredited NGOs to deliver humanitarian aid under agreed conditions to civilians living or located in war zones. Established in April 1989, with UNICEF as the lead agency, Operational Lifeline Sudan (OLS) was the first of this type of operation (Karim et al. 1996). Other early examples include the Special Relief Programme for Angola (SRPA) and the Southern and Northern Operations in Ethiopia, both beginning in 1990. The lead agencies were UNDP and the World Food Programme (WFP) respectively. In 1992 the UN involvement in Bosnia and Herzegovina also took the form of negotiated access, with the United Nations High Commissioner for Refugees (UNHCR) in the lead role (Duffield 1994). On this occasion, however, the UN-negotiated humanitarian operation for accessing civilians also received military protection.

In terms of charting the biopolitical underpinnings of the transition to the post-Cold War period, negotiated access is historically important. At a time when the number of internal wars peaked, in the early 1990s, it signalled a normalization of the international condition as one of ongoing conflict and political instability. It marked a step on the road to unending war. During the Cold War not only was the demand for UN-led peacekeeping operations relatively infrequent, they were usually mounted only after a ceasefire or formal withdrawal had been agreed by the parties concerned (Goulding 1993). UN involvement was used to 'seal the peace' that Third World governments and warring parties had usually agreed. Accepting to work in unresolved internal war normalized political instability, elevated the moral authority of the West and established the right of aid agencies to access all sides and populations in such conflicts. As one reflective UN official put it, 'recent years have witnessed a kind of double lifting of inhibitions that had been largely suppressed by the Cold War's rules of the game: the inhibition to wage war and the inhibition to intervene' (Donini 1996: 7).

Within negotiated access programmes, lead agencies would typically agree a humanitarian action plan with warring parties. This might have included convoy routes and airfields to be used and the days and times involved, together with schedules and means of agreeing cargoes or verifying manifests. Negotiated access also involved codifying protocols governing the neutrality and impartiality of participating aid agencies. NGOs, for example, would be expected to sign letters or memoranda of understanding accepting the terms and conditions agreed by the lead agency. Fearing a loss of autonomy, many NGOs were initially reluctant to become involved in such operations (Duffield et al. 1995). Given the logistics resources and funding that these operations unleashed, however, together with the diplomatic protection they conferred in war zones, NGOs soon became a regular component. Consent was always fragile, however. Governments and rebel groups concerned respectively over the loss of sovereignty or Cold War patrons were reluctant fellow-travellers. In Somalia and Bosnia and Herzegovina, the military protection of the humanitarian operation saw the beginnings of what would become an expanding and changing civil–military interface (Williams 1998; Weiss 1999). In this respect, the ability to work in the context of ongoing conflict through negotiated access initiated the start of complex, system-wide forms of international intervention (Brahimi 2000). Such operations would create new possibilities in terms of centralizing relationships between Western states, UN agencies, NGOs, militaries and private companies.

Negotiated access and the ability of aid agencies to work within ongoing conflicts led to a boom in official humanitarian assistance. While the total humanitarian aid donated by Western governments had been growing slowly since the 1970s, it peaked in the mid-1980s at around US$2.4 billion, reflecting the war- and famine-related emergencies in Ethiopia and Sudan. The main take-off, however, occurred at the end of the 1980s, when, over the next several years, humanitarian assistance more than doubled, to reach an initial post-Cold War peak of $5.5 billion in 1994. Although this fell back a little over the next few years, beginning in about 1997 there was a second surge, which, by 2003, had reached an all-time high of $7.8 billion (Development Initiatives 2005: 5). This increase has been relative as well as absolute; growing steadily as a proportion of total overseas development assistance, in 2003 humanitarian aid accounted for 11 per cent of all Overseas Development Assistance. One can interpret the first, early 1990s, surge as a response to the new humanitarian market opened up by negotiated access. The second surge reflects the post-interventionary opportunities realized through pacification and reconstruction. Regarding the initial surge, the UN system-wide operations that emerged in Sudan, Angola, Mozambique, Somalia, and Bosnia and Herzegovina, for example, acted as an administrative sponge to soak up this new spending. Between 1987 and 1995, peace-keeping operations (both UN and non-UN) saw a sevenfold increase to thirty-five. At the same time they grew in depth and complexity (Macrae and Leader 2000: 9). Supporting civilians within war zones created unprecedented demands for expensive logistical support including lorries and, especially, airlift capacity. Compared with the personnel, organizational and logistical costs, the food aid, medical supplies and shelter materials distributed were relatively cheap.

The rising expenditure on relief with the ending of the Cold War is shown in the aid budgets of donor governments, UN agencies and NGOs. During the early 1980s the total emergency spending by the UK's Overseas Development Administration (ODA), the predecessor of the Department for International Development (DFID), for example, was between 2 and 3 per cent of its total aid programme; by the early 1990s, it had increased to 11 per cent. About two-thirds of the £90 million involved was being directed through the UN and NGOs. The same trend holds for the European Union. In 1986, 15 per cent of the EU's total aid expenditure concerned emergencies. By 1991 this had risen to 21 per cent (Borton 1993). With regard to UNICEF, the humanitarian boom was marked. Between 1989 and 1992, expenditure in emergencies increased by nearly 350 per cent to $167 million (UNICEF 1993). At the same time the proportion of emergency spending increased from around 7 per cent to 23 per cent of total expenditure. Increased humanitarian spending also led to the creation of new institutional means for its coordination. As a response to the difficulties surrounding humanitarian coordination in the first Iraq war (Duffield 1991), important administrative departures occurred within both the EU and UN. In 1991, for example, the European Community Humanitarian Office (ECHO) was formed to better coordinate European disaster assistance. The following year, the UN established the Department of Humanitarian Affairs (DHA, the predecessor of the Office for the Coordination of Humanitarian Affairs, or UNOCHA).

Contingent sovereignty and the external frontier

Frontiers present themselves in several different forms (Hirst 2005). Besides the fixed and mutually recognized borders of countries, frontiers can also be fluid and relational zones of interaction, for example the shifting lines of conquest, exchange and identity that marked the changing fortunes of ancient empires. These were spatial frontiers capable of advancing and retreating over time as they traced shifting political, economic and cultural spheres of influence. Development and underdevelopment can be seen as establishing a similar relational and anthropological frontier zone. As practitioners of a technology of security, development practitioners are able to decide the exception – that is, distinguish the life to be supported from that which can be disallowed. The relational zone that interconnects development and underdevelopment is a sovereign frontier. Chapter 8 argues that this zone can be understood as having both 'internal' metropolitan and 'external' overseas sites. As a technology of security, development interconnects the two. That is, it acts across and blurs the conventional national/international dichotomy. The internal frontier is associated with race, identity and entitlement, together with attempts to foster social cohesion and integration. Regarding development's external zone or frontier, using the example of the World Bank in Africa, Graham Harrison describes such a frontier as breaking with conventional narratives of intervention and statehood. He develops an historical understanding of a changing ethnographic space of interaction and negotiation that brings together international aid organizations, donor governments, recipient states and local institutions (Harrison 2004: 26–32). While in one way or another the West has always been present in this zone, it is a relational, negotiated and contested frontier that can work both ways, so to speak, with the balance of power able to shift between national and international actors. Development and underdevelopment demarcate a complex and changeable sovereign frontier.

The external sovereign frontier is a zone of unequal interactions and power-effects interconnecting the institutions, agencies and actors of the West with the states, representatives and populations of the near- and non-West. It is a space of opportunities as well as resistance and threats. In this shifting and contested frontier, while continuities exist, forms of identification and exchange, degrees of interpenetration, bridging modes of discourse and the relative power and influence enjoyed by the West can vary. The colonial expansion at the end of the nineteenth century represented a major deepening of the West's external sovereign frontier. The nationalist anti-colonial struggle and independence weakened and pushed this relational frontier back. During the Cold War, respect for territorial integrity and recognition of sovereign competence favoured non-interference in domestic affairs. In Africa, for example, nationalist elites were able to dictate in large measure their terms of engagement with the international community. Today, however, following the increased interventionism of the post-Cold War period, the West's external sovereign frontier has once again deepened and become more intrusive. While territorial integrity is respected, within post-interventionary societies sovereignty over life is now internationalized and contingent. The frontier in Africa, for example, has 'irrevocably moved from national developmentalism to neoliberal conditionality' (ibid.: 32). In such places as Uganda, Tanzania and Mozambique, for example, donor governments, international financial institutions, UN agencies and NGOs now exercise significant control over the design and delivery of core economic and welfare functions of the state. This is examined in more detail in chapter 7.

While debt has been an important factor in the emergence of contingent sovereignty (ibid.), humanitarian emergency has been crucial in establishing the parameters and international architecture of post-interventionism as an enduring political relationship. Building on how the NGO movement had earlier expanded in the world of peoples, the discretionary post-Cold War ability of leading Western powers to declare states of humanitarian emergency had profound implications for the character of the external sovereign frontier. In a humanitarian emergency, ruling beyond the law means governing beyond international law, especially the post-Second World War settlement that supported non-intervention and *de jure* sovereign equality of states (Douzinas 2003). The ability of leading states to declare a humanitarian emergency – irrespective of the views of the state involved – has rendered its sovereignty contingent. Within post-Cold War development discourse, liberalism's recurrent dichotomy between civilization and barbarism reappears as the humanitarian differences between *effective* and *ineffective* states. This division, which highlights the differing capacities and political will of states, is the essential basis of human security and the responsibility to protect (ICISS 2001). While this is discussed in more detail in chapter 5, this distinction is the moral basis which the West has used to strengthen its external sovereign frontier and, at the same time, to justify the reimposition of a post-interventionary developmental trusteeship.

Most of the early UN-led negotiated access programmes were established as time-limited operations. That is, they were temporary 'corridors of tranquillity' or limited ceasefire arrangements to allow vital humanitarian access. During the course of the 1990s, however, there was a growing tendency among Western governments and UN agencies to redefine humanitarian programmes as more or less open-ended commitments to working in unresolved crisis situations. Like the NGO movement in early decades, the extending of the West's external sovereign frontier on the basis of emergency has produced countervailing post-interventionary pressures to consolidate through development. During the 1990s, however, the mutual conditioning between protection and betterment took a different form. Previously, in moving from relief to a developmental trusteeship, the NGO movement had faced a recurrent moral dilemma: the choice between the starving child who will die tomorrow and the many poor children who will lead wretched lives unless helped. By the mid-1990s, the strengthening of the sovereign frontier reflected by the pacification of internal war produced a similar consolidatory urge among Western governments and multilateral aid agencies. Rather than being couched in moral terms, however, reflecting the involvement of effective states, the need for post-interventionary development was now based on security grounds. Arguments concerning the negative effects of relief assistance, for example its creation of dependency, distortion of markets or, through diversion, prolongation of conflict, once again became common (UNDP 1994b; Buchanan-Smith and Maxwell 1994; Anderson 1996). The argument at the time, sometimes known as the 'development continuum', was that relief and development should be linked and that the former should not undermine the latter's goal of self-reliance. Towards the end of the 1990s, with humanitarian emergency having served its expansionary aims, this type of thinking coalesced into a consquentialist 'new humanitarianism', in which the alleged negative effects of relief were instrumental in producing a more limited and conservative view of humanitarian action (Duffield 2001).

4 Mozambique, Governmentalization and Non-material Development

Mozambique is now numbered among the donor-elected success stories of Africa. Together with such countries as Uganda and Tanzania, it is regarded as one of the continent's 'good performers'. Since the end of the 1990s a relatively stable donor–beneficiary government funding relationship has emerged in these aid dependent countries which Graham Harrison (2004) has called the 'governance state'. This is discussed in more detail in chapter 7. A governance state can be briefly described as a form of contingent sovereignty in which the international community exerts a good deal of control and oversight over the core economic, environmental and welfare functions of the state, that is, its core biopolitical functions. Of particular importance in this post-interventionary relationship has been the shift in donor funding away from project support through NGOs to funding through a jointly agreed donor–beneficiary government budget. This chapter, however, is concerned with another aspect of contingent sovereignty in Mozambique, that is, the donor-led shift from relief to development during the 1990s. Together with providing an example of the previously discussed role of emergency in extending the West's external sovereign frontier, this chapter also examines how, through the spread of public-sector management and auditing techniques, NGOs involved in rural rehabilitation and development work were increasingly aligned with emerging donor preferences through the latter's growing influence over project design and implementation. Premised on an economically undifferentiated African peasantry, although sustainable development involves a search for new forms of social organization, it remains committed to maintaining that non-differentiation. What emerges from an analysis of the documentation and views of practitioners associated with this process are the ambiguities, contradictions and silences that constitute non-material development in a post-interventionary setting.

The background to a 'complex emergency'

The civil war in Mozambique between the Soviet-leaning Mozambique Liberation Front (Frelimo) government and the Western-backed Mozambican National Resistance (Renamo) rebels gathered momentum during the early 1980s and reached its peak around 1987. It is estimated that by the time of the 1992 peace accords more than a million people, either directly or as an indirect consequence of the conflict, had lost their lives in this former Portuguese colony. Over 1.5 million refugees had sought safety in neighbouring countries, while 4 to 5 million were either war affected or internally displaced within Mozambique. The cost of material destruction is thought to have been in the order of US$18 billion (Hanlon 1991: 42). While the work of Richard Gursony for the US State Department (Gursony 1988), the FCO analyst Margaret Hall (Hall n.d.) and Alex Vines (Vines 1991) are exceptions, until recently there has been little examination of the war in Mozambique from the point of view of its local origins. On the contrary, the early involvement of the then Rhodesia and then, especially, South Africa in fomenting the Renamo rebellion has shaped the abiding impression of the conflict: an externally orchestrated by-product of the Cold War which had little purchase or political meaning within Mozambique itself (Hanlon 1991: 36). As the war grew in intensity, Frelimo was reluctant to acknowledge the extent of Renamo's reach and its destructive capacity. Indeed, there was a palpable tension between regarding the war as arising from internal tensions and wrongs, as opposed to seeing it as an externally supported programme of destabilization. These were not simply academic differences; in Mozambique they were tests of political allegiance. The view that the war arose from internal causes, for example, was ascribed to the political right, tacit support for apartheid and taken to imply hostility to the Frelimo government (Hanlon 1991: 69). Aware of these sensitivities, donor governments and NGOs tended to shy away from publicly commenting on the nature of the conflict, preferring simply to address its humanitarian effects. As the havoc wrought by Renamo grew, however, the need to find some way of recognizing the war's existence increased.

When the war did find its way into public debate, rather than through direct acknowledgement it was through the fabrication of a new way of speaking about conflict. Since this new diplomatic language addressed the war, it was an advance over the past. However, it also respected political sensitivities and, especially, it was careful not to apportion blame or responsibility. Thus in many respects it addressed the war without really mentioning it. From the late 1980s, Mozambique was increasingly being described in UN, donor and government circles as suffering from a 'structural' or 'complex emergency' (ibid.: 78; Borton 1994). Similar thinking emerged in UNICEF in Angola at the beginning of the 1990s. A complex emergency is understood as having multiple causes – economic, historical, environmental, social and so on. At the same time, in terms of shaping a policy response, it questions relief orthodoxy and embodies a move in conflict situations from relief to consolidating development. Rather than basing this shift on moral considerations, reflecting the interests of donor governments the idea of a complex emergency demands that development replaces relief on security grounds.

In what would become mainstream policy during the early 1990s it was argued in Mozambique that a complex emergency involved the conscious destruction of infrastructure and dislocation of population. Moreover, the destruction was not only physical; it included the dismantling of public institutions and, through the loss of productive capacity, poverty was increased. Although elements of this malaise were present before the war, it was being deepened and accelerated by it. Institutional decay and poverty were independent structural problems that, while intensified by the war, would persist even with its end. A complex emergency therefore required a different approach to relief assistance. After a decade of destabilization, relief assistance should be used developmentally to stimulate the economy and rebuild public institutions. Destabilization, for example, had forced people away from rural areas, rendering them dependent on food aid. Rather than prolonging that dependence, the displaced should be assisted to regain or establish productive self-sufficiency, even if the war was still ongoing. These ideas, current in Mozambique in the late 1980s, reflect how development and security would be reunited in the post-Cold War period – that is, how emergency was providing a bridgehead for more comprehensive and finely tuned interventions at the level of population. Compared with the 1950s, when poverty and underdevelopment were thought to invoke communist sympathies among the poor and alienated, this viral and adaptive way of thinking was now reworking development and security as a cause of internal conflict and institutional collapse that demanded new forms of trusteeship.

Since a complex emergency is multi-causal, political instability is understood as the product of the various expressions and modalities of underdevelopment. Emerging from many mutually reinforcing causes, complex emergencies are essentially apolitical; no special blame or responsibility is assigned to one party or cause. Although the notion of a complex emergency acknowledged the actions of the warring parties, their responsibilities were subsumed beneath the permissive mantle of a pervasive developmental malaise. As we shall see, one consequence of complex emergency thinking was for aid agencies to view the effects of the war largely in terms of cultural breakdown. At the same time, however, its radical contribution was effectively to abolish the political opposition between internal versus external views of the origins of the war in Mozambique. If negotiated access was the first significant post-Cold War tool of Western intervention, then complex emergency was its lingua franca. By April 1989, the term 'complex emergency' can by found in the documentation regarding the formation of the UN's Operation Lifeline Sudan (OLS). The following year, it emerged in connection with the establishment of the Special Relief Programme for Angola (SRPA) where seconded OLS officers had acted as advisers. It took the Gulf War, however, and especially the formation of the Department of Humanitarian Affairs (DHA) at the end of 1991, for the idea to enter the public domain properly. If the conflict was multi-causal and rooted in poverty and underdevelopment, then blame and responsibility were dissipated. A good example of this relates to Sudan. On several occasions in the early 1990s, the fundamentalist National Islamic Front government, in attempting to deflect criticism of its human rights record, argued on the floor of the UN General Assembly that it too was a victim of a complex emergency. In Mozambique this conceptual innovation allowed diplomats to make progress in both securing peace and gaining humanitarian access to non-government-controlled areas. Its economy of purpose was to make progress on access issues without, in effect, mentioning the war or exorcising its ghost. At the same time, it helped to extend the West's external sovereign frontier.

Reflecting Cold War restrictions, humanitarian aid was confined to government-controlled areas except for the closing stages of the war. Frelimo argued that providing assistance to civilians in Renamo areas legitimized the latter's destabilization policy (Hanlon 1991: 72–3). The multi-causal poverty-based language of complex emergency, however, eased this deadlock and supported the peace process. Helped by region-wide drought, by 1991 discussions for a ceasefire were already well under way. In April 1992 the UN called for a doubling of food aid over previous years to support the nearly 4 million estimated to be either war or drought affected. The emergency was now regarded as so severe that, on humanitarian grounds alone, Renamo-controlled areas had to be brought within the emergency operation. Among other things this required open negotiation between all parties concerning safe conduct for road convoys (Simkin 1992). The negotiating of humanitarian access, since it brought Frelimo and Renamo together, was seen as pivotal to the peace process (Edis 1994: 1). In April 1992 the government agreed for the first time that the UN could negotiate directly with the army and Renamo regarding humanitarian access. Both sides also requested the presence of the UN at talks in Rome to establish joint principles of humanitarian assistance. By the time the war ended, in October 1992, a number of agreed cross-line relief routes under UN and ICRC supervision were already in operation. Unlike other negotiated access programmes, for example Sudan and Bosnia and Herzegovina, which were decoupled from a peace process, that in Mozambique was firmly attached to it.

Since humanitarian aid had been confined to government-administered areas, it was felt that a new and impartial UN body was needed to administer the transition from war to peace. Following the Rome conference in December 1992 on the demobilization and reintegration of military personnel, the UN Office for Humanitarian Assistance Coordination (UNOHAC) was established. This created its own bureaucracy in which all parties were represented. During the reintegration phase these committees were important sites of humanitarian diplomacy, since opening up Renamo-controlled areas was a key aim. Initially having a planned life of one year, UNOHAC did not close until December 1994. By this time UNOHAC had overseen the return of 1.5 million refugees and 3 million internally displaced people. At the same time, around 80,000 military personnel had been demobilized. In providing relief assistance to both sides through the agency of joint administrative bureaucracies, it was seen by the UN and donor governments as establishing the ground in which peace could take root. Indeed, it is one of the few negotiated access programmes generally regarded as a success.

The changing relationship with NGOs

Throughout the war and during most of the 1990s, British aid to Mozambique was managed by the UK government's Overseas Development Administration (ODA). In 1997, following New Labour's election victory, it was replaced by the Department for International Development (DFID). While ODA was a section within the Foreign and Commonwealth Office, DFID was established as a separate ministry. However, most of the managers, field officers and advisers working for ODA transferred as a matter of course to DFID. Although names and overall organizational structures changed in 1997, during the latter half of the 1990s there were continuities in both policy and personnel regarding Mozambique.[1]

The war and its associated humanitarian emergency provide the essential background for the growing number of NGOs involved in Mozambique, increasing from about 70 in 1985 to around 180 by 1990 (Hanlon 1991: 90). By this time, encouraged in particular by the United States, the EU and Britain and reflecting the post-Cold War changes discussed in the previous chapter, increasing amounts of food aid were being channelled through NGOs. Following Frelimo government policy, NGOs were regionally concentrated according to their national origins. (Indeed, donor assistance generally is subject to a high degree of geographical zoning.) Most British NGOs, for example, found themselves in Zambezia province in northern Mozambique. Through what was then the ODA, UK humanitarian aid was concentrated in Zambezia and distributed through such agencies as Oxfam, ActionAid, Save the Children and World Vision UK. Since relief operations were only conducted in government-controlled areas, in Zambezia this meant coastal areas and government towns where the displaced had sought refuge.

Although ODA relief assistance during the war was significant (for example, £12.7m alone was spent during 1993/94), no proper evaluation of its use or effectiveness was ever completed. However, in the mid-1990s, ODA officials were of the opinion that past relief was 'widely believed to have been a success' (BDDCA 1996b: 3). There was an evaluation, however, of the ODA's response to the 1991–2 drought in the southern Africa region. Mozambique figured as one of several

---

[1] The fieldwork for this analysis was carried out in Zimbabwe and Mozambique between April and May 1998. Previously unpublished, it was part of a multi-country DFID consultancy to help formulate its general poverty alleviation strategy.

case studies (Clay et al. 1995). While the ODA's overall performance was judged as timely, an important concern was its reliance on British NGOs for the delivery of food aid. Since these NGOs were concentrated in Zambezia – among the least drought-affected provinces – the ODA's relief assistance was similarly concentrated (ibid.: 5). The problem was known among ODA and embassy staff at the time and, with little success, NGOs were encouraged to operate in more drought-affected areas.

This lack of control is indicative of the loose, arm's length subcontracting that characterized the relationship between the ODA and NGOs during the relief phase. Compared with today, in programme matters NGOs had a good deal of autonomy. Indeed, the independence of NGOs during the late 1980s and early 1990s, and its alleged negative effects on government capacity in Mozambique, has received much criticism (Hanlon 1991). During the relief phase British NGOs were supported by the ODA's Mozambique desk in London. For emergency and rehabilitation projects several funding arrangements were available (Fleming and Barnes 1992: 22). In all cases, the support was generally regarded as flexible and non-bureaucratic. Moreover, until 1995, when the management of its central and southern Africa programmes was decentralized and based in Harare, Zimbabwe, contact between ODA London-based regional officers and the headquarters staff of British NGOs was relatively easy (interview, *World Vision*, 9 March 1998). Funding for relief and rehabilitation projects was usually provided on the basis of information supplied by the NGO concerned. The same NGO would then monitor and report on how the funding was used. For emergency assistance, no analysis of social impact was required (Holden 1993). Through this arm's-length subcontracting NGOs maintained significant independence. While this had been politically useful to Western governments during the Cold War, in the changed conditions of the early 1990s it was increasingly less so.

Following the end of the war and the move to rehabilitation and subsequently to development work, the position of British NGOs and their relationship with the ODA changed markedly. While the ODA's assistance kept its Zambezia focus, NGOs switched from food aid to rehabilitation and reintegration inputs as displaced people returned to their original homes, for example focusing on de-mining, road rehabilitation, bridge repair and the distribution of seeds and tools to returning farmers. At the same time, however, through the extension of public-sector management techniques to NGO projects, the development work that emerged from these interventions signalled an increasing centralization and governmentalization of the petty sovereignty of the NGO movement.

As soon as the war ended in October 1992 there was a general acceptance by the national government and aid agencies in Mozambique of the need to move towards development work as soon as possible. For many agencies the advent of peace was a sufficient condition in itself to allow development to resume. In April 1993, on the occasion of the Tenth Annual National Emergency Meeting, the national government declared an official start to rehabilitation and development work (UKHC 1993). Moreover, it called for steps to be taken to end the free distribution of food. During the 1992–4 period, based on its pre-existing connections with British NGOs in Zambezia, the ODA quickly moved away from providing food aid into support-ing reintegration and resettlement activities through its emergency budget. In all, in the four years from 1992, the British government spent around £20 million under its emergency budget; the majority of this, however, went to support NGO resettlement and rehabilitation activities.

As part of the British post-war aid programme, the ODA began to look towards supporting rural development work. As early as April 1993, for example, preliminary discussions took place on what would become the Scott-Wilson Feeder Road project. This shift of emphasis, however, involved a major change in Britain's relationship with NGOs. During Mozambique's emergency phase, NGOs had attracted some criticism, including donor allegations of confusion, poor coordination and lack of social analysis (BDDCA 1994a; Holden 1993). Funding for development would see a decline in the arm's-length subcontracting that characterized humanitarian assistance during the 1980s. A much closer relationship emerged between the ODA and the NGOs it sup-ported. In December 1993, in the first initiative of its kind, the ODA organized a workshop for British NGOs working in Zambezia to estab-lish common aims and explore the possibility of joint initiatives. As a result of this meeting the ODA funded World Vision's Zambezia Agricultural Development Programme (ZADP) in April 1994. In moving from relief to development, ZADP was initially conceived as strengthening food security through agricultural extension based on the research and multiplication of improved crop and seed types. In October 1994 the Scott-Wilson Feeder Road project started. Implemented by the engineering consultancy company Scott-Wilson, this project aimed at encouraging the emergence of local contractors

by training them in the use of labour-intensive methods of road rehabilitation. ActionAid, another British NGO actively involved in the
emergency, began its ODA-funded Participatory Extension and
Household Food Security Project (EPSAM) in January 1995. It was the
first time in Mozambique that the British government helped a col-
laborating NGO to design a development project from scratch. The
project also attempted to improve food security through agricultural
extension work, animal re-stocking and support for small enterprises.
These projects fed into the ODA's first formal development strategy
for Zambezia, which was agreed at the end of 1995 (Barrett et al. 1995:
Annex 2).

In order to increase the interaction of headquarter staff with the
field, around this time the ODA decentralized its management structure, moving many programme functions from London to its overseas
regional offices. Reflecting the strengthening of the external sovereign
frontier, Mozambique now came under the British Development
Division for Central Africa (BDDCA) based in Harare, Zimbabwe.
Borrowing and adapting public-sector management techniques associated with the privatization and marketization of the welfare state, the
ODA was able to formalize its new managerial control over what were
now NGO implementing partners. Procedures governing joint project
design, commissioning and implementation, together with protocols
for monitoring and evaluation, were established. Log-frame analysis,
allowing progress to be measured against agreed benchmarks, has
been particularly important. While not all NGOs would enter such
contractual arrangements, these moves were consistent with the
wider changes taking place. There was the parallel development of UN
system-wide emergency responses in Sudan and the Balkans, for
example, involving NGOs accepting UN operating conditions in
exchange for access. At the same time the EU was similarly tighten-
ing the management of its humanitarian assistance.

In April 1995, commenting on the recent elections and improving
economy, an ODA official remarked that Mozambique 'is rapidly
becoming a "normal" country. This is the background against which
we should consider our strategy' (Aicken 1995). Given that other
donor governments had replicated in other provinces Britain's move
in Zambezia, that is, expanded their influence through NGO-
implemented rehabilitation work, the idea of returning to normal is
misleading. Western states were for the first time in Mozambique able
to work at the level of population. NGO autonomy declines in relation
to their realignment and openness to state aims and objectives. The

same official, for example, went on to argue that the ODA should now think proactively in terms of 'how we should encourage NGOs in roles that go beyond service provision' (ibid.). It was also felt that NGOs operating independently of the state should no longer be encouraged. Rather, their 'development priorities must increasingly be consistent with those of the government' (Barrett et al. 1995: Annex 2). In July 1995 an ODA technical coordination officer was attached to the provincial Ministry of Agriculture in Zambezia to help better co-ordinate local government and NGO activities. Increasing donor involvement included encouraging implementing partners to deepen the social and gender aspects of their work, better target the poor and tackle such issues as communal land registration. At the same time, ODA sought to align these activities with government require-ments, indeed, to see NGOs as a means of strengthening government capacity.

In this context, governmentality (see Foucault [1978]), or the art of government, involved the drawing together of the plurality of autonomous aims represented by Western states, recipient govern-ments and aid agencies into a shared web of mutual interests and overlapping objectives. During the Cold War NGOs had distanced themselves from both donor and recipient states in the name of pro-moting an independent 'bottom-up' community-based development as opposed to the 'top-down' prescriptions of states and multilateral development agencies. Mozambique provides a case study in how, almost imperceptibly and for the best of reasons, that relationship irrevocably changed. An enduring post-interventionary terrain has emerged where NGOs, while remaining independent, self-acting and capable of respectful criticism, have come to see their own interests and those of their beneficiaries as overlapping with those of donor and recipient states. Through a process of mutual enmeshment, the administrative sovereignty of the NGO movement now works in new ways with and between donors, recipient states and beneficiary groups. In acting on the poor to encourage new patterns of behaviour and forms of social organization, for example, NGOs make surplus population visible and prepare it for capture and governance by the state (Bryant 2002). All of these changes, interconnections and power effects come together within the frontier zone of contingent sover-eignty. By the latter half of the 1990s, as the following account of non-material development suggests, in terms of political outcomes the differences between NGOs and states had become blurred and atten-uated. With regard to post-interventionary societies it is often difficult to tell when one ends and the other begins. In politically charged environments such as Iraq and Afghanistan, the result has been the deliberate targeting of NGO workers by insurgents.

War and the destruction of culture

The thinking that informed the ODA's initial development strategy for Zambezia is reflected in a 1991 agreement between the World Bank and the Mozambique government. Compared with the narrow economic focus of 1980s' structural adjustment, poverty reduction would henceforth take place through a more focused package of compensatory and enabling measures within the framework of continuing macro-economic reform. Government strategy now embraced a twin track policy of strengthening labour productivity and the provision of basic services (Fleming and Barnes 1992: 11). It focused on employment creation and income generation for the poorest people, including labour-intensive industries, family-based rural development and informal urban micro-enterprises. Given the ubiquitous assumption that African peasantries are essentially self-reproducing, the thrust of this policy was that basic services, together with associated enabling and compensatory measures, would *inter alia* improve the general welfare of the surplus population by encouraging small producers to participate more effectively in the market economy. This set of assumptions was reflected in the ODA's 1994/5 Country Strategy Paper which made the case for poverty reduction through fostering household food security in agriculture and fisheries by improving market access. To further this aim the ODA had 'approved two sizeable new projects in Zambezia to be implemented by NGOs' (BDDCA 1994a: E9). At this stage local social cohesion was then not an issue and, provided that the external market environment improved, increased production was felt to be sufficient to offer the prospect of sustainable development (BDDCA 1995: 15.2).

However, even as the ODA's Mozambique rural development strategy got under way, it began to attract in-house criticism. This came from the growing number of therapeutic social advisers within the ODA. Since the early 1990s their influence has been increasing within the agency's management structure at the expense of more traditional agriculturalists, engineers and economists. With the formation of the DFID in 1997 this trend has continued. The concern was that the ODA's strategy continued to rely on an economy-led view of development. It was argued that increased market access and support for labour productivity would not, on their own, necessarily reduce poverty nor, importantly, improve the welfare of the wider community. At issue was the extent to which the strategy either encouraged the better off, or was blind to the potential for worsening the situation of the most vulnerable. The solution was greater social analysis and the need to stimulate new forms of social organization, collective identity and behaviour that would strengthen community-wide welfare. Paradoxically, through the governmentalization of the petty sovereignty of the NGO movement, rather than embarking on a new departure, what was being reconfirmed as the solution to the problem of surplus population was a Schumachian, homeostatic vision of non-material development.

The project documentation relating to ODA/DFID support for rural development in Mozambique in the latter half of the 1990s offers a sobering glimpse of how non-insured communities are experienced through the doctrine of sustainable development. From the outset, however, it should be emphasized that this experience is shared with other Western donors, UN agencies, NGOs and government elites. It is part of the common discourse that supports and justifies contingent sovereignty. At the same time, as discussed in chapter 8, it reflects the Enlightenment tradition of equating a people's social character with its possibilities for political existence. Compared with the insurance-based welfare technologies of mass consumer society, there is a widespread and persistent assumption that non-insured communities are essentially self-reliant. Indeed, through community mutuality and local reciprocity self-reliance provides a viable alternative to centralized forms of insurance and tax-based welfare (see Deacon et al. 1997: 64). According to this ingrained viewpoint, African society has a high degree of family-based social cohesion and is largely self-reproducing in terms of satisfying basic subsistence needs. As a result, the extension of formally constituted welfare systems and safety nets is not only difficult, given the relative absence of regular employment, it is also unnecessary. Whereas earlier dependency theorists had problematized self-reproduction as encouraging backward forms of exploitation (Wolpe 1972), neoliberalism welcomes it. Self-reproduction is synonymous with communal reciprocity and high levels of social cohesion. Consequently it provides a virtually free social security system offering the possibilities of adaptation and strengthening in order to manage the risks of market integration. This distinguishes African rural society not only from life in the developed world, but even the fragmented and less cohesive milieu of African towns, including those of Mozambique (World Bank 1995: 4).

Reflecting these widely held assumptions, a review of World Bank and government policy statements for Mozambique by Cramer and Pontara suggests that

> Most of the literature is informed by an archetype of the African peasant smallholder, conceived as a stable family that produces on a small scale, virtually entirely on the basis of the labour inputs of family members, and that consumes a significant proportion of own farm output, having no access to other sources of consumption. (Cramer and Pontara 1997: 4)

Moreover, regarding the literature's representation of surplus population,

> [T]he poor live in extremely isolated and self-contained households with little access to productive inputs and little incentive to increase production; most of the poor live on small land holdings with great insecurity of property rights; in spite of some evidence of differentiation and apart from regional differences it is possible to characterise the poor as members of a fairly homogeneous peasantry. (ibid.: 8)

Perhaps unsurprisingly the ODA/DFID and their implementing partners subscribed to this general view. A World Vision representative, for example, described even the wealthiest people in the ZADP II project area as being poor by regional standards. Although World Vision attempted to target the poorest, 'it was agreed that everyone is poor so we really ought to consider the whole of the population. If the whole population improves, the poor will have improved' (interview, 14 May 1998). Some donors, for example USAID, took the view that because of this lack of economic differentiation in Zambezia, attempts specifically to target the poor are an unnecessary and complicating factor (interview, 14 May 1998). During the latter half of the 1990s, the prospects for sustainable development, especially the need to strengthen community mutuality, was largely addressed in terms of how the war and population displacement had impacted upon this allegedly relatively undifferentiated and self-reliant peasantry. As part of Mozambique's complex emergency, the war was understood to have weakened, if not destroyed, the social cohesion of an otherwise homeostatic rural society. In this respect aid agencies in Mozambique reflected the general policy consensus on the relationship between development, social cohesion and conflict (Collier 2000). The World Bank-supported Mozambique Participatory Poverty Assessment put this consensus particularly well and is worth quoting at length.

At the level of the household, mutual support networks work so as to reduce vulnerability to shocks such as food scarcity, seasonal stress periods, drought, or the illness of a family member. In many instances, these community-based mechanisms have been placed under considerable strain from household impoverishment. Conflict between traditional social structures and post-independence structures . . . has weakened community level networks and the effects of the civil war dealt a further severe blow to safety nets based on social and institutional relations which were already in a state of readjustment. The capacity to make claims of kin and community members is as much dependent on the holding of assets of supporting households and informal safety nets begin to break down when these households are forced to roll back their charity. (MPPA 1996: 9)

From ODA/DFID social commentary, the impression emerges that the war has not only weakened traditional social structures and thus local resilience, but through the mixing of culturally attenuated life-forms a socially ersatz peasantry has emerged. The following quote is from an ODA gender consultant studying the position of widows in Zambezia.

[T]he intense destabilisation of society through the war, the movement of people away from their ancestral villages through internal displacement, urbanisation and modernisation, ethnic inter-marriage, the introduction of a cash crop economy in traditional communities, has resulted in much less homogeneity within one ethnic group . . . The social organisation of the countryside has changed enormously because of the war years and it is not possible therefore to state precisely what is the custom and practice of either a patrilineal group or a matrilineal group. (Owen 1996: 5–6)

Not only has culture and social cohesion broken down, the resulting surplus population is, culturally speaking, so intermixed as to be almost beyond knowing. The inability to 'be precise' ethnographically, rather than reducing the involvement of social advisers and development consultants, appears to grow with their increasing engagement. It is as if their status as advisers is to confirm that rural society cannot be fully known. Consider, for example, a review of customary land rights in the Scott-Wilson Feeder Road project area. This revealed

a lack of information about the very diverse systems of inheritance and land ownership in the customary sector in Zambezia. There are different ethnic groups within the Zambezia province (e.g., Chuabo, Sena, Lomwe) each with different cultures and customary laws and institutions. In some areas patrilineal inheritance and land ownership systems prevail and in others matrilineal customary systems are the norm. These systems are not monolithic and are neither static nor simple to understand. (Nelson 1997: para 28)

Continuing the theme of social breakdown and anomie, in supporting World Vision's ZADP II project the DFID noted that sixteen years of civil war had

effectively destroyed most of the previous community structures through out-migration to avoid the conflict and removal of traditional social hierarchies and relationships. Following the Peace Accord of 1992 many people returned to their home areas to find almost complete destruction of housing, physical infrastructure and services and therefore in many areas communities started to emerge afresh from family units to help meet basic needs (DFID 1998: Annex 1: 1).

Not only did war weaken and mix cultures, rendering them beyond full understanding, but this loss forced a spontaneous rebirth of rural society in order to continue meeting basic welfare needs. Through war and displacement the countryside has returned to a natural state of family-based simplicity. Cleansed by the fire of war a surplus population, indeed, an Agambenian bare life has emerged, carrying little or no historical or cultural baggage. Although such assumptions would not stand up to serious ethnographic examination, that is not the point. To experience surplus population as devoid of culture and history is entirely functional for aid agencies in the business of creating new forms of social organization and identity: a blank page is all the better to write on. What we glimpse in these shared impressions is a surplus life destined for developmental trusteeship. It is a population that carries the burden of continually being tested on and valued for its ability to contribute to collective self-reliance. Rather than questioning the feasibility of self-reliance as a basis for existence, the aim of development is to reconstitute it through a monotonous process of rediscovering 'new and improved' varieties of the same thing.

The re-emergence of social cohesion

Among many NGOs the breakdown of social cohesion and increased anomie was associated with the deepening of ignorance and suspicion among the peasantry. In the Maganja de Costa district of ActionAid's EPSAM project, for example, an NGO official commented that 'people say that the community was fragmented during the war and that they are suspicious' (interview, 5 May 1998). A consultant evaluating EPSAM observed that

> [It is] difficult to develop trust. When you ask them about agriculture, the farmers think that you are trying to take their produce or land. This is common. In order to build confidence farmers have been taken to other districts to see what ActionAid is doing there. On one occasion some did not turn up. Later it was found out that they did not come because they thought that they would be sold as slaves. Work is slow in Maganja due to this feeling. (interview, 17 May 1998)

Similar problems were reported in World Vision's ZADP project area. In Gurure district, for example, a social survey had to be abandoned in 1997 due to the 'extreme suspicion' of the local inhabitants. World Vision mainly attributed this to political competition in the area and its failure to get agreement from the parties concerned that it could go ahead with its investigation (World Vision 1997: 11). Such experiences of cultural collapse, suspicion and lack of cooperation establish a background of low expectation against which signs of improving social cohesion can be watched for.

An indicator of the strengthening social cohesion is the extent to which project work was claimed to have encouraged the reappearance of traditional forms of mutuality and welfare support. An independent review of World Vision's ZADP project, for example, claimed that by helping to strengthen farmers' groups, the project 'is promoting the traditional system of "mutual help" with its associated role as a social security mechanism, of particular importance to the weaker members of the community. This programme is also helping to improve community cohesion' (World Vision 1996: 3). This view was reflected in the ODA's subsequent argument in favour of a ZADP II at the beginning of 1997. A second phase was necessary because, among other things, community cohesion 'is only slowly emerging, with limited development input, supply, credit and marketing services' (BDDCA 1997: 1.4; see also Hansell et al. 1996). This was reiterated by the DFID with the claim that traditional forms of self-help, for example collective agricultural practices in land clearance and seed exchange between households, have begun to reappear in parts of Zambezia (DFID 1998: Annex 1).

NGOs and donors, however, are not in the business of strengthening tradition; of greater importance for development is the creation of new forms of social organization and collective identity. By 1996 a fresh note had entered the documentation with the donor observation that for non-insured rural communities development projects 'will also encourage the creation of groups which may reintroduce a social security network of mutual assistance important for ensuring food security in times of stress' (BDDCA 1996a: 3). In this respect, the degree to which peasant farmers accept NGO trusteeship and pre-scribed methods of collective working is of great significance. In the words of a World Vision consultant,

> Through training programmes in group organization, activity planning, the allocation of responsibility and financial management, farmer groups . . . are learning that they can achieve more as a group than as individuals, thereby having a positive effect on community empowerment. (World Vision 1996: 3)

Beginning from a condition of cultural collapse and suspicion, NGO trusteeship is important on two accounts. Rural development projects help to restore confidence and, among an essentially autochthonous and self-reproducing peasantry, encourage the reappearance of tradi-tional forms of local mutuality. Since culture has been weakened, however, it is more important for development to create new and better forms of self-reliance based on more egalitarian social institutions and inclusive reciprocities among the non-insured. This, after all, is the business of project design and the reason why ethnographic precision is not that important. About this time – towards the end of the 1990s – the Washington consensus, based on structural adjustment and the assumed automatic trickle-down effects of macro-economic reform, was abandoned by the World Bank and leading states (Stiglitz 1998). In its place, poverty reduction through the transformative effects of increased social penetration and population management has emerged. Regarding rural Mozambique, the governmentalization of NGO petty sovereignty placed the promise of such transformative power in the hands of Western states, and with it the prospect of forging new collective identities and greater resilience. Rather than continuing to leave things to chance and the anonymous workings of the market, the focus moved to the positive encouragement and inclu-sion of those marginalized groups, such as the elderly and women, who might otherwise be left out.

Opposing economic differentiation

The abandonment of the Washington consensus did not so much create an antagonism between those favouring market mechanisms and those supporting greater social intervention; both accepted the primacy of the free market. It was more a question of the organizational competition and replacement of the old with the new; the economic and technical with the social and gendered. Regarding ODA/DFID development work in rural Mozambique during the latter half of the 1990s, this tension was reflected in the in-house competition between economic and social advisers. The emerging emphasis on social and cultural factors manifested itself in a tendency to oppose the involvement of rich peasants, merchants and commercial groups in development projects in support of more marginalized and excluded groups – that is, to oppose the social categories that the ODA's initial economy-led development strategy had, albeit indirectly, often encouraged. The emphasis now was on creating countervailing anti-elite, collective and egalitarian arrangements. As argued in chapter 6, a similar strategy evolved around the role of international aid in Taliban-ruled Afghanistan. From the beginning, the ODA development projects agreed with NGOs in the mid-1990s were criticized by internal advisers and outside consultants as lacking an adequate social dimension. The alterations demanded sought to counter any impetus the projects might have given to the widening of wealth differences within the communities concerned. The two examples given below illustrate different aspects of this process – that is, the opposition to rich peasants and inclusion of more women within the ZADP project and, in the case of the Feeder Roads programme, measures to help peasants manage the external commercial pressures stimulated by improved transport access. Alternatives were sought in the promotion of more inclusive forms of community identity and organization.

When the World Vision ZADP project began in April 1994, it was driven by immediate concerns to 'kick-start' the rural economy (Hansell et al. 1996). Like ActionAid's EPSAM and Scott-Wilson's Feeder Road project, while framed in terms of poverty reduction it lacked the social protection measures that subsequent project redesigns would demand. The ZADP project was intended to help the smallholder sector through use of research and agricultural extension to promote improved crop varieties and practices. It also had two wider aims; first, to improve food security and reduce poverty at the household and provincial level and, second, to enhance the potential for sustainable agriculture in central Mozambique. Although they were difficult to separate from the general improvement in agricultural production following resettlement, an independent evaluation in October 1996 formed a reasonably positive view concerning the technical achievements of ZADP's initial phase (World Vision 1996). It was less convinced, however, with regard to its institutional impact including strengthening local government capacity and, especially, its possible negative social consequences.

In the early stages of the project, despite the declared intentions of World Vision, the ZADP project included relatively few women and old people. The reason for this, it was argued, was that the original extension model relied on a number of contact farmers. These tended to be 'the more senior and respected members of the community' (ibid.: 2). With the encouragement of the ODA, World Vision took on a sociologist to work with the extension workers (interview, 17 May 1998). In early 1995 the extension approach was changed from contact farmers to contact groups. Consequently not only were more women involved, but also a wider community cross-section was included. In terms of ZADP II, the key objective included paying attention to the ability of different groups to mobilize labour and, at the same time, finding means of helping women reduce the burden of domestic work. In this way the project was seen as attempting to help all disadvantaged groups and ensure that 'a widening of social and economic differentiation and increase in local food insecurity is avoided' (DFID 1998: Annex 1: 2). It was argued that avoiding social differentiation helps to foster the collective ownership of the project (BDDCA 1997).

When the Scott-Wilson Feeder Road project began in October 1994, like the initial ZADP and EPSAM initiatives it followed an economy-led logic. By reopening roads and injecting some cash into the locality it aimed to provide a boost to the rural economy. While framing the project in terms of poverty reduction, the project designers were reluctant to include a clear social dimension. Poverty alleviation was regarded as flowing naturally from the promised economic upturn. It was assumed, for example, that most of the labourers employed by the contractors would be poor local people. However, apart from offering encouragement and suggestions, it was felt best to leave actual recruitment to the contractors themselves (BDDCA 1994b: 10.3). A similar hands-off approach related to the implications for the environment and land rights that improved road access implied, despite increased timber extraction and commercial land acquisition being acknowledged as possibilities. The prevailing attitude was that the potential benefits to the poor of improved road access outweighed any possible negative consequences of increased commercial penetration (ibid.: 11.2; Annex B, 2.3).

Over the next couple of years, as the Washington consensus weakened, entrusting poverty reduction to the market came under increasing criticism. In September 1996 an ODA consultant reviewing the Feeder Roads project argued that the improved road access, far from benefiting the poor, could actually exacerbate their condition. The evidence suggested that greater access was leading large commercial companies and politicians to apply for land concessions for agriculture and timber extraction. With the possibility of increased land values, local people's rights could be threatened and, in particular, land ownership could shift from the poorest to the richest classes. This 'may push original tenants back from the roadside into undeveloped areas and this could have various negative impacts such as pushing people onto more fragile and less fertile land' (Nelson 1996: 10). These risks led to the recommendation that a number of 'mitigating projects and . . . supporting community development projects' should be developed as a matter of urgency (ibid.: 10). The main recommendation was that ORAM, a local NGO specializing in land issues, should be contracted to work with the Feeder Road project. In particular, those local communities adjoining the improved roads should be encouraged to form rural associations to register a collective 'community land title' (ibid.: 11). This would allow local communities to negotiate with and, if necessary, resist pressures from commercial companies trying to gain land concessions. Similar mitigating work in relation to land rights was also incorporated in the ZADP project.

Non-material development

There is a tension in the concept of sustainable development as a privately administered small-scale trusteeship. While it might be possible through socially inclusive measures to benefit a relatively undifferentiated community in one locality, can similar welfare benefits be extended to the wider region or province? What prevents any benefiting local group from using its new skills or resources to increase the economic gap between itself and its non-project neighbours? How can more powerful outsiders be prevented from exploiting the infrastructure that development has created in one location? To elevate one particular group above its non-project neighbours is, like not wishing to strengthen the forces of tradition thereby widening social and economic differentiation, not an appropriate aim of a sustainable development project. Sustainable development frowns on measures that widen economic disparity and upset the undifferentiated nature of surplus population. It is a poverty reduction strategy based on creating new forms of social organization. At the same time, however, it wishes to keep everyone the same. This impossible tension is evident in the NGO and donor documentation. Consequent on the opposition to social differentiation, projects that leave non-insured groups and communities untouched, so to speak, are, paradoxically, singled out for support.

The initial aim of the Scott-Wilson Feeder Road project was to rehabilitate roads using labour-intensive techniques. Although the employment was temporary as the project passed through their areas, it was thought that the cash earned by local labourers would provide a useful boost to household incomes. In order to monitor the effect of the project, Scott-Wilson had collected socioeconomic data using its own social advisers since the project's early days. The data were used to establish a base-line against which improvements in the welfare of participating households could be assessed and compared with non-participants. This evidence suggested that some economic differentiation had appeared between project and non-project households. These differences, however, are played down by arguing that they are small and that, in general, rural society remains undifferentiated.

> Modest degrees of socio-economic differentiation at the household level are evident at present in terms of hectares currently being cultivated, cropping patterns, hiring of labour for agricultural tasks, commercialisation of items extracted from forests, production of small livestock, food reserves and consumption, expenditures and ownership of selected articles of value. Overall, project and non-project households are similar in most of these essential characteristics; in other words, the project households seem fairly representative of the larger population of the community. (SW 1997: B7)

An independent evaluation of the first phase of World Vision's ZADP project commented that since the end of the war in 1992 the province had generally experienced a slow economic recovery. Resettlement had spontaneously improved household food security and lessened poverty. Peasant farmers had been able to recultivate former farms and take advantage of the emerging rural markets. Indeed, given 'the general economic recovery, it is difficult to isolate the effect of the ZADP on food security and poverty' (World Vision 1996: 1). Not only was project impact difficult to discern regionally, even within the target communities its contribution to widening economic disparities was described as minimal. For example, a household survey revealed that many of the contact farmers with whom World Vision worked over the preceding two years had purchased bicycles, radios, beds, doors and so on. However, 'no real differences were detected in the ownership of household items selected as proxy indicators of wealth between Contact Farmers and Non-Participants' (ibid.: 24). The only partial exception was the 'Old Contact Farmers'. These were the rich peasants with whom ZADP had initially worked and had been criticized for doing so. That this group had made more investments than other farmers reflected 'the fact that they represent the better-off members of the community *rather than reflecting the impact of ZADP*' (ibid.: 24, emphasis added).

Paradoxically, development appears in this context to be valued in relation to its lack of economic impact and to the fact that it did not promote visible social differentiation. This is less surprising, however, when one is reminded that sustainable development is not a modernizing strategy of economic catch-up. It is more a means of improving the resilience of self-reliant life through new forms of social organization. This tension is reflected in development's longstanding opposition to industrialization and fear of its anarchic social effects (Cowen and Shenton 1996). Sustainable development critiqued and eventually replaced nationalist attempts to reduce the international income gap through state-led industrialization. The Schumachian people-centred development that emerged in the 1960s has never been concerned with strengthening economic performance per se. More important is the creation of new forms of collective ownership and identity geared to spreading welfare benefits through improved self-reliance. It is a homeostatic doctrine of non-material development.

If the aim of sustainable development is to reduce poverty without increasing economic differentiation, it suggests that poverty is understood in a non-economic way. Associated with the idea of a complex emergency, by the end of the 1980s the idea of structural poverty had gained prominence in Mozambique (Fleming and Barnes, 1992). Structural poverty in rural areas had depended on the isolation of those households that were landless or had inferior land, were female-headed or headed by aged or disabled persons, and were lacking in labour, assets or skills. Understanding the relative distribution of such disadvantaged households would suggest ways in which poverty could be reduced. Ideas of structural poverty emerged as a critique of earlier views of poverty based on measuring differences in income and consumption. By the mid-1990s, it was increasingly accepted that poverty resulted from a series of relative disadvantages, for example, access to assets or the role of gender or age. While attempts to measure inequality in terms of income and consumption remained important, there was growing criticism of this approach as misleading and narrow. Policy discourse was increasingly adopting the view that rural poverty, like a complex emergency, was a multi-causal phenomenon in which non-economic factors are equally, if not more, important in defining this status.

> Poverty is not simply a matter of low incomes and expenditures. Clusters of non-material disadvantage make up deprivation traps that have powerful resonances in community and household life. For example, physical weakness, isolation, vulnerability and powerlessness are aspects that are likely to be relevant to Mozambique's current situation. *The value placed by the poor on such non-material values as dignity may reflect the importance of their membership of social institutions through which they gain access to welfare.* A multidimensional analysis of poverty illuminates the complexity of causality at the local level and the shortcomings of unifocal poverty alleviation strategies. (World Bank 1995: 2; emphasis added)

This view directly complements the experience of rural society as economically undifferentiated. Only by thinking that everyone is equally poor can you argue a case for the non-material nature of poverty. Its corollary is non-material development that promotes new and inclusive forms of community mutuality. Rather than increasing income per se, poverty reduction becomes a process of managing and changing 'social status'. While this relates to economic status it highlights 'differential entitlements in respect of local social institutions and economic opportunities' (MPPA, June 1996: 6). Structural or multi-causal views of poverty highlight the importance of a household's or an individual's physical capacity, together with their social capital including an ability to control assets or mobilize labour. The growth of qualitative research methods, such as participatory rural analysis (PRA), has broadened the understanding of such factors.

> Cross-cutting all of these are issues of social status in terms of aspects such as gender, age, family and disability. Factors that could cause poverty are associated with vulnerability – notably lack of a partner, old age, lack of family or kin-based support, and disability. In farming systems where access to land is not restricted, a key issue in determining poverty is the labour capacity of the individual and household. (Ibid.: 6)

Reflecting this view, as already noted, the Scott-Wilson Feeder Road project viewed the peasantry as relatively economically undifferentiated. However, some of the stratification that did exist 'can be understood in terms of differences in family life cycle stage (i.e., age of the household head, family size, number of adults, etc.) which typically correlates with capacity to cultivate effectively a larger field' (SW 1997: B7). The view that rural society is economically undifferentiated does not contradict the assertion that disparities in social status do exist. While these differences can have economic effects, they are essentially non-economic in nature. They arise from the natural life-cycle of the family and the differential, and often discriminatory, entitlements and opportunities that rural society provides. For example, in terms of mobilizing labour, households can grow, mature and decay, with the status of its members changing along the way. At the same time, gender and age can be disadvantageous in terms of gaining access to resources, such as land, or maximizing local opportunities and commanding respect. Poverty and vulnerability are particularly associated with the inability to mobilize labour and work land. Consequently, questions of age and especially gender are of central importance. However, household growth and the differential access to entitlements often intersect, rendering poverty a multi-causal and complex phenomenon. This same quality also means that poverty cannot be regarded as a fixed condition. Even a woman's status can vary over the lifetime of a household. While rich and poor (relatively speaking) exist side by side in rural society, there is no intrinsic or fixed relationship connecting them. Rather than being mutually reinforcing, they appear almost accidental and subject to change. This multi-causal and transitory experience of poverty belongs to the domain of *natural economy* rather than *political economy*. A generation ago, a political economy view formed the basis of Third Worldism and defined Frelimo's founding liberation ideology. In this case, not only was rural society seen as structured by internal relations of power and exploitation, the same was argued for the external relations between North and South.

Gender, natural economy and land

Within a natural economy women epitomize all the obstacles and difficulties facing sustainable development. They have low social status and limited entitlements, and their position can vary greatly during the life-cycle of the household. As a consequence, in the project documentation women are represented almost exclusively in terms of the various impediments and restrictive social practices preventing them becoming effective and independent economic agents. If gender has become a potent symbol of the development challenge, it is also a motif of everything that is oppressive and backward in traditional society. In

Zambezia the gender issue has primarily been addressed in terms of its implications for food security and market integration (DFID 1998: Annex 1: 2). Thus for World Vision widows and female-headed households are unable to command much labour 'which results in the cultivation of small fields of poor quality . . . Helping the poor develop alternative sources of income would allow them to keep more of the food they produce, increasing their food security' (World Vision 1997: 1–2). Regarding Scott-Wilsons's Feeder Road project, out of a total labour force of around 1,500 only about 17 per cent were women (interview, 28 April 1998); moreover, the clear majority of these were unmarried (SW 1997: B1). The main reason given was that married women were expected by their husbands to remain in the household to take care of children, to do the housework and help in the fields. Moreover, the rapid transition from school to marriage 'significantly reduces the scope for women's participation in road rehabilitation work. Combined with practical constraints in terms of domestic obligations in both productive and reproductive spheres, cultural proscriptions limit married women's patterns of social interaction' (ibid.: B9).

For married women, their situation is a demanding cycle of food preparation, cleaning, child care and farm labour. In this role, apart from working in the fields, they seldom leave the homestead (Cuppens 1998: 8–11, 14). They therefore have few opportunities for off-farm income earning activity. In terms of agriculture, men take responsibility for the heavy work of land clearance, together with food storage and transportation. Women share in land preparation, weeding and transplanting. At the same time they take the main responsibility for harvesting, winnowing and crop processing (World Vision 1997: 26). In its support for World Vision's ZADP II proposal, the DFID argued that ergonomics could be used to free the labour of married women from household work. By this means, 'the project should ensure that all disadvantaged groups benefit and that a widening of social and economic differentiation and increase in local food insecurity is avoided' (DFID 1998: Annex 1: 2). The documentation argues that for female-headed households and widows their disadvantage is further compounded by not being part of a male household plus the wider discrimination inherent in community practices. Regarding the former, this is largely discussed in terms of the absence of male labour to clear new land, thus confining female-headed households and widows to small and infertile plots. Discriminatory practices mean that women also tend to be allocated inferior land (ibid.). Widows in particular, following the alleged destruction of customary rights during the war and the weakening of social cohesion, find themselves especially vulnerable. Indeed, protected neither by the law, custom or kinship, such women have little to rely on but themselves (Owen 1996: 5–6).

Gender is a powerful symbol of both conservatism and isolation within rural society; it operates to magnify all the previously identified problems of backwardness, cultural collapse, lack of social cohesion and so on. In this respect, it also relates to the issue of land tenure. Much of the land in rural Mozambique is held under customary law. In the late 1990s few households had legal title to the land they worked. Since the end of the war there has been a growing pressure by specula-tors and commercial companies to gain large land concessions. This has generally been treated with concern by the aid community. From research commissioned by World Vision, in 1997 nearly 4 million hectares of land in Zambezia had title claims pending. This represented about a third of the province's total area and, more significantly, two-thirds of its arable land (Myers and Eliseu 1997). The ODA and then the DFID responded to this situation by encouraging their NGO partners to build into existing projects the encouragement of communities to embark on collective forms of land registration and legal titling. Importantly, the thinking involved reinforced the overall aim of these projects: to encourage new forms of equitable social organization and identity while at the same time opposing the internal economic differ-entiation of rural society. Collective titling was seen as giving a measure of legitimacy to the new social bodies that project-centred trusteeship was attempting to form. Legally titled rural associations, for example, would be better placed to deter speculators and, at the same time, nego-tiate more effectively with outside commercial interests.

Aid agencies followed the liberal consensus on the relationship between production and land ownership as reflected by the World Bank and the government of Mozambique (MAF 1998: 2). Basically, secure tenure encourages farmers to invest, increase production and protect the land. In Mozambique the assumption was that quasi-markets already exist (ibid.: 9). The main task was to secure formal title for community associations, to bring them into the light so to speak, so that they would then be free to make whatever arrange-ments their members wished in a globalizing world. Such neoliber-alism exists in tension with customary land tenure practices which, in the British-supported project areas in Zambezia, remained strong (World Vision 1996: 29). Abrahamsson and Nilsson express this tension well:

[T]he norms which today control daily life for very large numbers of the population have deep roots in African society. A paradoxical situation has thus arisen where the legal systems have weak legitimacy, while there are legitimate systems for the distribution of resources and the administration of justice in local society which are not legal. *It is crucial for the state's future legitimacy that this paradox is resolved.* (Abrahamsson and Nilsson 1995: 180; emphasis in original)

The dualism between a formal and legalistic system suggested here, as opposed to a traditional and customary one, is presented as a problem for the state's legitimacy. The ethnographic deficit within aid policy has already been mentioned. Regarding land, it is argued, for example, that not only are there a large variety of traditional land tenure systems, they are also difficult to understand (Nelson 1997: para 28). Rather than more ethnographic research, however, reflecting the views of the Wisconsin Land Tenure Centre (Myers and Eliseu, June 1997), the Ministry of Agriculture and Fisheries believes that, essentially, there is no need to understand customary land tenure. What is required is that 'land policy and law need to create mechanisms which allow the two systems to interact' (MAF 1998: 8). In practice this means that it is up to the state, through the legal system, to decide how it wants to relate to rural society. Rather than understanding customary systems of land tenure as such, it is more important to examine their discriminatory and exclusionary effects, including their impact on women. According to a specialist land consultant working for Oxfam, organizations need to focus on land tenure systems that interact with wider political and economic processes to influence communities. In particular, 'how are local level systems influencing processes of social differentiation within communities and what has been the impact on particular groups such as women or non-natives?' (Kloeck-Jenson 1998: 2).

Together with the operation of customary household and agricultural practices, traditional land tenure systems are also problematized in terms of discriminating against women and preventing them from becoming effective, that is, free economic agents. While acknowledged to be varied and capable of adaptation, traditional tenure systems are also depicted as inherently conservative. Vested in lineages and households, they can exclude just as well as include. Moreover, for aid agencies, if the tenure systems pose a constraint, it cannot be treated as a technical issue. Both the government and NGOs need to work with local communities 'in developing a more gradual strategy designed to induce changes in the rules and practices governing access to land and natural resources as well as how a particular group or individual may use them' (ibid.: 8). Traditional land tenure systems and the subordinate position of women represent a challenge to the donor/NGO vision of new collective forms of community organization that promote equity without encouraging economic differentiation. They problematize existing rural society as resistant to non-material development.

In summary, sustainable development in rural Mozambique has a number of characteristics. It assumes a relatively homogenous African peasantry that is conservative in nature and isolated from the market. The position of women, however, disturbs this natural sameness by flagging what is backward and discriminatory in traditional society. While development strategies such as improving transport, credit schemes and other incentives to integrate rural communities better into external markets are supported, two main challenges present themselves: first, to discourage, by promoting new and inclusive forms of community organization and identity, exacerbating economic differentiation; second, to provide these new communities with a measure of protection against the more rapacious tendencies of the markets within which they have to secure their self-reliance. In addressing these challenges, gender is a prime concept. Since rural society is economically undifferentiated, social change is mainly a question of changing social status. This is shaped by the bio-social rhythms of the family, household and kinship – that is, the changing nature of natural economy. Because women form half the population, new and more egalitarian forms of community organization, especially those that free women from the unmediated demands of family and tradition, provide an important boost for sustainable development. While productivity and welfare gains increase, importantly, the community as a whole is lifted without increasing economic differentiation. Additionally, if these new communities are able to secure collective legal title to land, this affords protection against both exploitative market forces and the conservative bias of customary tenure systems. In this manner, gender and the position of women have been absorbed as a formative aspect of non-material development.

Concluding remarks

The above summary is constructed from the policy discourse examined in this chapter. As far as is known, it does not exist as an actual project or even as a rationale for a project proposal. It summarizes the urge to govern in a liberal manner, through the invocation of people, freedom and rights, that was shaping sustainable development in Mozambique during the 1990s. It reflects a biopolitics of population that not only takes community-based self-reliance for granted, it insists on rediscovering it within new and improved forms of community organization, new social structures better able to manage life's risks and contingencies. At the beginning of this book, attention was drawn to the glib axiom now current among Western politicians: you cannot have security without development, while development without security is impossible. It is a sobering thought that for hundreds of millions of non-insured people the only 'development' available to them – that is, those external interventions that seek to protect and better life at the mass level of population – is largely reflected in the experiences and practices outlined above. At the same time, for the West to stake its own security on such 'development' is, to say the least, hoping for a lot. The next chapter develops this analysis further by examining the idea of human security. Although human security prioritizes the security of people rather than states, it also holds that states remain vital for providing and protecting human security. In this respect, its examination indicates how the state has once again moved to the foreground of post-interventionary development discourse. In different ways, this state discourse forms the basis of subsequent chapters. It is not the modernizing state as previously discussed, however. It is a state more in tune with transforming the trusteeship of post-interventionism into an enduring political relationship.

5 Human Security and Global Danger

The idea of human security embodies a mobilizing relation of governance able to bridge the worlds of sustainable development and international security. It is usually defined as prioritizing the security of people rather than states. From this perspective, instead of conventional military threats, international security is menaced by the modalities of underdevelopment – such as poverty, health crises, environmental collapse or migration. Using more analytical terms, security is threatened by the permanent emergency of non-insured or self-reliant life and the surplus population it continuously throws off. Less frequently remarked in the literature is that human security also demands that states play a central role in protecting and securing people (Boutros-Ghali [1992]: 44; ICISS 2001: 8). In privileging states to prioritize the security of people, human security displays its credentials as a biopolitical technology. Since it seeks to highlight a 'human' dimension of security, it is often thought as having a universal or even progressive connotation. One has only to scratch the surface of human security, however, to realize that it remains wedded to the architecture of the territorial nation-state. In terms of the capacity and will to provide the public goods that support human security, it embodies a practical distinction between effective and ineffective states. Reconstructing ineffective states to better support the human security of the people living on their territories has moved into the foreground of development policy: the state is once again at the centre of development. Rather than yesterday's modernizing or industrializing state, however, it is a state that seeks to secure humans more in terms of sustainable development. This chapter also examines the related idea of the 'responsibility to protect' which, since the mid-1990s, has defined the moral grounds for international intervention. At a time of pacification, post-interventionary occupation and the deepening of contingent sovereignty, the responsibility to protect opens the way to a responsibility to reconstruct.

This chapter concludes with a consideration of the way in which the advent of unending war has impacted on the notion of human security, including throwing into relief the governmentalization of the petty sovereignty of NGOs that occurred during the 1990s.

Human security as a technology of governance

Human security is a biopolitical category.[1] It seeks to understand a world in which the geopolitical concerns of Northern states have been overlaid with a more diffuse and multiform threat associated with alienation, breakdown and insurgency emanating from the nominal populations of Southern states. Human security – the ability of the people of former protectorates and colonies to enjoy complete and fulfilled lives – has moved from the shadows of domestic affairs onto the international political agenda. Failure to achieve human security risks disillusionment, internal war and the mobilization of transborder networks and flows that threaten the cohesion of borderland states and hence the weft of global order itself (Carnegie Commission 1997). The need to secure humans, both for their benefit and ours, has attracted increasing policy interest over the past decade. Especially since the end of the 1990s, this interest has developed an institutional depth, accompanied by a growing number of related government, practitioner and academic networks,[2] university centres, courses and research initiatives,[3] publications,[4] official reports[5] and international commissions. Noteworthy examples include 'The Human Security Network', launched in 1999 at foreign ministerial level and involving thirteen different governments.[6] Also

---

[1] Some of the research for this chapter was made possible by an ESRC grant (RES-223–25–0035) within its New Security Challenges programme. I would also like to acknowledge and thank Nicholas Waddell for his work on the original grant.

[2] For example, the UNESCO Forum on Human Security (www.unesco.org/securipax/) and the Human Security News Association, bringing together freelance journalists and web-builders (www.humansecurity.org.uk). The Development Studies Association also has a Conflict and Human Security study group (www.devstud. org.uk/studygroups/conflict.htm).

[3] The universities of Harvard, Oxford and Tufts, for example, have established major institutes, centres or programmes dedicated to human security.

[4] For an extensive bibliography see Paris 2001.

[5] Key official reports include Boutros-Ghali (1992); UNDP (1994a); OECD (1998); ICISS (2001); Collier et al. (2003); CHS (2003); HSC (2005).

[6] Austria, Canada, Chile, Costa Rica, Greece, Ireland, Jordan, Mali, the Netherlands, Norway, Slovenia, Switzerland, Thailand and South Africa as an observer (www.humansecuritynetwork.org/).

significant has been the establishment in 2001 of an independent International Commission on Human Security,[7] co-chaired by Professor Amartya Sen and the former UN High Commissioner for Refugees, Sadako Ogata. In 2001 a separate International Commission on Intervention and State Sovereignty, in its report *The Responsibility to Protect*, suggested that human security is not only providing a conceptual framework for international action; 'there is growing recognition world-wide that the protection of human security, including human rights and human dignity, must be one of the fundamental objectives of modern international institutions' (ICISS 2001: 6).

While the effects of 9/11 initially overshadowed the work of the International Commission on Intervention and State Sovereignty (ICISS), its general thrust has proved to be of growing influence and, among other things, is shaping the ongoing process of UN reform. As a final indication of the now embedded nature of human security, in 2005 the Human Security Centre at the University of British Colombia published its first *Human Security Report* (HSC 2005), modelling it on UNDP's annual *Human Development Report*. While subsequent editions are planned, the first volume examines the broad relationship between human security and conflict. Within the literature, the rise of human security is often portrayed as resulting from a growing humanism within international relations that draws on the increasingly accepted norms and conventions associated with, for example, the UN Declaration of Human Rights, the Geneva Conventions, and the founding of the International Criminal Court (ICISS 2001). Human security appears as an enlightened way of thinking that broadens security beyond states to include other threats to life, for example, poverty, environmental pollution, population displacement and infectious diseases such as HIV/AIDS. Importantly, it involves 'a growing recognition of the role of people – of individuals and communities – in ensuring their own security' (CHS 2003: 5). In the words of Astri Suhrke, human security 'evokes "progressive values"' (quoted by Mack 2002: 3).

Rather than look at human security from a humanistic viewpoint, however, it is examined here as a relation or technology of governance (Duffield and Waddell 2006). Similar to sustainable development, with which it is related, as a concept human security is able to bridge divisions, blur established interests and bring together erstwhile separate sectors and actors. Being able to enmesh, order and coordinate different loci of power, human security is an important governmentalizing

---

[7] www.humansecurity-chs.org/.

technology within the post-interventionary frontier of contingent sovereignty. While quickly entering the lexicon of policy makers, human security remains somewhat controversial. Due to continuing realist concerns with state security, like the neglected study of civil or non-state wars, the idea of human security has made slow headway within mainstream international relations and security studies (Mack 2002: 3–4). At the same time, in bringing together development and security, human security has been criticized for its vagueness and capacity for wide variations of meaning, indeed, for even being 'slippery by design' (Paris 2001: 88). Even many of human security's proponents 'recognise that it is at best poorly defined and unmeasured, and at worst a vague and logically inconsistent slogan' (King and Murray 2001: 591). However, it is important to realise that human security 'is less an analytical concept than a signifier of shared political and moral values' (Mack 2002: 3). It is precisely its vagueness and lack of precision that enables it to work as a technology of governance within the external frontier zone.

Human security has the ability to work across boundaries, simplify complex ideas, create alliances and tie independent administrative or petty sovereigns together. In other words, rather than an empirical condition to be measured or compensated for, human security is more a mobilizing, integrating and colonizing concept of post-Cold War international governance. Achieving the aims of human security represents a vast, almost visionary, undertaking. As its keenest proponents recognize, to succeed requires complex forms of global coordination involving multi-levelled state–non-state agreement and extensive divisions of labour between governments, UN agencies, NGOs, private companies, civil society groups and militaries (CHS 2003: 130, 143). Moreover, these different networks require new global data sets, decision-making bodies and forms of centralization such that their discrete and scattered interventions to protect and better surplus life globally can achieve a coherent design. While development and security have always been interconnected, human security reflects the contemporary reworking of this relationship. In particular, it unites these terms on an international terrain of non-insured groups, communities and peoples.

The global envisioning and practical enactment of novel forms of centralization and interconnection between development and security are made possible by human security. These terms, however, are themselves the outcome of earlier constructions and mergers. In the case of development, human security relates to the already discussed notions of people-centred, human or sustainable development (King and Murray 2001). While emerging earlier, sustainable development, in bringing together ideas of community development and the environment, is also a bridging or mobilizing concept. Sustainable development emerged as a critique of state-led modernization strategies. It reiterated a self-reliant, people-centred view of development that decoupled betterment from any direct connection with economic growth (UNDP 1996: iii). Sustainable development is about creating diversity and choice, enabling people to manage the risks and contingencies of their existence better and, through regulatory and disciplinary interventions, helping surplus population to maintain a homeostatic condition of self-reliance. This has been examined in detail in relation to Mozambique.

If the 'human' in human security signals and values an entrepreneurial life that strives for self-management and self-reliance, then 'security' relates to those risk factors that threaten or menace the homeostasis of self-reliance. Human security embraces a liberal, people-centred problematic of security. It reflects the optimism of sustainable development with its promise of freedom and rights while also drawing attention to the 'downside risks' relating to 'the conditions that menace survival, the continuation of daily life and the dignity of human beings' (CHS 2003: 10). The 'security' in human security embodies the idea that underdevelopment is dangerous. It highlights those factors such as poverty, health crises, environmental collapse, conflict and population displacement that threaten and undermine the homeostasis of self-reliance. While appearing to be new it is, as already described, a view of security that can be found in nineteenth-century fears of social breakdown as well as the claimed link between poverty and communism at the time of decolonization. Such fears were then, as now, to be assuaged through a developmental trusteeship over the surplus population concerned. Since decolonization, however, as will be examined in chapter 8, fear of social breakdown has been increasingly connected with an urge to contain its international effects, in particular the spontaneous and destabilizing forms of global circulation associated with poverty, conflict and migration that the permanent emergency of self-reliance continuously unleashes. In this respect, internal war and political instability have a special significance for human security.

Internal war and the crisis of containment

Restrained by the certainty of nuclear annihilation, a liberal peace reigned in Europe during the Cold War. At the same time, however, superpower rivalry was displaced to the Third World, which became a cockpit of violent conflict. In this respect the end of the Cold War saw a brief period of international optimism. The decline of superpower rivalry, and with it the external sponsorship of competing factions within internal conflicts, brought hope that the founding values of the UN would at last be realized and the world reap the benefits of peace (Boutros-Ghali, 1992]). The break up of the former Yugoslavia and the international debacle in Somalia, however, soon changed perceptions. During the early 1990s, at a time when the number of civil wars globally was reaching its peak, a new consensus emerged within policy discourse. Not only was conflict continuing, its nature was changing. It quickly became accepted that today's wars, unlike the past, were increasingly 'within States rather than between States'; moreover, they were 'often of a religious or ethnic character and often involving unusual violence and cruelty' largely directed against civilians (ibid.: 7). Emerging at the same time as the idea of human security, this 'changing nature of conflict' theme became an established part of 1990s conventional wisdom (Kaldor 1999). It holds that these new wars, unlike traditional interstate conflicts, are largely civil in character, where warring parties not only show little restraint regarding civilians and human rights, they deliberately target essential infrastructures, livelihood systems and cultural institutions for political advantage, psychological oppression and criminal gain (International Alert 1999; Collier 2000; DFID, FCO and MoD 2003).

The 'changing nature of conflict' motif was an important part of the West's moral justification for the increased interventionism of the 1990s. It also helped to establish the problematic of human security. However, as an explanation of what is 'new' in the nature of war, it does not stand up to serious examination. As discussed in chapter 2, the Clausewitzian idea of contained warfare that functionally distinguished people, army and state never applied outside Europe and even there had visibly broken down by the time of the Second World War (Schmitt [1963]). Given this history, contemporary internal wars are in no way singular. Moreover, contrary to popular assumptions that most past wars were between states, since the end of the Second World War the clear majority of all conflicts have been civil or internal. As already discussed (chapter 1), from a peak in the early 1990s the number of such conflicts has halved under the impact of increased international activism (HSC 2005). In distinguishing conflicts of the Cold War period from those of today, what is important is not that the former were restrained regarding civilians and human rights while the latter are not. Although important for the West's own self-image at a time of international intervention and pacification, it is not the case. As part of the general erosion of the political status of non-Western states (Tamás 2000), the real difference is that the international community of effective states now denies any legitimacy to warring parties within ineffective ones. By the time of the Spanish Civil War in the late 1930s, internal war had become an established feature of international conflict. During the Second World War an earlier reluctance by states to foment insurgency movements in each other's territories gave way before a new-found legitimacy in supporting partisan forces operating in countries occupied by Axis powers. During the anti-colonial struggle, nationalism provided a framework in which the terrorism of insurrectionary violence could be recouped as politically legitimate (Seshadri-Crooks 2002). As a follow-on, supporting conflicts waged by irregular armies became an accepted, if often covert, part of Cold War superpower rivalry (van Creveld 1991: 58). These civil conflicts disrupted lives, displaced millions of people and, during the 1960s, coalesced to form an emerging global refugee crisis (Suhrke 1994).

Compared with the present period, the geopolitics of the Cold War bestowed legitimacy on the leaders of these civil insurgencies. Through funding, arms supplies and political patronage, the superpowers and their allies attempted to utilize the hopes and fears of colonial and newly independent peoples for their own strategic purposes. With the end of the Cold War, however, while civil conflicts continued under the weight of their own momentum, they rapidly lost their international political function. Indeed, those same aspirations, national hopes and dreams of freedom that had formed the contingent basis of a changing and destabilizing pattern of geopolitical alliance soon became a local policing problem for the victors of the Cold War. By the beginning of the 1990s, violent conflict, its leaders and, by association, their related forms of government had lost international legitimacy. Or rather, they awoke to find that their legitimacy had been withdrawn (Tamás 2000).

Reflecting the critical move from states to people, rehearsed since the 1960s in sustainable development, understanding conflict has also moved its locus from wars between states to conflicts within and across them. Like sustainable development, households, communities and populations furnish the terrain on which such conflicts are fought. Within this continuation of total war by non-industrial means, both development and war take communities, livelihood systems and social networks as their point of reference. For the former they are sites of entry, protection and betterment; for the latter they are the objects of attack and destruction, as well as providing the means of defence and resistance. In other words, both sustainable development and internal war – albeit for opposing purposes – take life or population and not the state as their reference point. Regarding their contribution to homeostatic self-reliance, policy discourse positions them as opposites. Where sustainable development supports and strengthens community-based self-reliance, and hence legitimate political identity, internal war attacks and destroys it. In other words, not only has conflict been delegitimated, political violence has been cast as a systemic threat to development itself and consequently, the ability of the West's moral trusteeship to contain the destabilizing effects of non-insured surplus population.[8] In a radically interconnected world, no matter how distant or seemingly insignificant the conflict, the security of the West itself is now threatened.

Sustainable development establishes an identity between community and security. During the 1990s conflict was rediscovered by policy makers as a threat to sustainable development. Secure non-insured people are those able to manage their poverty within the limits of self-reliance. Such a self-reproducing community is proof against the aleatory nature of life. Based on strengthening coping mechanisms and the encouragement of new forms of collective identity, a self-reliant community minimizes feelings of alienation and exclusion, and is thus a bulwark against the spread of political instability and internal conflict. Secure humans are able to resist the illicit rewards and dangerous enticements of violent leaders (Saferworld 1999: 69). At the same time, secure communities are less likely to provide recruiting grounds for terrorist networks (DAC 2003). For policy discourse, political violence destroys the homeostasis of self-reliance, wrecking public infrastructures, tipping livelihood systems into disequilibria and increasing the risk of enduring cycles of poverty, conflict and displacement. For the World Bank, a 'conflict trap' now interconnects poverty and state failure (Collier et al. 2003). Political violence, internal war and ineffective states undermine and destroy the ability of sustainable development to

---

[8] There is a counter-literature that has emerged as a critique of the conventional view of conflict in terms of breakdown, chaos and excess. Its contributors have variously attempted to rescue the rational, innovatory and political nature of insurgency. Rather than a form of social regression, conflict can also be seen as transformative, producing new flows, interconnections, modes of legitimacy, alternative systems of protection and claims to rights. See, for example, Chingono (1996); Duffield (2001); Keen (1998); Reno (1998); Nordstrom (2001); Richards (1996); Roitman (2001); Tishkov (1997); Schierup (1992).

contain surplus life. From this liberal perspective, political violence, indeed, political alterity becomes 'development in reverse' (ibid.: ix).

The inverse relation between self-reliance and political violence in development discourse is the basis of the monotonous truth of the post-Cold War era: you cannot have security without development, while development without security is impossible (DFID 2005b). Rephrased more analytically, without self-reliance *you cannot be free of political violence,* and freedom from political violence *is impossible without self-reliance.* Conflict destroys social cohesion and legitimate political identity based on community-based self-orchestration and the small-scale ownership of property. Set in place by decolonization, it is part of a general crisis of containment that has been deepening since the 1980s. This not only relates to displaced populations, migrants, refugees and asylum seekers, but also to the shadow economies, illicit commodity flows, international criminal networks, terrorism and so on that flow across and emanate from the world's crisis zones. These bad forms of global circulation typically associated with non-insured surplus population penetrate the porous borders of mass consumer society, damaging its social cohesion and destabilizing its way of life (Strategy Unit 2005). Framed by a crisis of containment, these concerns and interconnections are captured within the idea of human security.

Globalizing versus containing tendencies

Human security emerged as an organizing concept in the early 1990s, and had already developed a significant institutional depth prior to the formal commencement of the unending war on terrorism. As part of a biopolitics of self-reliance, human security interconnects security and development concerns – that is, both 'globalizing' and 'containing' tendencies respectively. While these terms are interconnected and mutually conditioning, much of the literature on human security exhibits either a globalizing security or containing development bias. Boutros-Ghali's (1992) *An Agenda for Peace* and the International Commission on Intervention and State Sovereignty's (2001) report *The Responsibility to Protect,* for example, are concerned with human security as an adjunct of an expansive and interventionist approach to international stability. On the other hand both UNDP's *Human Development Report 1994* and the Commission on Human Security's *Human Security Now* (2003), while sharing similar concerns over international security, focus more on the developmental and consolidating or containing side of human security.

The globalizing/containing distinction can be seen as reproducing

the mutual conditioning between protection/betterment already discussed in relation to humanitarian emergency. Regarding ineffective
states, *The Responsibility to Protect* uses threats to human security to
argue that sovereignty should now be regarded as contingent. It
moves the debate over humanitarian intervention from the realm of
international law to the terrain of moral duty (Pupavac 2005). In contrast, *Human Security Now* is more concerned with strengthening and
consolidating the resilience of self-reliant populations. While taking
for granted the moral case for intervention, it seeks to strengthen sustainable development through advocating a comprehensive programme of international coordination and centralization that will
ameliorate the risks and contingencies endured by surplus life in conflict, post-conflict and migratory situations. In general, however, the
immediate effect of 9/11 has been to emphasize the globalizing
security tendency within human security.

The different but interconnected globalizing/containing dimen-
sions of human security are also reflected in the international comportment of donor governments, for example Canada and Japan.
Both countries are at the forefront in promoting the idea of human
security. Canada, however, has been mostly concerned with human
security from a perspective of violent conflict, protection and
humanitarian intervention. In axiomatic terms, in a radically interconnected world, those states that threaten the human security of
their citizens threaten everyone. This particular human security focus,
in freeing defence from a traditional 'military threat' view of national
interest, has been argued to have rescued Canadian foreign policy
from irrelevance (Jockel and Sokolsky 2000–1). Along with Norway,
Canada was a prime mover in the thirteen-nation Human Security
Network established in 1999 at foreign ministerial level. It is also the
main sponsor of the ICISS. Japan, on the other hand, rather than
advocating intervention per se, has used its influence to address
human security from a containing or consolidating development
perspective, for example by advocacy on the various menaces threatening human survival: environmental degradation, violation of
human rights, international crime, drugs, population displacement,
poverty and so on. Japan is the main sponsor of the independent
Commission on Human Security that began its work in 2000; this
body has no Canadian commissioner. At the same time, Japan
declined to join the Human Security Network (DFID 2005b: 3; King
and Murray 2001: 590). These institutional preferences reflect the
globalizing/containing tendencies within human security. Just as

these tendencies are interconnected, however, institutional preferences are neither fixed nor immutable. With the advent of unending
war Japan, for example, has recalibrated its aid rules in order to fund
security-related activities (Christian Aid 2004: 22).

Reinstating the state

While human security embodies security and development inflections,
it is security that informs a state-oriented technology of intervention.
Although using the term 'human security' only once, one of the first
intergovernmental elaborations of the idea that threats to human well-
being rather than interstate conflict define global danger in the post-
Cold War era was UN Secretary-General Boutros Boutros-Ghali's
Agenda for Peace ([1992] 1995). As a prelude to the pacification of the
global borderland, *Agenda for Peace* was primarily concerned with
laying the foundations for a new international and governmentalized
regime of conflict resolution and peacekeeping. In this respect, it sets
the scene for the ICISS's *The Responsibility to Protect* (2001). In what is
today a well-established view of human security, *Agenda for Peace*
argues that the referent object of security is now the individual rather
than the state and that this broadens the definition of security to
include wider environmental, health, demographic, economic and
political issues (Boutros-Ghali [1992]: 42–3). At the same time, to
address these issues an extensive international division of labour is
necessary that includes not only states but also UN agencies, NGOs
and civil society groups working within 'an integrated approach to
human security' (ibid.: 44). However, from a biopolitical perspective,
the enduring importance of *Agenda for Peace* is that while prioritizing
the security of people rather than states, the ultimate responsibility for
securing humans is *passed back to the state*. While speaking on behalf
of people, freedom and rights, human security positions that state as
the ultimate guarantor of those rights. Consider the following quota-
tion concerning the achievement of an integrated approach to human
security:

> The foundation-stone of this work is and must remain the State. Respect
> for its fundamental sovereignty and integrity are crucial to any common
> international progress. *The time of absolute and exclusive sovereignty,
> however, has passed; its theory was never matched by reality.* It is the task of
> leaders of States today to understand this and to find a balance between
> the need for good internal governance and the requirements of an ever
> more interdependent world. (Ibid.: 44, emphasis added)

The italicized sentence is frequently quoted in isolation as testimony to the post-Cold War emergence of contingent sovereignty. The preceding two sentences, however, often omitted, qualify this idea. The paragraph as a whole appears to contain a paradox: *the state remains fundamental* although *the time of absolute sovereignty has passed*. While human security is about people rather than states, its enjoyment is conceived as unevenly divided between states. Some states are better able, or have more incentive, to support human security than others (Abiri 2001: 4). When Boutros-Ghali refers to the 'leaders of states' in this context, he is not thinking of the developed world. He is implicitly addressing the underdeveloped world, especially the incumbents of weak and failed states. He is addressing those zones of instability where the crisis of containment is deepest. One has only to scratch the surface of human security to realize that, in terms of capacity and political will, it embodies a distinction between effective and ineffective states. It is the absolute sovereignty of the latter which has passed. Human security thus overlaps and interconnects with ideas of state failure (Maass and Mepham 2004). The distinction between effective and ineffective states, with its associated delegitimation of the latter (Tamás 2000), is part of what Vanessa Pupavac has argued to be a normative change in the nature of post-Cold War international relations – that is, a shift from a Cold War system based on the *de jure* equality of states and its related principle of non-interference to one of *de facto* inequality associated with international intervention and contingent sovereignty (Pupavac 2001; van der Pijl 2002).

While implying a progressive, universal or cosmopolitan ethic, like human rights before it (Arendt [1951]: 229–31), human security has been reinscribed within the juridico-political architecture of the territorial nation-state. While the common definition of human security is prioritizing people rather than states, it can be more accurately understood as *effective states prioritizing the well-being of populations living within ineffective ones*. This distinction between effective and ineffective states, which is synonymous with the biopolitical separation of insured from self-reliant species-life, is central to *The Responsibility to Protect* (ICISS 2001: 5). In an interconnected and globalized world 'in which security depends on a framework of stable sovereign entities' the existence of failed states that either harbour those that are dangerous to others, or are only able to maintain order 'by means of gross human rights violations, can constitute a risk to people everywhere' (ibid.: 5). Indeed, there is no longer such a thing 'as a humanitarian catastrophe occurring "in a faraway country of which we know little" ' (ibid.). When a state is unable or unwilling to ensure the human security of its citizens, the Commission argues, 'the principle of non-interference yields to the international responsibility to protect' (ibid.: ix). However, while the security of people rather than the state is, like human rights and human security with which it interconnects, prioritized, the Commission remains wedded to reinstating the state. In this respect, a cohesive and peaceful international system 'is far more likely to be achieved through the cooperation of effective states confident in their place in the world, than in an environment of fragile, collapsed, fragmenting or generally chaotic state entities' (ibid.: 8).

Human security is but one indication that the state has once again reclaimed the centre ground of development policy. This time, however, it is not a modernizing or industrializing state concerned with reducing the wealth gap between the developed and underdeveloped worlds, it is a post-interventionary human security state tasked with containing population and reducing global circulation of non-insured peoples through promoting the developmental technologies of self-reliance. As Daniel Warner (2003) has pointed out, while the Commission talks in terms of interventions to protect human security, this is not taking place in the name of a universal or global citizenship and the need to create its supporting and inclusive institutions; instead, the responsibility to protect is a short-term international substitution for a failed state until a local substitute can take over. The responsibility to protect is part of what Michael Ignatieff (2003) has described as *Empire Lite*. In this respect, the Commission does not propose 'a responsibility to protect beyond the original state and it is in this sense that the Report is insufficient' (Warner 2003: 113). While emphasizing that human insecurity weakens state sovereignty, it does so 'without finding a responsible alternative' (ibid.: 114). Instead, it is assumed that a functioning state will follow from a failed state once transitory assistance is no longer needed. While this reflects the justifying rationale of post-interventionary reconstruction, as the situation in the Balkans, Afghanistan and Iraq suggest, winning the peace among the world of peoples has proved to be difficult, complex and long-term.

Containing underdevelopment

As a liberal technology of security, human security distinguishes between effective and ineffective states in order to assert an interventionist responsibility to protect. At the same time, the development inflection of human security is concerned with the practicalities of improving the resilience of non-insured groups and communities through ever more concerted efforts to support self-reliance (Chen et al. 2003). While these tendencies are distinct, they interconnect through a number of shared assumptions, for example the axiom that we now live in a radically interconnected world where the security of one person, 'one community, one nation rests on the decisions of many others, sometimes fortuitously, sometimes precariously' (CHS 2003). Moreover, while states are capable of menacing people and communities, for both they remain 'the fundamental purveyor of security' (ibid.: 6). Differences largely exist in relation to the nuances given to the interconnectedness and homeostatic nature of global existence. Building on these shared assumptions, globalizing security is more concerned with issues of international circulation – for example, how disasters or conflicts in one region have the ability, through population displacement, shadow economies or terrorist networks, to impact on other regions or countries. While accepting such risks, containing development focuses on creating a coherent and comprehensive international division of labour able to establish and support homeostasis; it seeks to secure the non-insured through the disciplining and regulatory effects of self-reliance. Development aims to embed security within the world of peoples by making it sustainable.

An early containing expression of human security is found in UNDP's *Human Development Report* (1994a). Here human security is defined as 'freedom from want' and 'freedom from fear' – that is, safety from chronic threats such as hunger and disease, together with protection from damaging disruptions 'in the patterns of daily life' (ibid.: 23). UNDP divides life's contingencies into seven interconnected areas of security: economic, food, health, environment, personal, community and political. Critics have argued that this list is descriptive and gives little explanation of how they relate to each other. However, UNDP's initiative has been influential, indeed, it was a 'unifying event' (King and Murray 2001: 589) in terms of launching human security as a governmental assemblage bringing together security and development. It has stimulated others to suggest more inclusive definitions (Thomas 2001) or more rigorous cross-cutting data sets in order to measure it (ibid.; Mack 2002). To date, the most comprehensive developmental evocation of human security is the Commission for Human Security's *Human Security Now* (2003). This report holds a holistic and interdependent view of human security similar to that of UNDP. Its division of the contingencies of population, however, is more dynamic and integrated with conflict and its effects (see also HSC 2005). It signals for special consideration, for example, human security in relation to conflict and post-conflict recovery, the protection of people on the move, economic insecurity, basic health needs and the need for non-inflammatory education.

The Commission defines human security as the protection of the vital core of human life through 'protecting fundamental freedoms – freedoms that are the essence of life' (CHS 2003: 3). Rather than presenting a particularly new definition or set of innovative ideas for the measurement of human security, however, the emphasis of *Human Security Now* is on encouraging the complex and extensive forms of coordination and centralization necessary for an international biopolitics of self-reliance to take institutional root. Important here is ensuring protection through the building of a coherent international infrastructure that shields people's lives from menacing threats. This requires working institutions at every level of society, including police systems, the environment, health care, education, social safety nets, diplomatic engagements and conflict early warning systems (ibid.: 132). In achieving such an ambitious vision of coherence, it is noted that there already exist numerous loose networks of actors including UN agencies, NGOs, civil society groups and private companies that are currently operating such agendas independently of each other. Rather than inventing something new, the task is more that of governmentalizing what exists – that is, ordering, structuring and tying these independent loci of petty sovereignty into a coherent governmental assemblage of overlapping aims and objectives.

> To overcome persistent inequality and insecurities, the efforts, practices and successes of all these groups should be linking [*sic*] in national, regional and global alliances. The goal of these alliances could be to create a kind of horizontal, cross-border source of legitimacy that complements that of traditional vertical and compartmentalised structures of institutions and states. (Ibid.: 142)

Human Security Now argues for an ambitious global framework for coordinating and integrating existing aid networks, programmes and data sets in order to ameliorate the risks and contingencies faced by non-insured peoples. Effective states have a moral duty to call forth and help coordinate these disciplinary and regulatory cross-border networks and relations. Since they would be collective public/private assemblages of protection and betterment, however, and not the design of a single state, the Commission on Human Security argues that when formed, these assemblages would have the international legitimacy to work with weak and ineffective states. It has already been argued that human security signals the return of the state to development discourse. The state in question, however, is effectively a post-interventionary human security state concerned with containing the effects of permanent emergency through strengthening the self-reliance of the peoples concerned. In this regard, the Commission has supplied an ambitious, multi-agency and cross-border vision of how this might be achieved. In a world of contingent sovereignty where the traditional national/international dichotomy has blurred, the future lies in the enmeshing of ineffective states within international public/private governmental assemblages having the developmental technologies and ability to work directly at the level of population.

Unending war, human security and NGOs

The post-9/11 political acceptance that combating terrorism commits the West to a war of indefinite length and depth has impacted upon human security as a technology of governance (Duffield and Waddell 2006). While already well under way during the 1990s, the fore-grounding of homeland security concerns means that issues of illicit and uncontrolled circulation – of people, weapons, commodities, money or ideologies – emanating from or flowing across the global borderland have reinforced development as a technology of containment. While development and security have always been interconnected, security considerations are increasingly evident in pressure to increase the amount of development resources directed to measures, regions and sub-populations deemed critical in relation to the dangers of radical global interdependence (Woods 2004). As President Bush's *National Security Strategy* (2002) sees it, the fruits of liberal democracy are under threat from a new global danger. In today's radically inter-connected world, in which national borders are necessarily porous, enemies are no longer the massed armies of opposing state encampments but their opposite – transnational global terrorist networks 'organised to penetrate open societies and to turn the power of modern technologies against us' (Bush 2002: v). Securing freedom necessitates stopping the spread of terrorist networks through closing home bases, preventing new sanctuaries from forming and stemming the proliferation of weapons, funds and recruits.

In achieving security, addressing the ungoverned space of failed and fragile states has been identified as pivotal. Whereas ineffective states were treated with relative neglect during the 1990s (Newburg 1999), they are now the subject of renewed policy interest; this theme is taken up more fully in chapter 7. While ineffective states continue to be associated with the criminality, breakdown and chaos that emanates from a sovereign void, that space is now regarded as vulnerable to colonization by forces opposed to the West and able to grow on the poverty and alienation of the non-insured peoples encountered. The new-found concern over fragile states indicates that unending war is not primarily a military concern. It is more an indefinite and globalized counter insurgency campaign that utilizes the civilian petty sovereignty of aid agencies to engage with questions of poverty and political instability. The *National Security Strategy* of the United States, together with the EU (Solana 2003) and the OECD states (DAC 2003), highlight development assistance as a strategic tool of unending war.

The OECD's DAC (2003) report, *A Development Co-operation Lens on Terrorism Prevention*, for example, suggests that while containing the effects of poverty and underdevelopment remains important, current policy has broadened to address issues of global circulation and inter-penetration. Insurgent populations, shadow economies and violent networks are the new global danger in a world 'of increasingly open borders in which the internal and external aspects of security are indissolubly linked' (ibid.: 5). Echoing the 1990s' 'the poor are attracted to violent leaders' argument (Duffield 2001: 127–8), the *Lens on Terrorism* sees terrorist insurgency as stemming from a sense of anger arising from exclusion, injustice and helplessness. In this situation, terrorist leaders, who may themselves be motivated by grievances and resentment, 'feed on these factors and exploit them, gathering support for their organisations' (ibid.: 11). The package of developmental measures designed to reduce alienation involves a set of interventions with the ultimate goal of building 'the capacity of communities to resist extreme religious and political ideologies based on violence' (ibid.: 8). Education and job opportunities become key, reflecting the concern that the new global danger does not lie with the abject poor, who are fixed in their misery; instead, it pulses from those mobile sub-populations of the non-insured capable of circulating and bridging the dichotomies of North/South, modern/traditional and national/international.

The privileging of the state in its role of guaranteeing human security has been reinforced by indefinite war. Indeed, the function of development in securing self-reliant populations has attained a new strategic importance. The shift from negotiated forms of UN intervention at the beginning of the post-Cold War period to the more coercive 'integrated mission' of the post-interventionary encounter is part of these changes; this theme is taken up in the next chapter. The international community is closing ranks and is now prepared to take on spoilers in the move from war to peace. Some NGOs, however, stress that there are problems in trying to harness development as a tool of homeland security. Arguments based on 'enlightened self-interest' often gloss over contradictions between domestically oriented security interests and South-oriented development priorities. The concern is that a situation is emerging where 'their' development is only important in so far as it contributes to 'our' security. Areas or sectors where such links are less apparent are liable to fall by the wayside. As the Commission on Human Security argues, current approaches to political instability 'focus on coercive, short-term strategies aimed at stopping attacks by cutting off financial, political or military support and apprehending possible perpetrators', rather than 'addressing the underlying causes related to inequality, exclusion and marginalisation, and aggression by states as well as people' (CHS 2003: 23–4). Similarly, the NGO members of the Global Security and Development Network have argued in a joint statement to the DAC that, despite flagging the importance of poverty reduction, the *Lens on Terrorism* can be interpreted as calling for 'the redirection of aid away from poverty reduction and towards a counter-terrorism and security agenda' (BOND 2003: 1; see also Christian Aid 2004; Woods 2004). While these shifts in policy are of real concern for many NGOs, that discourse now emphasizing the security role of aid has also reconfirmed the consolidating or containing effects of development. In this respect, the advent of unending war has thrown into relief the governmentalization of the petty sovereignty of the NGO movement during the 1990s. The shift from outside the state to being a central component of an enduring post-interventionary relationship has meant an uncomfortable period of adjustment for many agencies.

A number of NGOs and other critics have invited comparison between the securitization of development and the Cold War. The reappearance has been noted, for example, of official assistance, including arms sales and trade concessions, as a reward for political allegiance in the war on terror (Christian Aid 2004; Cosgrave 2004; BOND 2003; CHS 2003). In what Christian Aid has dubbed 'the new Cold War' it sees '*terrorism* replacing *communism* as the bogey' (Cosgrave 2004: 15). While this is an apt comment on the recurrent nature of the liberal problematic of security, a direct replacement is not taking place. During the Cold War, Western powers armed Third

World states in order to help them resist liberation movements seeking to remake the state in the image and requirements of the people. While today strategically located states facing Islamic insurgency are again being reappraised in assistance terms, this is taking place within a new interventionist front – that is, direct Western involvement in the reclamation of sovereign voids and the reconstruction of ineffective states in order to satisfy the basic needs of population. This is a post-Cold War phenomenon. Reflecting the discussion above on the containing tendency within human security, governance assemblages are emerging within post-interventionary societies in which the international community now has control of the core economic and welfare functions of the state, that is, its core biopolitical functions. This is discussed further in chapter 7. It is an aspect of contingent sovereignty in which the NGO movement is deeply implicated and involved.

Despite the fears of some NGOs that poverty reduction is being downgraded in order to combat terrorism, within policy discourse – if not aid flows generally (Woods 2004) – unending war has reconfirmed the central role of poverty reduction. The frustrations and alienation of the poor, although not causing terrorism, is positioned as providing a fertile breeding ground for recruitment. While reducing absolute income poverty remains important, 'approaches to inequality and exclusion should be given increased priority' (DAC 2003: 8). What is also being restated is that poverty reduction, as reflected in sustainable development, remains focused on creating new and inclusive forms of social organization among the poor. In this respect, there is a good deal of common ground within NGO concerns and criticism. At the same time many agencies have rediscovered at first hand the paradox of liberalism – that is, the ability to invoke freedom and rights while at the same time accepting the necessity of despotism. For some NGOs unending war has reversed the progress made during the 1990s in affirming human rights. The threat of terrorism has given states the opportunity to derogate from existing human rights treaties on the grounds of security (Cosgrave 2004). Not only has the practice of detention without trial reappeared, many members of the global 'coalition of the willing' have used existing legislation or have passed new national security laws which, critics argue, have used terrorism as a pretext for suppressing legitimate internal opposition. Human rights organizations have raised such concerns, for example, in relation to India, China, Thailand, Pakistan, Nepal, Zimbabwe, Bangladesh, Afghanistan, South Africa, Nigeria, Uganda, Kenya and

Tanzania (ibid.: 27–35). This repressive climate has had a negative impact on those NGOs working to empower civil society groups to claim rights and express legitimate political concerns. As reflected in the proscribing of organizations in the 2000 Terrorism Act (Fekete 2001), many groups that even a decade ago would have been regarded has having legitimate grievances over the arbitrary use of state power have now been outlawed.

Since the end of the 1990s many aid agencies have also been concerned with the post-interventionary closure of 'humanitarian space' (Macrae 1998), a concern that has again deepened in the aftermath of 9/11 (FIFC 2004). During most of the 1990s, military involvement in humanitarian emergencies was mainly in the form of providing logistical support and helping to protect civilian aid workers. Soldiers were not directly involved in providing humanitarian assistance. Since Kosovo and Afghanistan, however, this situation has changed (Donini et al. 2004). Due to the depth of insecurity and insurgency violence, as a hearts-and-minds force protection measure, the military has become directly involved in activities it calls humanitarian. This includes repairing essential infrastructure and delivering basic supplies (Gordon 2006). As some NGOs argue, however, such undertakings 'are more properly described as military intervention in pursuit of a political goal' (Christian Aid 2004: 23). However, to the discomfort of many aid agencies, military hearts-and-minds campaigns have highlighted the longstanding relationship between development and counter insurgency (Slim 2004b). Within crisis states generally, aid policy has increasingly been shaped by the political objectives of the intervening powers. In Kosovo, Sierra Leone, Afghanistan, East Timor and Iraq, for example, relief and development assistance has been given the job of strengthening the legitimacy of weak and fragile states and remaking such countries into showcase examples of the benefits of Western involvement. These post-interventionary demands place great responsibility on civilian aid personnel and draw them directly into volatile and exposed political processes.

At the operational level, in highly polarized societies such as Iraq and Afghanistan the most obvious casualty has been the *neutrality* of aid organizations. That is, their ability to lift surplus population above the political fray and to treat that rescued life solely on the basis of human need. The extent of polarization within these countries is now so great as to expose the secret relationship between neutrality and sovereign power. Unending war has collapsed the liminal space between state and society which the NGO movement had previously inhabited. An important consequence of governmentalization is that, from the perspective of their prospective hosts and beneficiaries, NGOs are now indistinguishable from the occupying forces with which they have often arrived or on which they rely for protection (Vaux 2004). Attempts by the NGO movement to draw a line between itself and the military within integrated missions has usually involved the agreement of codes of conduct separating respective spheres of responsibility (Gordon 2006). The bombing of the Baghdad head-quarters of the UN and the ICRC in August 2003, however, are graphic illustrations of the new and indistinct situation that NGOs now occupy in post-interventionary societies. Many have begun to ask whether the benefits that aid workers bring is 'now outweighed by the price that they are being asked to pay' (Foley 2004). Through the ambushing of convoys, rocketing of premises and booby-trapping of vehicles, more than forty aid workers have been murdered in Afghanistan in the twelve months to August 2004 alone. Currently, whole swathes of Afghanistan and Iraq are no-go areas for aid agen-cies. The shameful killing in Baghdad of the head of Care International, Margaret Hassan, illustrates the dangers that NGOs now face in defending the sovereign frontier.

Concluding remarks

Human security emerged during the 1990s as a centralizing and gov-ernmentalizing technology of international governance. In securing non-insured communities and peoples, it envisages bringing together existing practices, institutions and networks of sustainable develop-ment – that is, a horizontal and coordinated system of cross-border interventions, indeed able to complement, or temporarily replace, the efforts of ineffective states. Indefinite war confirmed this vision while giving it a new emphasis. Rather than simply prioritizing the security of people living within the territories of ineffective states, unending war has moved the security of homeland population, livelihood systems and infrastructures to the fore. It has privileged the role of effective states in deciding the security needs of others. In a radically interdependent world, defending the West's way of life is now premised on securing the global borderland of crisis states. While con-firming the consolidating and containing aspects of development, it has given an impetus to the urge to globalize security that human security also embodies. Complementing containment, a sharper focus on sub-populations and strategic territories distinguished by their potential to circulate and interconnect has gained ground in policy discourse.

Unending war has also made visible the governmentalization of the NGO movement. From being outside the state, the enmeshing web of mutual interests and overlapping objectives that was welcomed by many NGOs as a way of continuing to expand following the end of the Cold War now marks them out on the streets of post-interventionary societies, especially politically charged ones. Once the champions of 'grass-roots' solidarity within the liminal space between 'top-down' official development and donor complicity, some agencies now fear that they have become the accomplices of Western foreign policy (Woollacott 2004). Such concerns, however, are somewhat disingenuous. As discussed in relation to Mozambique, many NGOs supported the deepening of state–non-state linkages. Agencies that now endorse the 'new Cold War' position, for example, were encouraging greater coherence between aid and politics during the 1990s (IDC 1999). At this stage the issue was not that aid and politics were too close or incompatible, it was that in many emergencies, notably Rwanda in 1994, there was a tragic lack of international political will and involvement (Macrae and Leader 2000). While the NGO movement now fears that it may be too close to intervening powers, in the past it has often called for more state intervention. To continue this discussion of the relation between aid and politics, and the difficulties of achieving coherence between them, the following chapter considers the UN's Strategic Framework for Afghanistan. Initiated during the period of Taliban rule, it was a conscious experiment in getting aid and politics to work together.

6 Afghanistan, Coherence and Taliban Rule

By the mid-1990s UN-led consensual or negotiated approaches to humanitarian intervention were in a state of crisis and eclipse. Negotiated access had emerged as an initial post-Cold War humanitarian response to ongoing conflict. Within a few years, however, growing humanitarian and peace interventionism had created a new situation – that is, the need to police the transition from war to peace and to reconstruct war-affected societies. Together with the decline in the number of open and ongoing wars, the consensual basis of negotiated access was also increasingly out of tune with the emerging situation (Jones 2001: 2). As indicated in relation to Mozambique, as a way of securing humanitarian access a negotiated consensus conferred political recognition, and hence responsibilities, on all sides in internal or civil wars, that is, on state incumbents and, informally at least, non-state actors as well. Negotiated access bestowed recognition on existing territorial nation-states, together with their incumbents and claimants. While UN-led humanitarian interventions allowed aid agencies to pioneer new technologies of international security, including ways of containing and supporting population within conflict zones (Duffield 1994), as a way of reforming ineffective states and strengthening international stability they were of limited use. Their consensual basis now jarred with a liberal will to govern that defined its role as 'catalysing change and transforming *whole* societies' (Stiglitz 1998: 3). While humanitarian intervention opened up the political space of contingent sovereignty, such a radical vision of post-interventionism would require a much more thoroughgoing integration of development and security than humanitarian assistance allowed for.

From negotiation to coercion

Following the early post-Cold War hopes for a rejuvenated UN, the setbacks in Somalia, Bosnia and Herzegovina, and Rwanda produced a malaise within the international system. Building on the first Gulf War, from the mid-1990s more militarized forms of international intervention began to develop. While contributing to the decline in open civil wars, these interventions have been associated with Western-led 'coalitions of the willing' that typically brought together effective states and/or regional associations. Examples of such post-negotiation interventions include NATO's Kosovo campaign (1999), Britain in Sierra Leone (2000) and Australia's intervention in East Timor (2000), together with the more explicit regime change operations by US-led international coalitions in Afghanistan (2001) and Iraq (2003). All form part of a pacificatory trend and the emergence of a post-interventionary political terrain. Characteristically, such Western-led interventions have usually taken place either without formal UN agreement or with the UN's agreement but independent of UN management, or UN endorsement or involvement have been sought retrospectively. However, while the interests of effective states, often cited as reflecting a turn towards bilateralism (Macrae et al. 2002), have predominated in such interventions, the UN itself has also matched the move away from consent to more coercive forms of involvement. This shift is reflected in the advent of the UN 'integrated mission'.

A key event in this history was the report of the multi-agency Joint Evaluation of Emergency Assistance to Rwanda, which examined the West's response to the 1994 genocide and its immediate aftermath (Eriksson 1996). This evaluation was unprecedented in its scope and international involvement, the like of which has not been seen since. Its Steering Committee included, for example, representatives from nineteen OECD governments, the EU, all the relevant UN agencies, the International Committee of the Red Cross and five major NGO networks. Its main finding was that the international response to the genocide suffered from a lack of policy coherence between the actors involved. In particular, humanitarian action 'cannot substitute for political action. This is perhaps the most important finding of this evaluation' (ibid.: 46). In the absence of international intervention, aid agencies had been left to face a catastrophe that it was beyond their abilities to deal with (Macrae and Leader 2000: 9). Such criticism encouraged the UN to embark on several years of experimentation with various forms of strategic coordination. The aim was not only to bring aid and politics – that is, development and security – together in more effective and practical ways, but, at the same time, to craft an institutional framework more relevant to supporting the complex transition from war to peace.

Compared with earlier consensual and negotiated approaches, the trend has been towards a more robust model of UN intervention based on the integrated mission (Jones 2001). This has been defined as 'an instrument with which the UN seeks to help countries in the transition from war to lasting peace, or address a similar complex situation that requires a system-wide UN response, through subsuming various actors and approaches within an overall political–strategic crisis management framework' (Eide et al. 2005: 14). Moreover, in contrast to earlier approaches, 'the United Nations of today does not shy away from taking a side in a peace process, for instance in favour of an internationally recognized transitional government and against "spoilers" trying to undermine the transition process' (ibid.: 7; see also Wheeler and Harmer 2006). It is thus a post-interventionary move from negotiation to coordination, backed by a more coercive political stance in the interests of supporting the transition from war to peace. Emerging first in Kosovo in 1999, variants of the integrated UN mission currently exist in Afghanistan, Burundi, Ivory Coast, Haiti, Iraq, Sierra Leone, Sudan and East Timor. Moreover, within such post-interventionary societies, the UN is often no longer the main focal point of external assistance and support for the emerging state. This role is now commonly divided between the UN and new donor financial and security arrangements. Some of these new arrangements are reviewed in the following chapter. In this respect, the idea of an 'integrated' mission is, in many theatres of operation, a misnomer.

The emergence of the UN integrated mission, together with the associated turn towards 'coalitions of the willing' and pre-emptive regime change, is symptomatic of the deepening since the mid-1990s of the political space of contingent sovereignty and the emergence of post-interventionary occupation as an enduring political relation (Crombe 2005). The halving of the number of ongoing wars since 1992 (HSC 2005) invites interpretation as a significant process of international pacification. However, while ending open conflict within ineffective states has proved to be relatively easy, winning the peace among the world of peoples has presented a more intractable problem. Many countries now find themselves hosting large foreign contingents of donor representatives, UN specialists, aid workers, consultants, private contractors and foreign militaries. They have become the laboratories of the new liberal imperium that Michael Ignatieff has called *Empire Lite* (2003). In helping to secure the peace, in the case of post-interventionary societies new strategic demands have been placed on aid. Trying to win hearts and minds in the politically polarized worlds of Iraq and Afghanistan, for example, has led to the rediscovery of the link between development and counter-insurgency (Slim 2004b). Harmonizing and strengthening the inter-connections between development, politics and military force has been the essence of counter-insurgency since decolonization (Thompson 1966). It is perhaps unsurprising, therefore, that the current term of art describing the main policy challenge within the contested political space of contingent sovereignty is once again that of achieving *coherence* between aid and politics (for an overview see Macrae and Leader 2000; Leader and Colenso 2005; Gordon 2006).

By the end of the 1990s, many donor governments (ODA 1996; DFID 1997; MFA 1997) and multilateral organizations (EC 1996; OECD 1998) had produced their own, essentially similar, visions of the desired practical coherence between development and security, that is, between the varied humanitarian, development, commercial, diplomatic, security and military activities which constitute the institutions of contingent sovereignty. A common feature of such post-interventionary peace and reconstruction schemes is the declared intention to move from ad hoc interventions in favour of more collective planning; from concerns with delivery to those of measuring impact; and from exclusiveness to partnership arrangements with aid recipients. They reflect a recurrent theme within aid policy that the reactive and dubious aid responses of the past must give way to proactive forms of engagement where performance improvements are planned into project design and outcomes are measured in a transparent way. The development–security nexus is not just a theoretical proposition. Through such institutional arrangements as strategic coordination, strategic frameworks, compacts and global plans, that is, through the search for coherence, it also involves a practical programme of institutional reform, merger and hybridization.

Coherence reflects the manner in which state power is currently being governmentalized. While the chapter on Mozambique illustrated aid as social engineering among rural groups and communities, this chapter is more concerned with aid in a counter-insurgency role – in this case as a set of civilian interventions to create the conditions for internal political change. In a zone of indistinction where public/private differences have blurred, in order to coordinate and order multiple administrative sovereigns, discourse has shifted from law and the juridical to what is morally right and desirable (Douzinas

2003). Aid and politics are coherent as long as politics claims the moral high ground and decides the rights and wrongs of intervention. If petty sovereigns are not to be excluded, they have to adjust and reorder themselves to the right that might now decrees. To paraphrase President George W. Bush's declaration of unending war, *you are either with us or against us.* This is not a programme of state expansion as such; it is the deepening of the West's sovereign frontier through setting the moral standards and desired forms of comport-ment against which other actors must now measure, adjust and orchestrate themselves. As a result, the state seeks to govern at a dis-tance through a matrix of self-organizing civil, non-state and private actors (Abrahamson 2004). The search for coherence is also, however, a process that constantly throws up sites of resistance, demands for autonomy and acts of desertion and sabotage. Governmentalization is never one-way or complete. The recent pacification and occupation of the global borderland has necessarily been international in scope and involved a complex division of labour between multiple state and non-state actors, each having their own motives and agendas. Broadly speaking, the main characteristics of the fragmented and privatized aid environment within ineffective post-interventionary states are best described as *anarchy.* While presented as a search for synergy and efficiency, coherence is better understood as an attempt to strate-gize sovereign power in an anarchic environment of resistance and opposition.

This chapter critically examines the first conscious attempt to achieve coherence between aid and politics internationally – that is, the UN's Strategic Framework for Afghanistan (SFA) launched in 1998. At its most basic, the SFA attempted to harmonize the UN's political attempts to secure a region-wide peace agreement involving the ruling Taliban regime with its development efforts to strengthen communities and foster peace from below. Even before the US-led removal of the regime in November 2001, however, this experiment had failed. With the advent of indefinite war, the search for coherence has deepened. While embodying an urge to govern in a globalizing and centralizing way, coherence exists in a world that is largely inde-pendent of its feasibility or actual results.

The strategic framework for Afghanistan

The SFA was a conscious attempt to bring together development and security, or, in more practical terms, aid and politics, in the interests of local peace and international stability.[1] It ran between September 1998 and December 2000, when it effectively ceased to function as a result of the insurmountable tensions and contradictions it had generated. The US-led insurrection of November 2001 that quickly toppled the Taliban regime, however, has overshadowed the experience and implications of this experiment (HDC 2003: 4). The SFA is worth considering, since many of its problems have been carried over into the UN Assistance Mission in Afghanistan (UNAMA), set up in December 2001 (Stockton 2002). Conceived as an experiment, the SFA has also left a paper trail. There are several accounts, for example, of the SFA's background and establishment (such as Witschi-Cestari et al. 1998), as well as UN and practitioner interpretations of its functioning and implications (UNOCHA 1998; Newburg 1999; UNOCHAA 1999; UNCO 2000; Donini 2001; Donini et al. 2004). Moreover, then as now, Afghanistan continues to be a site of experimentation in governance and regime consolidation in conditions of crisis and insurgency (Costy 2004; Suhrke 2006). Rather than regarding the collapse of the Taliban regime as a year zero, examining the SFA is an opportunity to reconnect the continuities between past and present. Indeed, the rekindling of the Taliban insurgency only adds to this endeavour.

The Strategic Framework initiative is part of the already mentioned move from negotiated access to the more coercive form of the integrated mission. Indeed, the SFA can be seen as a stepping stone between the two. Lakhdar Brahimi, for example, who headed the UN political mission in Afghanistan between 1997 and 1999, also authored the *Report of the Panel on United Nations Peace Operations* (Brahimi 2000), usually known as the Brahimi Report. Apart from producing this document shaping the emergence of the integrated mission, between October 2001 and December 2004 Brahimi himself was Special Representative of the Secretary-General for Afghanistan and head of UNAMA. The basic aim of the SFA was to bring the activities of the UN's 'political' wing (reporting to the UN Department of Political Affairs – DPA) into greater coherence with its 'aid' wing (UNDP, UNICEF, WFP, etc.). While human rights was later added as a 'third pillar', the aim remained that of reducing disconnects and improving harmony across all of these activities. While no formal

---

[1] The fieldwork for this research was undertaken in Pakistan, Afghanistan and New York in May and July 2001 with the support of the Afghanistan Research and Evaluation Unit (AREU), Kabul and Islamabad. See Duffield, Gossman and Leader (2002).

merger of the various agencies was involved or envisaged, the guiding principle of the SFA was that political, aid and human rights actors and concerns should 'inform and be informed by each other' in the interests of achieving peace and stability in Afghanistan (interview, UNOCHA, 16 May 2001).

As will be argued below, the subsequent failure of the SFA to achieve coherence can be explained in relation to the UN's political mission and its development wing taking the 'state' and 'people' as their respective and opposing reference points. During the SFA phase, although both were formally accorded equal status, in practice the development wing occupied the dominant position. The toppling of the Taliban regime, however, and the expansion of contingent sovereignty following occupation, have caused the positioning to be reversed, with 'politics' now predominating over 'aid'. Not only does this characterize the reconstruction efforts in contemporary Afghanistan and Iraq (Costy 2004), it is reflected more widely in the advent of the UN integrated mission (Sida 2005). As discussed in the previous chapter, the urge to take a globalizing security view of human security also signals this shift. Unending war has lent urgency to the search for coherence. Effective states have found a new ability and legitimacy to order, structure and coordinate – that is, governmental-ize – other independent sites of power, including the creation of new hybrid and cross-departmental organizations (see Lockhardt 2005).

Following the seizure of the Afghan state by pro-Soviet interests, the then Soviet Union intervened militarily in 1979 to offer its support in the face of the growing Islamic opposition the seizure had encouraged. The UN first became involved in Afghanistan politically in 1981. It was instrumental in negotiating the eventual withdrawal of Soviet forces in 1988, following their defeat by what rapidly became a US- and Pakistan-supported rural insurgency. Despite the ending of the Cold War, however, and a high level of international support, the UN was unable to prevent Afghanistan descending into vicious factional warfare between competing Mujahideen groups in 1992. On gaining a reputation as a failed state, Afghanistan slipped down the international agenda of priorities. The loss of superpower patronage re-emphasized the importance of regional economic and political linkages. From being a dependent rentier state, Afghanistan fractured into a series of transborder political systems that, through the pursuit of extra-legal economic activities, enjoyed varying degrees of independence from the circuits of Western aid and diplomacy (Rubin 2000; Fielden and Goodhand 2001). The Taliban emerged in September 1994 with a leadership largely of southern Pashtun origin with strong links to Pakistan. Within two years they had consolidated their position, situating themselves as a militant Islamic solution to the political fragmentation they encountered. The Taliban captured Kabul in September 1996 and by the end of 1998 had extended their authority over much of the country, bringing relative security to the areas under their control. They expanded through consolidating some ethno-political and religious networks while eliminating others. Despite being ousted from state control at the end of 2001, at the time of writing, there has been a resurgence of Taliban rural opposition to Coalition occupation and the state-building project currently under way.

By the time the Taliban had consolidated their position in the mid-1990s, both the UN's political and aid missions in Afghanistan were in a state of crisis. With the disappearance of a legitimate or recognized government, the role of the political mission had been challenged. In addition, during the 1980s and early 1990s, humanitarian and development assistance had been politically partisan, with many NGOs, for example, working directly with Mujahideen commanders (Baitenmann 1990). There was growing criticism that, in part at least, humanitarian endeavours had helped to fuel the conflict. At the same time, outside Afghanistan the UN was itself in the process of thinking through its organizational role and improving strategic coordination (Jones 2001). The outcome of these pressures was that in 1997 Afghanistan was chosen as a laboratory to test a new UN approach to conflict and humanitarian crisis. While not formally approved until September 1998, what became known as the SFA was intended to chart a new path for the UN system.

While the emergence of the Taliban precipitated an aid crisis in Afghanistan, the UN's humanitarian and development agencies had already begun to improve coherence before the advent of the SFA. In 1992, for example, UNDP established a Rehabilitation Strategy for Afghanistan. In 1996 this programme was refocused as a peace-enhancing initiative based on strengthening community cohesion as a means of promoting dialogue and good governance. It developed into UNDP's inter-agency programme for Poverty Eradication and Community Empowerment (P.E.A.C.E.). This was linked to plans to improve aid coordination based on the collection and study of socio-economic data and governance patterns (UNDP 1997: 1). Responsibility for relief and development in Afghanistan was split between the United Nations Office for the Coordination of Humanitarian Assistance to Afghanistan (UNOCHAA) and UNDP respectively. Reflecting the growing trend to integrate UN country management as part of the wider move to improve strategic coordination, these functions were merged under the leadership of a Resident Coordinator/Humanitarian Coordinator (RC/HC) in January 1997. This merger gave rise to a number of other coherence-type measures, including the formation of new programme and policy oversight bodies staffed by aid agency and donor representatives. At the same time, NGOs were more fully integrated into the estimation of need, and administrative measures were taken to improve the complementarity and coherence in the provision of assistance.

This process of field-level reform in Afghanistan fed into a similar dynamic of change and competition occurring between UN agency headquarters. At this level the feeling was such that 'some reform was essential just to keep aid in business' (Newburg 1999: 24). With the DPA playing a lead role, the result was an inter-agency mission (which included Oxfam) to Afghanistan in October 1997. Responsibility for its recommendation to establish a shared strategy changed hands several times, reflecting a certain discomfort among agency heads 'about the degree to which a framework for assistance would force their compliance with policies outside their control' (ibid.: 24). As a result, it finally ended up in the office of the UN Deputy Secretary-General. By the time of the formal launch of the SFA in September 1998, the nature of the framework had changed considerably. Initially the intention had been to create a common programme for Afghanistan. This would have been a radical endeavour in which different agencies would have merged their identities and drawn resources from a common fund. However, rather than integrating, this 'was quickly replaced by an effort to engage in common programming' in which 'politics' and 'aid' retained their institutional identities (ibid.: 24). It was felt that the former would help *directly* through peace initiatives while the latter contributed '*indirectly* by creating the conditions that make recovery and reconstruction a viable option for those who, at present, see no option other than war' (UN 1998: 3). Through this alignment it was felt that the opportunities for peace could be maximized.

Since political and aid actors both shared the same liberal aims of peace and prosperity, the SFA promised a 'common conceptual tool' to identify different but complementary and mutually reinforcing ways of facilitating the transition from war to peace (ibid.: 4). Such a peace-building strategy demanded that there be 'no "disconnects" between political, human rights, humanitarian and developmental aspects of the [international] response' (ibid.: 3). The day-to-day operation of the SFA was to be informed by a number of operational modalities, the most important of which was the agreement that aid and politics should speak with one voice on all important issues and agree collective action when human rights were violated. As will become clear below, a weakness in the strategic framework approach is that any number of actors can claim to share the same aims, provided that the level of abstraction is high enough. Even the Taliban, for example, at some point in the programme would probably align themselves with 'peace and prosperity'. While sharing similar broad objectives, aid and politics within the SFA, for example, had different approaches, so different in fact that each regarded the other as antagonistic, not complementary, and a direct threat to its own institutional survival.

Development and security in practice

In bringing 'aid' and 'politics' together through the SFA, it is important to understand what each of these terms meant in practice. Aid, for example, was mainly humanitarian and basic in nature, including nutritional support, shelter materials, health inputs, sanitation programmes, educational resources and agricultural projects. As in Mozambique, where possible its disbursement was also associated with the encouragement of self-reliance through new and more inclusive community-based organizations and networks. Among entrepreneurial aid workers this aid invoked a strategic possibility – that is, its deployment in support of non-elite and inclusive community-level conflict resolution and social reconstruction projects. UNDP's P.E.A.C.E. initiative mentioned above was an example of this thinking. It reflected a wide consensus among aid agencies that badly managed humanitarian assistance had negative effects, for example creating dependency, encouraging criminality and undermining self-reliance. If used properly, however, and in a way that brought people and communities together, it could have a more positive impact (Anderson 1996; CMI 1997; Uvin 1999), for example by helping to create overarching community or ethnic goals that improved social cohesion or helped to build 'peace from below'. Within the SFA this was how aid was understood as contributing indirectly to peace. 'Politics' on the other hand, embraced more traditional elite-based initiatives that, through diplomacy, mediation and confidence building, were designed to bring the various internal and regional actors into negotiation. These more direct attempts to secure peace had been the staple diet of the various UN political missions in Afghanistan since the early 1980s.

While both these spheres of activity shared the same aim of peace and stability, they are very different. Aid embodies a biopolitics of self-reliance harnessed to strengthening social cohesion in the interests of international security. It represented a different vision of the political compared with that within the DPA. Aid spoke in the name of people, rights and freedom, while the UN's political mission talked a realist language of elites, best efforts and compromises. Rather than the SFA providing a means of improving coherence between these approaches, it became a site of an increasingly bitter competition.

As discussed more fully below, the role of aid within the SFA was to rebuild civil society, create local constituencies for peace and, at the same time, encourage the acceptance of moderation and democratic representation among political actors – it was concerned with changing and modulating behaviour. The aim was not to support the state per se but, indirectly, to empower self-reliant groups and communities as responsible political actors – in other words, to create the conditions for internal political change. In comparison, the UN's political mission continued to reflect a more geopolitical mindset. Its elite-based interventions and confidence-building measures were constructed around the nation-state idea. In Taliban-ruled Afghanistan, however, building peace from below had greater affinity with counter-insurgency and regime change. It was an ambitious strategic vision beyond the capacity or legitimacy of individual donors, aid agencies or NGOs. It connected with the new and emergent contractual regimes linking state and non-state actors and requiring system-coherence, inter-agency coordination and effective networking; in other words, aid as politics invokes new forms of governmentality. Reflecting the mobilizing potential of human security already discussed, aid within the SFA envisioned a future international regulatory regime able to promote peace and security through modulating behaviour by rewarding positive attitudes and penalizing or ignoring negative ones.

Some NGOs felt that the imagined role of aid within the SFA was an exaggeration of its possible political effects, especially when, as now, the aid system was struggling to satisfy even the most basic welfare needs, let alone transform society as a whole (Wilder 1997; CMI 2005). From this cautionary perspective, rather than a programme of concrete social change, the SFA is better understood as embodying a will to power or, at least, several versions of the truth. In other words, it is better understood as *a framework of inter-agency positioning and competition*. While the SFA attempted to bring aid and politics together on the shared platform of peace, these dispositions took 'people' and 'state' as their respective points of reference. Since the Framework regarded them as equals within it, it proved incapable of resolving the differences and tensions that emerged between them. The two-year history of the SFA was one of an entrepreneurial developmentalism locked in competition with a realist political outlook. While politics was the underdog during this period, on balance not only was politics a better indicator of events in Afghanistan, but the removal of the Taliban would see politics take the driving seat in the new international administration.

From building 'peace from below' while ignoring the Taliban state, the aid industry would be rapidly reoriented to provide legitimacy for the transitional state. That is, it would adopt a more clearly defined 'aid pacification' (Stockton 2002: 25) or counter-insurgency role in justifying and supporting regime change. Today, as in the past, however, problems of coherence and difficulties of effecting political change through the aid programme remain (Suhrke 2006).

Aid and peace-building in a failed state

Since UNCO interpreted the SFA in developmental terms, rather than encouraging coherence, it problematized elite-based diplomatic and political confidence-building strategies. What was conceived as an 'indirect' contribution to peace-building became the driving force within the Framework. Because Afghanistan was not formally recognized by the international community, the SFA sought to provide a principled and accountable way of engaging the Taliban. The fact of non-recognition meant that external assistance, in order to be legitimate, had to be transparent, centrally controlled and thus subject to the will of Western states. The engagement of aid agencies through the SFA, however, was ambivalent. At a rhetorical level, it was confrontational and sought to promote peace and uphold human rights. At a practical level, however, by having to adjust to the forces and realities of local operating conditions, aid programmes tended to accommodate the Taliban. This ambiguity resulted in a tension between 'principles and pragmatism' within the SFA (UNOCHAA 2000).

The SFA defined the overarching goal of the UN in Afghanistan as facilitating the transition from war to peace through mutually reinforcing assistance and political strategies. Compared with the UN's earlier 'negotiated access' approach to complex emergencies, this was a significant change. The SFA can be seen as a halfway house to the current 'integrated mission' with its more coercive as opposed to consensual political stance. Enlarging the role of the UN through the Strategic Framework to include the direct and indirect promotion of peace moved the UN into a position of potential political opposition to the Taliban. This repositioning was not lost on the Taliban and, through the language of security, rights and, especially, gender, the SFA marked out a volatile terrain of competition, antagonism and compromise between the UN and Taliban (Fielden and Azerbaijani-Moghadam 2001). UNCO's moves to construct a framework of principled engagement intensified in concert with the Taliban's determination to resist.

How a crisis is understood relates directly to the measures that policy makers prescribe. The underlying assumption shaping the political role of aid within the SFA was that Afghanistan was a 'failed state'. The Framework documentation thus gives a brief description of an impoverished war-torn society characterized, for example, by community fragmentation, depleted social capital, collapsed basic services, disappearance of traditional coping mechanisms, avid gender discrimination and absence of effective government. This complex reality was seen as mixing a violent political crisis, a humanitarian emergency and two decades of missed development opportunities. The fragmentation of the country 'and the collapse of practically all institutions of state, also constitute an "emergency of governance"' (UN 1998: 3). This crisis of governance was reflected in the 'weakening of civil society', including the isolation of the countryside. For aid agencies the lack of Taliban legitimacy in many rural areas had produced a 'political vacuum' in which not only had citizen–state relations diminished 'but so, too, have the citizen–citizen relationships that are the foundation of communities and the state' (Newburg 1999: 11). In this situation the only thing that functioned was the 'criminalized economy'. With the conventional economy in crisis, war profiteering, poppy cultivation, drug trafficking and transborder smuggling provided 'opportunities for a [criminal] minority to thrive' (UN 1998: 3).

The idea of Afghanistan as a failed state was the conceptual and institutional driving force of the SFA. In this respect it stands comparison with the instrumentality of ideas of social breakdown and rural isolation already examined in Mozambique. At the same time, it provides a point of departure for the discussion in the following chapter of current approaches to fragile states. Within the Framework, the idea of state failure justified the strategic use of aid as tool for conflict resolution, social reconstruction and behavioural change. The aid programme became a series of interventions that promised to rejoin what had been fragmented, rebuild that which had collapsed and refill the void: where the state had failed, aid could succeed. Whereas this form of representation had been central to conceptualizing the role of aid in rebuilding social cohesion in rural Mozambique, in Afghanistan it was extended to the orchestration of peace and justifying the coordinating role of UNCO. To the extent that the Taliban presided over a fragmented and dysfunctional sovereign void, it was incumbent on the UN to fill this space with a coherent system that afforded 'no disconnects between the political, human rights, humanitarian and development aspects of the response' (UN 1998: 3). The absence of legitimate state interlocutors also demanded 'stronger working alliances among UN partners and a culture that places a premium on co-operation and coordination for effective action' (ibid.). Moreover, in the absence of a functioning government, UN agencies needed to perform 'essential strategic planning, resource allocation and other "surrogate government" functions'(UNCO 2000: 1). In other words, state failure in Afghanistan necessitated the UN assuming the role of a 'surrogate government'; given the eventual overthrow of the Taliban, in retrospect this was an international government in waiting.

The limits of principled engagement

The political use of aid is embodied in the founding principles of the SFA. Among other things, these established that assistance was provided as part of 'an overall effort to achieve peace', that capacity building activities had to advance human rights and not provide support 'to any presumptive state authority', and that assistance had to ensure 'indigenous ownership at the village, community and national levels' to help build the country as a whole. These principles were informed by operational modalities that included the aim of ensuring that assistance was used 'to significantly reduce structural discrimination by gender, tribe, ethnicity, language, religion or political affiliation' (UN 1998: 4–5). Opportunities for peace-building were to be sought at the level of the community, civil society and the promotion of self-reliance. How peace-building through aid was experienced within the SFA is first examined, before turning to the conflictual relationship with the UN's political mission.

The leading example of the attempt to build peace from below was UNDP's already mentioned P.E.A.C.E. programme. Repackaged in the mid-1990s from a number of existing activities, it represented 'the first deliberate effort to work to encourage non-institutional (and non-faction based) peace building' (Witschi-Cestari et al. 1998: 18). The failure of the state was claimed to have reinforced the importance of local community-based organizations. At the same time this failure gave aid agencies the opportunity to bypass political obstacles to promote 'a form of shadow development that creates alternative venues for local decisions, attempts to empower local leaders and their communities, and provides the first building blocks for post-war Afghanistan' (Newburg 1999: 16). Empowering local communities meant that 'communities would be able to form networks over larger geographical areas, with peace as part of their agenda' (Ostby 2000: 3). Community assistance thus creates the possibility of forming peace constituencies that can temper the violent actions of faction leaders. Strong community organizations can 'to some extent limit the anti-social behaviour of commanders, and safeguard local resources for use in constructive activities' (ibid.: 3). According to a senior UNDP informant interviewed in May 2001, the possibility of a return to the inter-factional violence and destruction of the early 1990s had been reduced in those districts where the P.E.A.C.E. programme was operating. In so far as aid was now consciously attempting to establish the conditions for internal political change in a fraught environment, it had vectored into a counter-insurgency role. Moreover, this civilian form of counter-insurgency – that is, unconnected with supporting military involvement – reflected the turn in aid programming more generally in zones of crisis during the 1990s (Anderson 1996).

Peace-building through the aid programme in Afghanistan was originally conceived as an indirect contribution to peace. However, reflecting its view that the UN's political mission was failing, UNCO called for a 'paradigm shift' within the Strategic Framework initiative involving 'a scaling up of efforts to engage civil society in the peace process' (UNCO 2000: 3). This signalled a growing competition with the political mission and, at the same time, attempts by UNCO to broaden the political role of aid within the SFA to include changing Taliban behaviour through 'principled engagement'. This was initially theorized in two UNOCHAA *Next Steps* documents (September 1998 and February 1999), which represented a significant intensification of the political role envisaged for aid. Arguing that aid can have a non-elite peace-building effect in its own right – claims absent from the initial Strategic Framework initiative agreed with the DPA – this 'paradigm shift' was consolidated in *The Three Pillars: Strengthening the Foundations* (UNCO 2000). As far as the UN's country programme was concerned, rather than being an indirect contribution to peace-building, exploiting the potential of aid to modify behaviour was what the SFA should be about.

Since all assistance can be used by recipients for purposes unintended by donors, earlier ideas of attempting to operationalize principled engagement with the Taliban by distinguishing 'life-saving' and 'capacity-building' activities were questioned. At the same time, not all community-level activity is 'good' and all state-based capacity building 'bad' (UNOCHAA 1999). The former can have negative consequences just as the latter, in the right circumstances, can improve matters. The SFA operating principles for engaging the Taliban stipulated that assistance should only be provided when it could be 'reasonably determined that no direct political or military advantage will accrue to the warring parties'. Furthermore, it must 'attain high standards of transparency and accountability [and] be appraised, monitored, measured and evaluated against clear policy and programmatic objectives'. Through technical sub-agreements, the Memorandum of Understanding (MoU) agreed in May 1998 between the UN and the Taliban was regarded as one way of making the relationship transparent, making progress amenable to measurement and helping to clarify the question of community and/or national ownership of programmes (UNOCHA 1998: 3). The main departure in the *Next Steps* documents, however, was to envision a regulatory carrot-and-stick aid system that could modulate the political behaviour of the Taliban.

The *Next Steps* recommended that aid should be used to reduce structural inequality and, while no conditionality was attached to humanitarian life-saving activities, assistance would depend upon meeting certain 'minimum standards' including non-discrimination among UN staff on grounds of gender and 'respect for humanitarian principles, including access to all segments of the population and in particular women, minorities and other vulnerable groups in need of assistance' (ibid.: 4). In achieving such minimum standards, *Next Steps* envisaged the UN adopting both positive and negative responses. Specific leverage points 'will be identified so that "sanctions" or "rewards" can be targeted and effective' (ibid.). Moving beyond trying to distinguish between 'life-saving' and 'capacity-building' activities was central to establishing points of institutional discipline and regulation. In particular, no direct assistance would be given to authorities in areas where SFA principles were being deliberately violated. At the same time, however, UN agencies would continue to work 'with the technical branches of public administration structures when there is evidence that these entities provide essential services to the civilian population in a non-discriminatory manner (e.g., health, solid waste disposal)' (UNOCHAA 1999: 2).

Next Steps outlines a vision of distinguishing 'good' and 'bad' parts of the Taliban regime according to whether or not they practised discriminatory behaviour. It is similar to establishing benchmarks of what DFID now calls 'good enough governance' in relation to fragile states (DFID 2005a); this is returned to in the following chapter. Regarding the Taliban, in order to encourage good institutional practice while discouraging bad, establishing a graded list of non-life-saving assistance was suggested. Donors could either reduce or increase the inputs on this list in order to modify Taliban behaviour. This could include, for example, the selected suspension of valued activities, such as providing projects with vehicles, or refusing to develop high-profile projects or initiatives. It might also involve decisions to remove expatriate staff so that 'ongoing humanitarian activities will be implemented through national staff and their local counterparts' (UNOCHA 1998: 4). Outside such suggestions, however, UNOCHA never did draw up such a list, let alone attempt to assess how effective this social engineering would have been. Given the anti-Western stance of the Taliban, the threat to withdraw expatriate project staff, for example, hardly seems convincing. Nevertheless, the *Next Steps* documents are a good example of the attempts being made by entrepreneurial practitioners to inter-connect development and security. In this case, the Resident Coordinator/Humanitarian Coordinator (RC/HC) was imagined as issuing an appropriate response to displays of good or bad Taliban behaviour and ensuring system-wide compliance with 'what should trigger it and its gradation' (ibid.: 5). In this way the SFA would provide the UN with the means to 'define the benchmarks and indicators to measure . . . progress and adjust its presence inside the country accordingly' (ibid.: 3).

The idea that the SFA could embody a principled set of sticks and carrots capable of socializing the Taliban rested on a number of contradictions and lacunae. While UNCO justified its role as a surrogate government by regarding Afghanistan as a failed state, the ability of the Taliban to prosecute a war and thwart international conventions suggested something different, that it was a responsive and cohesive political force. Ideas of failure and fragmentation, however, were central to the aid mission's division of the state into 'good' and 'bad' parts. The idea of social breakdown rests on little or no connection existing between these divisions. It therefore becomes possible to think of working in a principled way with the good while excluding the bad – that is, increasing the resources of the former while the latter either stagnates or changes its behaviour. The risk of such behaviourist instrumentality, however, is that rather than principled engagement, aid agencies find themselves in an accommodationist relationship with a political force they have consistently underestimated. As well as the present Taliban resurgence, this can also be seen in relation to gender, where the SFA conspicuously failed to develop a coherent or principled strategy of engagement.

The Strategic Framework's view of Afghanistan as a failed state was challenged by the November 1997 report issued by the UN Office of the Special Adviser on Gender Issues and Advancement of Women (OSAGI), *Report of the UN Interagency Gender Mission to Afghanistan*. Or, at least, its recommendations assumed that the Taliban was a cohesive political force. It argued that negotiation conducted 'at all levels and in all parts of the country to facilitate women's participation in relief, rehabilitation and recovery should be consistent. It should be pursued vigorously and continuously in order to ensure quality work as well as to educate authorities in the nature of international standards and practices' (OSAGI 1997: 16). Moreover, it suggested that joint technical committees be established to encourage dialogue with Afghan authorities. The Gender Mission argued for a consistent, multilevel framework of negotiation and advocacy with the Taliban. This broad framework of interaction was distinct from the selective, best-chance approach inherent in the idea of principled engagement. Indeed, the latter approach advocated boycotting and ignoring those ministries or institutions held to be discriminatory. As a consequence of this difference, the consensus within the aid community was that the Gender Mission had failed to get to grips with the issue (Witschi-Cestari et al. 1998). A selective and consquentialist approach to engaging the Taliban, as opposed to an open engagement at all levels, was the prevailing culture. Such principled engagement was tested in July 2000 following a Taliban edict restricting the employment of Afghan women by aid agencies. Not only was the SFA unable to 'speak with one voice', the general position among aid agencies was one of 'no disengagement, no confrontation, staying out of the political arena, approaching the Taliban through line ministries, keeping the dialogue open, moving slowly, keeping a low profile and adopting a wait-and-see attitude' (Fielden and Azerbaijani-Moghadam 2001: 7). Despite the subordination of women becoming a cause célèbre in the weeks preceding the removal of the Taliban in November 2001, gender has once again become a marginal issue within current attempts to reconstruct Afghanistan (CMI 2005: 127–130).

The problematization of state-based politics

In Taliban-ruled Afghanistan the UN Special Mission to Afghanistan (UNSMA) was the only body that formally defined its role as peace-building. Reporting to the DPA in New York and mandated by the Security Council, UNSMA's role was varied, and included mediation between regional actors and the Afghan diaspora (see Rubin et al. 2001). In this chapter UNSMA's activities in Afghanistan are the main focus. At its peak, its Civil Affairs Unit (CAU) had six regional offices within Afghanistan. However, in response to the imposition of UN sanctions in December 2000, the Taliban retaliated by significantly restricting UNSMA activities. With the exception of Kabul, the CAU offices in Taliban-controlled Afghanistan were closed, formal meetings were proscribed and, on the grounds that the sanctions were one-sided, the Taliban rejected further UN political mediation. By May 2001, UNSMA had been reduced to an office in Kabul together with a Civil Affairs Officer (CAO) in Faizabad (in United Front territory) and a liaison officer in Tehran. Interviewed that month, Abdul Rahman Zahid, the Deputy Foreign Minister, was clear that the Taliban regarded UNCO as the legitimate face of the UN and, in its role of facilitating humanitarian assistance, could, for the moment, continue operating. The political mission UNSMA, however, was now unacceptable.

While there had been a series of political missions in Afghanistan since 1981, the descent into civil war in the early 1990s broke that pattern. After an interruption of almost two years, UNSMA was created in December 1993 with a Security Council mandate to use its mediation efforts in support of a negotiated settlement leading to a broad-based government. It was not until towards the end of the 1990s, however, that UNSMA began to take on the shape it would have under the SFA. The Civil Affairs Unit (CAU), for example, was established in 1998. The Unit originated from frustration with the inability of the UNHCHR to conduct credible investigations into the violation of human rights in Afghanistan. During the two years that the CAU was operating, through its Civil Affairs Officers its role included official mediation with the Taliban, liaison with UN agencies and NGOs, observing and fact-finding, compiling reports on life in Afghanistan and monitoring human rights. Mediation with the Taliban included such things as raising questions on behalf of the aid community, fulfilling official instructions such as issuing *notes verbales*, and informal briefings with NGOs. In terms of monitoring human rights, officers interviewed informants, examined risks and looked for trends. If there was evidence of systematic abuse, the CAU decided the best way to take the matter forward, including referring matters to UNHCHR. UNSMA also compiled a database of all international treaties and agreements signed by former Afghan governments and, where possible, took up compliance issues with the Taliban. Rather than attempts at social engineering through aid, the general approach was that if the Taliban entertained hopes of formal recognition, it had to observe international law and conventions.

While the invocation of Afghanistan as a failed state justified the UN's aid mission adopting the role of a 'surrogate government', the same understanding problematized the more traditional elite-based UN approach to political mediation and peacemaking. Since the end of the Cold War generally, political elites engaged in internal or regionalized conflicts have lost international legitimacy. During the mid-1990s, the political mission in Afghanistan was variously charged with having no cognizance of the role that aid could play in promoting peace from below and with continuing to apply failed and outdated elite-based mediation strategies (Newburg 1999). It was argued that, despite producing few results, the UN political mission continued to seek partners inside and outside Afghanistan that were willing to forego military engagement in favour of political negotiations. Moreover, ordinary citizens were not included in such negotiations. In the words of one commentator, 'peace-building efforts – a task defined by some assistance actors – and peace-making – the mandate of the political mission – were often poles apart from one another, and both tasks seemed quite foreign to Afghan military leaders and civilians alike' (Witschi-Cestari et al. 1998: 5–6). Prior to the formation of the SFA, the aid community's view of UNSMA could be summarized as ineffective, unresponsive to change, only engaging discredited warring parties and ignoring ordinary Afghans.

The CAU was created a few months after the SFA's formal launch in September 1998. The SFA and the increasing depth of the political mission in Afghanistan emerged together. Despite the Strategic Framework, however, the negative views of the political mission, if anything, intensified with UNSMA's growing visibility. The DPA, for example, was widely held to be unaccountable and a law unto itself, while UNSMA was regarded as aloof and averse to sharing information ('rather than coherence there is a wall between political and humanitarian action'). In a continuation of earlier criticisms, UNSMA was accused of failing to understand the idea of peace from below, preferring instead to equate peace with a ceasefire ('it does not understand that peace is a process that permeates throughout society'). Moreover, it still only engaged with political elites, many of them war criminals. It needed to broaden its understanding of the peace process, for example by addressing the criminal economy. In this respect, the DPA provided no analysis and the peace process itself continued to be a missing pillar within the SFA. Aware of such criticisms, UNSMA had its own interpretation of the situation. Basically, the UN's aid mission had quickly come to the conclusion that it was not in its best interests to be closely associated with UNSMA and had actively kept its distance. Rather than UNSMA being aloof, the aid community never sought to involve the CAU or share information with it. Because UNCO had an accommodationist attitude towards the Taliban, UNSMA's work on human rights continually threatened its position ('UNCO just wants to be liked by the Taliban'). Moreover, aid agencies were able to claim 'success' through volumes of aid delivered or the number of training sessions held; in politics you only succeed when you succeed.

It is possible to lay these antagonisms at the door of poor coordination and liaison mechanisms, competing mandates, different funding regimes and so on. At the same time, several informants commented on the existence of personality clashes and a general ignorance about the role of opposite numbers within the SFA. In other words, incoherence arises from a combination of institutional failings and individual weaknesses. However, a 2005 study of the new and more coercive UN integrated missions in Burundi, Ivory Coast, the Democratic Republic of the Congo, Liberia, Sierra Leone and Sudan discovered similar friction between aid and politics. Although now in effective control, the political missions were variously accused, for example, of engaging in a one-way transfer of power, subordinating aid rather than including it and monopolizing planning exercises. In a neat reversal of the situation in Taliban Afghanistan, country aid missions were thought by political actors to be 'unwilling to adapt to new realities', especially the shift from 'impartial' to 'partial' UN support for an agreed transition process (Eide et al. 2005: 18). While it is possible to regard such differences as arising from 'institutional, structural, cultural and personal factors' (ibid.), and then proceed to recommend (yet another) reform of coordinating mechanisms, the recurrence of these antagonisms in time and space suggests that another explanation is needed.

The search for coherence is not a technical issue to be resolved by better coordination; it is a will to power that confronts and seeks to work through the multi-agency anarchy of contingent sovereignty. In the governmentalizing process of orchestrating and reordering independent sub-powers, the search for coherence inevitably produces sites of resistance and struggles to maintain autonomy. Some of these struggles, for example regarding humanitarian neutrality (Sida 2005), are central to liberalism itself. If humanitarian agencies are unable to hold the victims of disaster above politics and freely tend their needs, what sort of society have we become? Tensions between development and security are integral to the search for coherence. The greater the demands for alignment, the more such differences are encouraged. Reflecting the 'development' versus 'security' inflections within human security discussed in the previous chapter, the SFA was a stepping stone to the consolidating and containing effects of aid being fully subordinated to the globalizing security aims of politics within integrated-type missions – that is, from independently promoting peace from below to having this entrepreneurial counter-insurgency activity incorporated as a civilian component of politically directed pacification regimes within newly occupied zones of instability. Just as governmentalization involves the drawing together of self-managing sites of power and authority, it also creates new opportunities for non-cooperation, resistance and desertion.

UNSMA and the critique of aid

By 1999, UNSMA had established a three-track approach to peace-building, consisting of negotiations with the warring parties, work with the Afghan diaspora and dialogue with neighbouring regional states, including attempts to limit arms supplies (HRW 2001). While this framework remained fairly traditional, UNSMA's thinking bene-fited from the presence of the CAU in Afghanistan. In particular, it formed a view on the role of aid that contradicted the aid mission's views on building peace from below and principled engagement with the Taliban. While UNCO justified its existence in relation to the claim that Afghanistan was a failed state, UNSMA has been mandated to engage the warring parties. During the initial rise of the Taliban its ability to secure order had been noted by many observers. UNSMA's initial view was that, although conservative, the Taliban represented a cohesive political force. Following the capture of Kabul in 1996, the Taliban took over the remnants of the state apparatus. Mullah Omar was declared Commander of the Faithful, and the country was renamed the Islamic Emirate of Afghanistan (IEA). UNSMA assumed that the Taliban would keep the limited state infrastructure it had inherited and would build on it from an Islamic fundamentalist perspective. This assumption is reflected in the May 2000 *Report on Administrative and Judicial Structures of Afghanistan* (UNSMA 2000). Contrary to the failed state assumptions underpinning the approach of the aid mission, this report outlined the administrative structure of the IEA, including its tax system, judicial arrangements, courts and legal system.

By 2000, however, UNSMA was already changing its view of the Taliban. While it remained a cohesive force, a centralizing and expansionist tendency has emerged following the seizure of Kabul and its earlier successes in restoring order. Rather than building on the existing state institutions, it either deliberately eroded or side-stepped much of the inherited public administration. Authority was concentrated in the hands of Mullah Omar and, in effect, Kandahar rather than Kabul became the capital of Afghanistan. Those parts of the state for which the Taliban had little use, such as a secular police and schools, decayed even further; at the same time, as well as there being a growing reliance on foreign fighters, security institutions such as the military and intelligence, together with some commercial functions, were maintained. Rather than a failed state, UNSMA came to see the Taliban more in terms of a 'rogue state', in this case an internally ruthless, totalitarian political entity, linked to a transnational shadow economy and having destabilizing connections with opposition and terrorist groups on a region-wide basis, including al-Qaida.

While the official mandate of UNSMA remained that of seeking an elite-based negotiated settlement, for some months prior to the US-led intervention in November 2001 the informal view within the UN's political mission, which was shared by much of the donor community, was that the Taliban could not be reformed and, indeed, no attempt should be made to do so. Even if such an attempt were possible, it would simply legitimate a totalitarian and destabilizing regime. A dangerous political impasse had emerged in which the Taliban would never accept to be democratically tested by the Afghan people, nor would the majority of refugees return unless there was a change of regime. Rather than a negotiated settlement, UNSMA had formed the opinion that the likely future for Afghanistan was one of growing internal dissent leading to a popular anti-Taliban insurrection. With such thinking already existing within the UN's political mission, aiding and supporting such an insurgency was the key element in the Coalition military campaign that ousted the Taliban.

UNSMA's view of the legitimate role of aid followed from this analysis. In concert with a number of donor governments, it argued for international aid to be limited to, at most, basic humanitarian assistance restricted to the neediest. This view contradicted attempts by the aid mission to expand the role of humanitarian assistance to develop peace from below and modify Taliban behaviour through principled engagement. UNSMA questioned both the ability of what was, in effect, limited welfare and livelihood support to achieve such aims and, indeed, whether the Taliban could be reformed. An Afghani NGO representative (now a minister in the post-Taliban administration), interviewed in May 2001, supported an expanded role for aid. He argued that using aid to encourage or empower people to assert their rights, usually known as rights-based programming, was the opposite of limiting aid to basic humanitarian assistance. Among other things, the latter would be tantamount, for example, to 'removing the right to health'. Thus while the Strategic Framework assumed a complementarity between development and security, on the role of aid – an elemental issue within the Framework initiative – rather than complementarity there were two irreducible and opposing positions. This organic opposition was also reflected in the relationship of aid and politics to human rights.

The role of UNSMA in monitoring human rights was widely seen as problematic by the aid community. From the moment the CAU was established, it was subject to constant criticism and distancing, despite only a handful of officers being engaged in collecting human rights information. A particular concern was that attempts to monitor individual political or civil rights undermined the possibility of rights-based programming, that is, the empowering of communities to articulate collective social and economic rights. Rather than the identification and punishment of guilty parties, such monitoring was more likely to invoke Taliban retaliatory restrictions and thus provoke further UNSMA calls to limit aid to basic humanitarian assistance. Many aid agencies also found CAU attempts to collect sensitive information a threat to their own activities. In the view of one NGO informant, 'UNSMA claims to be the eyes and ears of the Secretary General, but what eyes and what ears? Is this an intelligence system? We have been asked to co-operate but many agencies refuse to meet them.' Many aid agencies regarded UNSMA as little more than a spy for the international community. On the other hand, the political mission regarded the aid programme as accommodationist and infiltrated by the Taliban. These contrasting attitudes and perceived threats led to moves by the aid community to distance itself from UNSMA. In order not to compromise the impartiality of humanitarian agencies, for example, Civil Affairs Officers were not allowed to travel with them on the same UN travel request. According to a UNOCHA official, 'the SFA does not mean we have to abolish the distance between the pillars. In fact, if they are not clearly separated it muddies the waters with the authorities.' As for UNDP, it never established any relations with UNSMA. While UNSMA would gain from linking with UNDP 'given the risks of collaboration, I'm not sure how we would benefit' (interview, UNDP, 15 May 2001).

When the Taliban curtailed the operations of UNSMA at the end of 2000 in response to the imposition of UN sanctions, it was a terminal blow to the SFA. Not only were the Taliban capable of distinguishing between 'politics' and 'aid'; they penalized one while allowing the other, after a fashion, to continue. Moreover, despite the SFA's call for 'one voice' in all matters of importance, the aid community made no formal representation to the Taliban over its actions against UNSMA. The general climate in Islamabad and Kabul in May 2001 was that of business as usual. Indeed, the attitude among many UN officials and aid workers to the demise of the UN's political mission was one of 'good riddance'. In all but name, the Strategic Framework effectively collapsed in December 2000. Faced with such restrictions, the Framework demonstrated the absence of coherence between development and security.

Concluding remarks

The division between aid and politics described above was not limited to the SFA. It was also replicated within and between donor governments and other aid agencies. As one DPA official put it in 2001, 'if you take a long view over the last ten years politics and aid have come together. However, if you take a short view of the last two years, then there has been a tremendous resistance.' At this time donor governments within the Afghanistan Support Group divided into a 'development/humanitarian group' and a 'politically orientated group' that usually wanted 'to discuss different things' (interview, former chair ASG, 21 May 2001). These groups reflected the divergent positions outlined above in relation to the SFA itself. Moreover, while the balance of force between development and security has now been reversed, regime change in Afghanistan has not resolved these differences.

Following the collapse of the Taliban regime, the first steps towards the creation of an integrated UN mission in Afghanistan came in

December 2001. Security Council Resolution 1401 made it clear that the UN's primary role is peace-building through 'the stabilization of the structures of the new state by political efforts and by using economic assistance to build legitimacy for the post-Taliban administration' (Costy 2004: 146). In some respects the United Nations Assistance Mission in Afghanistan (UNAMA) has a similar institutional structure to that of the SFA. For example, it has two main pillars, that is, 'Politics' and 'Relief, Recovery and Reconstruction'. However, rather than aid and politics being complementary, *politics is now in the driving seat.* Reflecting this situation, the establishment of the mission's political component proceeded quickly, with the appointment of a Special Representative of the Secretary-General (SRSG) for political affairs in December 2001. At the same time former UNSMA staff were speedily recycled into the new structure. In contrast, 'the absorption of human-itarian staff into the new structure became subject to lengthy and painstaking interdepartmental negotiations' (ibid.: 148). A deputy SRSG for aid was not announced until March 2002. Besides bringing the various components of the UN presence under political direction, the UN in Afghanistan has also found itself drawn into new relation-ships with the donor governments, NATO and the World Bank. In fact the UN is now involved in an international counter-insurgency role where 'international assistance has increasingly taken on the role of *regime consolidation:* feeding and servicing war-affected communities; regulating population movements; shoring up internal security systems; stimulating social and economic recovery; and rebuilding state institutions of new, more accommodating elites' (ibid.: 144 (emphasis in original). Within this post-interventionary structure, as the number of agencies, mandates and organizational preferences has increased, problems of coherence not only remain; if anything they have deepened (McNerney 2005).

7 Fragile States and Native Administration

This chapter is concerned with an important but unremarked paradox of the present period. During the Cold War the West often supplied arms to Third World regimes in order to help them to resist attempts by revolutionary groups seeking to remake the state in the light of popular demands and requirements. Today the West finds itself in the role of remaking states to meet the needs of people. Reflecting this post-interventionary shift, since the early 2000s a number of ideas relating to working in countries variously described as 'difficult environments', 'under stress', 'poor performers' or 'fragile states' have entered policy discourse (Torres and Anderson 2004; DCD 2004; DFID 2005a). They attempt to capture the development challenge at a time when many states are perceived to have failed in the protection of human security. Since the content of these terms is similar, the 'fragile state' is used here as a generic expression of this concern. While in some respects it is an updating of the earlier idea of the 'failed state', institutionally failed and fragile states have much in common. As expressions of state ineffectiveness they represent the antithesis of what policy makers and many academics conceive as effective, successful or robust states, especially in relation to supplying the public goods that support human security (Ghani et al. 2005). As examined in relation to the representation of the Taliban regime, state failure usually denotes such things as a chronic lack of state capacity, political fragmentation, collapsed public infrastructure and social isolation.

As part of this book's approach to development's various technologies of security – humanitarian intervention, sustainable development, human security, coherence – the fragile state is examined as a relation of international governance rather than a concrete thing. This chapter is not concerned with dissecting the innumerable typologies of administrative capacity and political will that discussions of state ineffectiveness throw up with eager regularity. As technologies of governance, the difference between failed and fragile states is not sought in variations on the absence of 'empirical' sovereignty (Jackson 1990); the difference is practical, and concerns the *sense of priority* and *policy tools* with which the international community addresses 'ungoverned' territory. Emerging before the concept of fragility, the idea of the failed state gained currency in the early years of the post-Cold War period. Throughout the 1990s, failed states, especially in regions of limited strategic importance to the West, generally ranked low on the international community's agenda of priorities. As a consequence and in contrast to today, the main policy tool associated with state failure was humanitarian aid (Leader and Colenso 2005: 38). It has already been argued that the collapse of the Washington consensus towards the end of the decade signalled the return of the state to the centre of development discourse. The argument that human security requires effective states, changes in the nature of aid disbursement and an improvement in its perceived effectiveness all encouraged this policy shift (McGillivray 2005). It was 9/11 and the perceived advent of indefinite war, however, that has made the need to rebuild ineffective states a central pillar in extending the West's external sovereign frontier.

Fragility and global instability

Since humanitarian assistance by its nature attempts to ignore or side-step states, it is of limited use in their reconstruction (Leader and Colenso 2005: 39). In contrast, the concept of the fragile state denotes a new willingness by the West to engage weak or defunct state entities developmentally. Unlike the failed state, the fragile state concept captures much of the current institutional experimentation occurring under the rubric of coherence in the post-interventionary transition from 'war to peace' in difficult environments (ibid.; PRDE 2004; DCD 2004; Picciotto et al. 2004). At a time of unending war and the dangers of surplus population circulating globally, state failure has gained a new significance. Building on the interventionary logic of the responsibility to protect, the fragile state takes up the post-interventionary challenge of the *responsibility to reconstruct* (ICISS 2001). While the failed state was a void, in many respects the fragile state denotes enduring technologies of governance associated with occupation and contingent sovereignty. The fragile state connects with the reinvention of development as a civilian form of counter-insurgency. As such, it also signals yet another reaffirmation of the connection between poverty and insecurity.

There is no agreed global list of fragile states; they appear, for example, in Africa, the Caribbean, the Pacific, south-east Asia and the Transcaucus region. Neither are they limited to countries that have been affected by conflict. The DFID defines fragile states as 'those where government cannot or will not deliver core functions to the majority of its people, including the poor' (DFID 2005a: 7). Although there is no accepted standard of measurement, there are thought to be about forty to fifty countries of varying combinations of weak institutional capacity and lack of political will that fall into this category. It is estimated that about 16 per cent of the world's population live in fragile states; collectively, however, they account for '35% of the world's poor, 44% of maternal deaths, 46% of children out of school, and 51% of children dying before the age of five' (Leader and Colenso 2005: 9). Fragile states are the most 'off track' with regard to achieving the UN's Millennium Development Goals (MDG), which include halving chronic poverty by 2015. Indeed, their existence threatens the achievement of these goals (Benn 2004). They are countries where people are statistically more likely to die early or live with chronic illness, where they are least likely to go to school or receive essential health care, and where economic growth is stagnant. World poverty and its associated negativities are concentrated and over-represented in fragile states.

Not only are fragile states an obstacle to reducing global poverty, they are also a source of international instability. Just as the fragile state has in policy discourse replaced the failed state, the idea of 'conflict', having held the ring for most of the 1990s, is now being replaced by 'instability'. In Britain, the Prime Minister's Strategy Unit report *Investing in Prevention* (2005), which complements the DFID's work on fragile states (Torres and Anderson 2004: 3), signals this important shift. It acknowledges the significant decline in open civil conflict since its 1992 peak, which is explained in terms of the major increase in post-Cold War international peace activism and enforcement (Strategy Unit 2005: 21). The report points out, however, that the decline in open conflict does not tell the whole story. Namely, most of the decrease in organized violence 'is due to its suppression or containment rather than its resolution' (ibid.: 22). The risk of future armed conflict consequently remains. Moreover, if a wider view of human security is adopted, the situation is far from comforting. While battlefield deaths may be declining, a broader view of security '*suggests that numbers of deaths are increasing*' (ibid.: 22 (emphasis in original)). In recent African conflicts, for example, on average only around 13 per cent of war-related deaths were directly attributable to physical violence. The overwhelming majority of fatalities result from the epiphenomena of conflict: mass displacement, lack of sanitation, disease, malnutrition or neglect (IRC 2003). Moreover, such epiphenomena merge into wider problems of generalized insecurity, sporadic violence, economic collapse and the absence of public health and welfare infrastructures. When other factors are taken into account, such as the future impact of HIV/AIDS, growing environmental stress, climate change, the strategic competition for oil and the economic isolation of non-integrating countries, it is likely that increased global instability *will be an enduring characteristic of the strategic landscape rather than a temporary phenomenon* (Strategy Unit 2005: 24 (emphasis in original)).

Because fragile states concentrate poverty and its effects, they pose great risks to global stability. Chronic poverty is not only a moral affront in today's world, global instability challenges the West's ability to achieve its strategic interests, including maintaining the integrity of mass consumption. In the case of Britain, for example, instability is seen as undermining many important national and international objectives, such as 'reducing global poverty, ensuring humanitarian protection and promoting human rights, fighting terrorism, managing immigration flows, reducing the threat of organized crime, and improving energy security' (ibid.: 20). Unstable countries are regarded as playing an important part in facilitating international terrorism. Exemplified by al-Qaida in Afghanistan, they can provide leadership havens and training grounds for recruits. In addition, within 'ungoverned' territory transborder shadow economies can operate freely (ibid.: 29). More generally, while poverty does not cause terrorism, the resulting alienation can serve as a recruiting ground and as justification for violence (DAC 2003). As a threat to national social cohesion, crises in fragile states are argued to be capable of triggering large flows of spontaneous refugees and asylum seekers. While migrants from unstable countries accounted for only 20 per cent of all migration to Britain in 2003, the same states 'yielded 65% of asylum seekers, and 90% of those granted asylum or leave to stay in Britain' (Strategy Unit 2005: 28). Given the policy of migrant dispersal discussed in the next chapter, importantly in 'already disadvantaged communities in the UK large inflows of transient populations can be damaging to social cohesion' (ibid.: 28). Regarding energy security, fragile states facing instability held 60 per cent of global oil reserves in 2003. That proportion is projected to rise over the coming decade. At the same time, Britain was predicted to become a net importer of natural gas in 2006 and oil in 2010 (ibid.).

Contingent sovereignty and non-material development

Within policy discourse, fragile states are a manifestation of modernity's failure; they are unable to reconcile the demands of progress with the need for order. Lacking various combinations of capacity and political will, they either ignore or menace the human security of their citizens. Simply by existing they threaten global stability. In calling forth a new and enduring post-interventionary era of developmental trusteeship, the fragile state signifies how development and security are being recombined at a time of global insurgency and unending war. Since the state has re-entered the foreground of development discourse, it is worth asking – what sort of state is being reconstructed? It is not the industrializing and modernizing state that emerged in the struggle against colonialism and sought to reduce the economic gap between the West and the rest. Apart from China, India and other parts of Asia, this project largely collapsed several decades ago. A clue as to what is being envisioned in those unstable territories where Western development policy remains instrumental is contained in the already discussed and related concepts of sustainable development, human security and contingent sovereignty. That is, a state is envisioned whose sovereignty over life is contingent on its delivery and support of *non-material development*. According to the DFID, for poverty reduction the most important functions of the state are 'territorial control, safety and security, capacity to manage public resources, deliver basic services, and the ability to protect and support the ways in which the poorest people sustain themselves' (2005: 7). In this and other accounts, the emphasis is on securing population by using 'the effective delivery of basic public goods' (Torres and Anderson 2004: 13) to *maintain the homeostasis of self-reliance.* Within policy discourse the idea that the collective welfare of millions of people entails little more than supporting essential infrastructure, primary education or basic needs is accepted without pause of criticism (see also Ghani et al. 2005). Even debt cancellation is framed in relation to improving self-reliance.

The metaphorical distinction between 'insured' and 'non-insured' life was used in the Introduction to contrast the biopolitics of development and underdevelopment respectively. The pervasive and ingrained assumption that non-Western peoples are largely self-reproducing in terms of their general welfare has also been commented on. This assumption is the occluded heart of development – habituated to the senses, never problematized in theory *but instrumental in practice.* You cannot describe this tendency as Eurocentric since this implies judging others by one's own standards or desires. The assumption of self-reliance says something different. It suggests that policy discourse experiences those defined by underdevelopment as a separate species-life. This is returned to in the following chapter, when racism and development is discussed. The instrumentality of self-reliance has already been examined in rural Mozambique. Such instrumentality can also be recognized in relation to the fragile state. Here it produces an experience of the state in which any centralizing bureaucracy dedicated to monitoring, disciplining or regulating population is absent. One does not encounter, for example, the centralizing or massifying welfare technologies associated with social insurance. In commenting on development in Lesotho, James Ferguson notes that the state's central role in the optimization of life, as evident in the biopolitics of mass consumer society, is here absent; given the salience of his comments, he is worth quoting at length.

> The growth to state power in such a context does not imply any sort of efficient, centralised social engineering. It simply means that power relations must increasingly be referred through bureaucratic circuits. The state here does not have a single rationality, and it is not capable of optimally ordering the biological resources of its population in the sense of the 'biopower' model. The state does not 'rationalise and centralize' power relations, [it] grabs onto and loops around existing power relations, not to rationalise or coordinate them, so much as to cinch them all together into a knot. (Ferguson 1990: 274)

Ferguson is here referring to the biopower associated with the emergence of European society. A contrary developmental biopolitics of self-reliance does not require the state to create centralized or comprehensive means for supporting and administering life. The absence of generalized wage labour means that there is no basis for conventional tax or national insurance schemes. Self-reliance pulls against the need for accounting, numbering and monitoring in depth, together with methods of estimating entitlements, rationing resources or assessing impacts on life and livelihoods. Within Europe, such technologies have encouraged increasingly refined methods of surveillance and behavioural modulation through a fine-grained calculus of risk (Ericson and Doyle 2003). In comparison, the idea of a 'surveillance society' in relation to rural Africa, for example, is out of place if not absurd. It is no accident that in many cases the most comprehensive forms of population monitoring are the coarse-grained surveys that came with the international aid agencies, that is, relatively crude, limited and often non-comparable surveys of basic biological need. The Darfur region of western Sudan, for example, has been subject to eight back-to-back humanitarian surveillance regimes since 1985 (Young and Jaspars 2006: 11–12). Rather than a coherent system, these mainly NGO initiatives have proved difficult to sustain, and few have attempted to gain a region-wide perspective, being mainly targeted on sub-regions and specific population groups. At the same time, they have differed in their objectives, moving through food-aid needs, famine early warning, monitoring food aid distributions, and so on, according to a changing perception of the crisis and the availability of funding. The methodologies involved have also varied and include random cluster surveys, anthropometric measurement, sentinel site monitoring, harvest assessments, and regional, village and household surveys. In the Horn of Africa, for example, several NGO-led attempts at long-term nutritional surveillance have collapsed because of funding problems, to be replaced by ad hoc surveys at times of crisis (ibid.: 13). It is a form of contingent surveillance befitting life that is otherwise surplus to requirements. That a fragile state can usually only guess the size of its population is not just a capacity problem; it is more the result of not needing to know.

The governance state

Indefinite war has made the threat of fragile states and ungoverned space more visible. In examining the practical technologies of development involved in their reconstruction, it is useful to begin with their opposite: the donor-declared success stories of Western aid, in particular those post-interventionary African societies such as Uganda, Ghana, Tanzania and Mozambique that have bucked regional trends and enjoyed robust levels of economic growth over the past decade. In order to offset the perception of African failure and exceptionalism, since the late 1990s such states have been used to showcase the fact that aid can work under the right circumstances. It can deliver economic growth, stability and the promise of poverty reduction (Torres and Anderson 2004: 10). The right circumstances are a strong institutional and policy environment in which states have the capacity to manage aid flows and elites have internalized neoliberal doctrine. Reflecting the high degree of international influence and control over the core economic and welfare functions of the state, that is, its core biopolitical functions, Graham Harrison (2004) has called such countries 'governance states'. During the 1990s, development aid became more selective, tending to concentrate on such 'good performers' at the expense of fragile 'poor performers'. At the same time, by the end of the decade a movement had begun away from supporting NGO projects outside the state to funding the good performers directly through their budgets. The governance 'state' is best understood as a funding regime or mechanism for chronically aid-dependent countries that provides stability to the donor–recipient relationship. It involves the latter in programme design and aid disbursement while giving the former ultimate authority. As a way of extending the West's external sovereign frontier, the value placed on this post-interventionary stability and interpenetration has shaped the emerging consensus on fragile states, or at least, what a fragile state should ideally become. Any linear assumption that fragile states will automatically evolve into 'good performers', however, has been questioned; the challenge is to create dedicated fragile state tools and aid frameworks that can act as intermediary stepping stones (Leader and Colenso 2005). Before examining these tools, the architecture of the governance state is examined in more detail.

Post-interventionary governance states began to stabilize in the mid-1990s after a decade of World Bank-led structural adjustment, that is, the rolling back of the state in favour of privatization and expanding markets. This stabilization was celebrated by the World Bank in its rejection of the so-called Washington consensus that had shaped the coercive and conditional ethos of structural adjustment. In a 1998 lecture, Joseph Stiglitz, then the Bank's senior vice-president and chief economist, publicly acknowledged fifty years of development failure. Structural adjustment and market reform had failed because 'they viewed development too narrowly' (Stiglitz 1998: 1). It had been assumed that progressive social change would mechanically follow from getting the economy right. Such change, however, had not been forthcoming, and traditional forces resistant to progress remained embedded. The situation required a new post-interventionary paradigm for 'catalysing change and transforming *whole* societies' (ibid.: 3 (emphasis in original)). Such a radical process, however, cannot be imposed. Stiglitz recognized that while you can force people do things against their wishes, you cannot make them think what they do not believe. Social change, therefore, has to be based on a comprehensive process of consensus building that encourages ownership and participation by aid recipients. The end of the Washington consensus heralded what Harrison has called the era of second-generation reform or 'post-conditionality' (Harrison 2001). Whereas structural adjustment had been concerned with reducing the role of the state, second-generation reform is more focused on the nature of state action and involves 'institutional capacity building; civil service (or more broadly public service) reform; the introduction of new forms of information technology, finance, management and human resource management; technical assistance and the facilitation of public participation in policy monitoring, evaluation and development' (Harrison 2004: 18).

These institutional reforms are concerned with constructing a stable and enduring system of accounting and management that allows aid-dependent states to absorb and operationalize external funding and technical assistance. A central plank in achieving such predictability within post-interventionary societies is having the 'right type' of state interlocutor. That is, those who believe in what they do and are part of the web of overlapping interests and shared objectives known as the international community. By the early 1990s the effect of structural adjustment on emerging governance states had typically been to divide nationalist elites into 'old' and 'new' factions, with the latter resigned to implementing Bank policies. Moments of conflict and tension between these factions were 'succeeded by the strengthening of the pro-reform elements within the ruling elite and a strengthening of support for those elements by the [international financial institutions] and others' (ibid.: 37). Since the 1980s, for example, the international community has consciously cultivated a pro-reform elite within Tanzania. Measures included establishing technical workshops bringing together expatriate and Tanzanian economists, as well as supporting selective secondments and training programmes. During the 1990s the World Bank and donor governments intervened to secure positions of influence for pro-reformers in key ministries and private consultancy companies. These Tanzanians would provide much of the momentum to sustain reform in the late 1990s (Pender 2005: 11). It has already been described how the UN also tried to use the aid programme to encourage the 'good' Taliban while excluding the 'bad' in Afghanistan. In Tanzania, the pro-reformers are sceptical towards local political elites and, at the same time, have a shared 'way of doing business' with international donors and NGOs. They have a common educational background (often in British or US universities), have been socialized in the same professional culture and share a conceptual vocabulary and understanding of authoritative knowledge. While this post-interventionary elite is small, its power and capacity is substantially bolstered by the presence and activity of external actors in the aid programme. Representatives 'of international institutions, donor governments, and international and domestic [NGOs] play a routine, intimate part in the regulation and management of the poverty reduction programme' (ibid.: 12).

Aid policy in governance states can be said to be post-conditional in that pro-reform elites have internalized international policy requirements and objectives. While all development assistance is by its nature conditional, within governance states conditionality loses its external or coercive edge. Poverty reduction is now *a shared project* on which donors, NGOs and governments all work together. An important means of strengthening this process of governmentalization has been the Poverty Reduction Strategy Paper (PRSP). Emerging from a lengthy and intensive period of negotiation, PRSPs are a post-interventionary successor to structural adjustment. Agreed between donors and the government, they are funded by the former but owned by the latter. They set out in some detail the programmes, responsibilities and monitoring methods for delivering pro-poor growth. The PRSP process is linked to the shift away from project support outside the state. Funding directly through the budget, which allows donors to harmonize and align 'behind country-led development approaches' (Leader and Colenso 2005: 11), has emerged as the preferred funding mechanism in governance states (Harrison 2004: 90). Reflecting the hegemony of neoliberalism, the ministry of finance emerges as the key institution within governance states. It is the main point of donor entry into the state, regardless of the service ministry with which they may be dealing. Through selective donor funding, the ministry of finance usually has the best buildings and offices, the newest management systems and more computerization, enabling it to 'ensure fiscal prudence throughout most of the state' (Harrison 2004: 84).

With the West's external sovereign frontier, the post-Cold War collapse of the national/international dichotomy takes on a physical form within the institutions of the governance state. Typically, groups or committees of donors and international NGOs meet either fortnightly or monthly to shadow the activities of the main service ministries. Depending on the service concerned, groups are usually chaired by a donor having a relevant specialist interest, and the appropriate permanent secretary or other government officials are counted as members. The groups discuss policy, monitor progress and consider new funding options. Such fora are an important means of governmentalization within the space of contingent sovereignty. They generalize new methodologies of government based on corporate plans, surveys, logical frameworks, time frames and funding requirements.

Not only does the civil service regularly produce information for these groups, they 'are a routine part of the way government works' (ibid.: 88). Donors also have their representatives working inside the state as counterparts, accountants and capacity builders. In these different ways, donors and NGOs 'work in a routine fashion at the centre of policy making' (ibid.: 90). In relation to Tanzania, to all intents and purposes it 'can be described as an internationally managed and regulated society' (Pender 2005: 13). Rather than thinking of the international community somehow acting externally on such states, 'it would be more useful to conceive of donors as *part of the state itself*. This is what distinguishes the sovereign frontier of governance states from those of other African states' (Harrison 2004: 87–88 (emphasis in original)).

If the 'state' has again moved to the foreground of post-interventionary development discourse, then the governance state provides the contours of what that ideal state might be. While its territorial integrity is respected, sovereignty over life is internationalized, negotiable and contingent. Since its population is regarded as essentially self-reliant, any centrally administered, comprehensive or insurance-based measures to compensate for life's contingencies are not required. At the heart of the governance state is a budget support mechanism allowing donors to harmonize and align their contributions and policies behind an active-citizen approach to welfare, based on market incorporation through the provision of essential infrastructure and satisfying basic needs. Periodic crises of self-reliance are addressed through humanitarian assistance. This aid-dependent and privatized model of development has placed Western donors, UN agencies and NGOs inside the governance state. In a world of growing instability, the influence that contingent sovereignty imparts is valued above the corruption or authoritarianism that such states often exhibit (ibid.: 93–4). As John Pender has argued, there is little popular demand for this level of international occupation. No one in Africa has ever voted for the current development regime: it came with the vote. Nor does it address the specific deprivation within these states. Sustainable development breaks with the notion of material improvement; as a model of poverty management its highest aim is a homeostatic condition of self-reliance satisfying minimal requirements. After a decade of international leadership Tanzania, for example, 'is showing little domestic dynamic to improving material standards of living' (Pender 2005: 16). When Stiglitz relaunched development nearly a decade ago by signalling a post-conditional future, he concluded his lecture by posing the question, 'transformation to what kind of society, and for what ends?' (Stiglitz 1998: 29). It was a question that he left unanswered.

The fragile state and liberal imperialism

In a radically interconnected world, the fragile state represents the threat of ungoverned space. Within policy discourse it exists as a set of technical prescriptions to bolster administrative capacity and strengthen international oversight, the aim of which is to transform the fragile state into a governance state. In contrast to governance states, which are funding regimes providing stability to the donor–state relationship in aid-dependent countries, fragile states are dangerous because they lack the capacity to become aid-dependent and thus a known part of the West's sovereign frontier. In creating specific development tools for fragile states, a starting point is the type of aid flow that is argued to have helped 'good performers' in the past. There are a number of difficulties, however. Because of the established donor preference to pick development winners, fragile states have a history of aid neglect and parsimony. Using a World Bank measure that ranks states according to capacity and performance, the bottom 40 per cent of aid receivers account for only 14 per cent of bilateral aid. The top 40 per cent, however, absorb nearly two-thirds (DFID 2005a: 12). Moreover, what aid fragile states do receive is volatile, crisis driven and lacking in harmonization (Ghani et al. 2005: 10–12). From an institutional perspective also, the aid received is ineffective. There is a tendency for donors and NGOs to establish parallel structures that replicate and undermine state systems rather than enhancing them. Much of it is humanitarian assistance that 'is delivered outside state structures' (DFID 2005a: 12). Lacking capacity, fragile states cannot meet donor-auditing and accounting requirements, nor can they absorb aid and disburse it in an accountable manner. In terms of conventional wisdom, fragile states are 'aid orphans' within an aid system that is now beginning to work. It follows that the problem of fragile states can be addressed by increasing flows of 'good' aid, that is, development assistance which is long-term, predicable and properly harmonized and aligned around appropriate mechanisms that work progressively to increase state capacity, local ownership and collective identity.

Before this approach is examined, it is worth mentioning what is absent from mainstream considerations of success. Fragile state discourse draws on Robert Jackson's *Quasi-States: Sovereignty, International Relations and the Third World* (1990), that distinguishes between *de jure* and *de facto* state sovereignty – that is, the gap between the state as a formal or legal entity and its organizational or empirical capacity to govern. The approach to fragile states has been conceived as 'implementing strategies to close this sovereign gap' (Ghani et al. 2005: 4). Important in this conception is the absence of any sense that donors, UN agencies, NGOs and other international actors themselves have a sovereign presence. In other words, there is no experience of such actors, or of state elites being part of a frontier zone of conflict, negotiation and identity. Although actively trying to close it, the West is curiously absent from the 'sovereign gap'. At the same time, also missing is any sense that success within this zone is less about the right policies and more about having the right local interlocutors, in this case a pro-reform elite that shares an economic and political vocabulary with the international actors that engage it. Given that public welfare is premised on self-reliance, rather than effecting a significant improvement in living standards, the notion of success in governance states speaks more to the degree to which the international community decides the core economic, social and security functions of government. Ideas of 'successful' development invariably ignore the political basis on which it is constituted (see also Ferguson 1990; Escobar 1995; Mitchell 2002).

It would be wrong, however, to see the 'sovereign gap' as simply an exercise in obfuscation. While obscuring the West's sovereign presence, through the urgent need to reconstruct the institutional basis for the exercise of freedom and rights it is simultaneously an international clarion call *for its assertion*. Reducing the gap between a *de jure* and a *de facto* authority in difficult environments is argued to require a 'global paradigm shift' involving the search for greater coherence between the existing forms of intervention (Ghani et al. 2005: 20). Fragile state discourse aims to improve international coherence around the design and management of core biopolitical functions of the state. If the governance state provides an ideal of ordered aid dependency, ungoverned space constitutes an acute challenge for international security. Apart from the selectivity and lack of coherence within the aid system, there is an absence of administrative capacity and, importantly, a dearth of the right type of state interlocutors. The threat posed by ungoverned space to an international problematic of security, however, is not something new. It is no accident that the difficulties encountered in attempting to reconstruct failed states, a duty arising from today's responsibility to intervene and protect human security (ICISS 2001), has led the West to rediscover colonial forms of liberal governance. While often presented as cutting-edge thinking, fragile state discourse is exemplary in this respect.

Reintroducing Native Administration

While the fragile state problem is part of the present conjuncture, the social assumptions and technologies of power being deployed in response resonate with an earlier liberal imperialism, in particular the late colonial practice of indirect rule or Native Administration already mentioned in earlier chapters. Native Administration involved the decentralization of administrative duties by the colonial state to tribal organizations according to their perceived level of social evolution. In mobilizing tribal authorities as administrative auxiliaries, nationalist forces dismissed Native Administration as a cheap and politically backward form of colonialism. For decades this pervasive view has confined indirect rule to the dustbin of history. Strengthening the power of traditional rulers is usually argued to have 'maintained a high level of tribal consciousness. In some cases, it accentuated regional differences' (Darby 1987: 44). From this perspective, rather than a liberal technology of development, Native Administration is more a reactionary form of 'decentralised despotism' (Mamdani 1996: 18). Such a nationalist bias tends to conceal the links between Native Administration and today's post-Cold War interventionism. Both indirect rule and fragile state discourse function as technologies of security concerned with the viral nature of global circulation. While the former was central to liberal colonialism's counter-nationalist strategy, the latter is concerned with the transnational nature of terrorist threats. Indirect rule and fragile state interventions both attempt to secure emerging state entities against minority and externally supported enemies. In this respect they bookend the nationalist project, the one resisting its onset, the other attempting to construct an international security regime out of the debris of its political collapse. Like indirect rule, supporting fragile states also involves a decentralization of administrative tasks, this time by the international community according to the level of administrative capacity of the state entity involved.

Indirect rule represented a radical break with the militarized, indeed often genocidal, direct rule that was common during the so-called New Imperialism of the closing decades of the nineteenth century (Hobson [1902]). It involved a rejection of a single, hierarchical model of progress that informed contemporary ideas of race-based social Darwinism. The virtues of indirect rule were cogently expressed, for example, in the early twentieth century work of such liberal imperialists as J. A. Hobson, Edmund Morel and Lord Lugard. Indirect rule emerged in parts of India towards the end of the nineteenth century, for example, in the restoration of Mysore to princely rule, before spreading ad hoc to other regions of the British Empire, such as the Basutoland protectorate in southern Africa and the development of West Africa's cocoa and palm oil industries. By the 1920s, however, spurred on by the formation of the League of Nations, indirect rule had been formalized in the theory and practice of Native Administration (Lugard [1922]). Variants of indirect rule were also encountered beyond the British Empire, for example, within the US Bureau for Indian Affairs during the 1930s and 1940s (Cooke 2003).

Until around the time of the First World War, the growth of Native Administration had been largely propelled by liberal concerns over the negative effects on the self-reliance of subject peoples of direct militarized rule, rapid urbanization and unregulated commercial exploitation (MacMichael 1923: 2). In attempting to strengthen communal organization against the unexpected and anomic consequences of progress, Native Administration was deployed as a counter-nationalist security technology. In seeking to strength social cohesion, Native Administration was used to mobilize 'traditional' rural peoples against this threatening new urban manifestation of the 'modern'. As a forerunner of counter-insurgency discourse (Thompson 1966), including the contemporary use of aid as a tool of conflict resolution (Anderson 1996), it was liberal colonialism's attempt to govern in the name of defending a vulnerable majority from the negative designs of a usually externally inspired elite. As a non-settler trusteeship, the evolution of Native Administration in Sudan is a good example. As a means of keeping the urbanized and transnational forces of nationalism in check, promoting Native Administration through conserving and mobilizing the tribal forces of the countryside became an increasingly urgent political task following the end of the First World War. Through indirect rule 'a solid barrier will be created against insidious political intrigue which must in the ordinary course of events increasingly beset our path' (MacMichael 1928: 4). During the latter half of the 1920s and most of the 1930s, the creation and amalgamation of tribal units into administrative structures through the devolution of local powers continued apace (MacMichael 1934). Although the colonial regime ultimately failed in its attempt to mobilize Sudan's tribal peoples in defence of imperial rule, as will be argued in relation to fragile states the discursive practices and forms of political comportment informing Native Administration continue to survive and replicate. To disclose the fragile state in this way, current policy prescriptions are discussed under three headings: 'Culture and the limits of government', 'The necessity of despotism' and 'Adjusting government to culture'. In order to illustrate the affinity between fragile state discourse and Native Administration, each of these sections opens with a few comments on liberal colonial practice.

Culture and the limits of government
Indirect rule emerged as a liberal alterative to the exterminatory impulse driving the New Imperialism of the late nineteenth century. When compared with Britain's Old Empire of self-governing colonies such as Canada, Australia and New Zealand, for its critics the New Imperialism bequeathed extensive territories containing 'large populations of savages or "lower races"; little of it likely, even in the distant future, to increase the area of sound colonial life' (Hobson [1902]: 124). In other words, it established a problem of government that, excepting the outwardly biological language of race, is still recognizable in failed and fragile state discourse. Indeed, despite an interlude of over a century, the geographical space of this 'unsound life' is still largely contiguous with today's fragile states. In addressing this problem of government, indirect rule was liberal colonialism's tool of choice. Native Administration embodies the principle that 'progress will take place more and more upon the qualitative plane, with more intensive cultivation alike of natural resources and of human life' (ibid.: 235). In what we now recognize as multiculturalism, rather than one model or standard of progress there are in fact many. Edmund Morel, for example, argues that the sociocultural differences in humanity must be taken into account when considering the stable growth of national identity. Moreover, encouraging 'the unfolding of the mental processes by gradual steps is the only method by which the exercise of the imperial prerogative is morally justified' (Morel 1920: 205). Central to indirect rule's evolutionary developmentalism was the conscious act of knowing the peoples concerned. The study of languages, customs and social organization through the emerging discipline of anthropology was encouraged. By promoting tolerance borne of understanding, such knowledge was seen as engendering trust. Knowledgeable colonial administrators could give 'wider concept to the latent mental powers and spiritual potentialities' of subject peoples (ibid.: 241).

The next chapter discusses the place of racism in development in some detail, in particular, while retaining its biological essence, the foregrounding of a culturally coded racism in the aftermath of the Second World War and the contested process of decolonization. Here it is sufficient to mention that, reflecting their liberal pedigree, both Native Administration and fragile state discourse reproduce the Enlightenment identification between culture, or social character, and the capacity for political existence (Jahn 2005). As already mentioned, both attempt to exert a trusteeship over a vulnerable majority in order to defend it against the avaricious, criminal or extremist designs of a usually externally inspired elite. For Native Administration the vulnerable majority was experienced in terms of population striated according to a multitude of dependent tribes, ethnic groups or castes, each identification imparting its own special group character, aptitudes or predilections. For fragile state discourse – reflecting development policy generally since decolonization – the vulnerable majority is now the 'poor' (Duffield 2001: 126–8). More accurately, it is the various 'tribes' of the poor that, according to their differing characteristics, behavioural traits and needs, are dependent on external assistance: the chronically poor, the landless, slum-dwellers, widows, the elderly, female-headed households or the internally displaced. The relativization of poverty has already been discussed in relation to Mozambique. In terms of indirect rule, the enemy against which the tribal majority needed defending was the educated urban elite. Within fragile state discourse, the poor have to be protected from state incumbents that are either unable or unwilling to support human security. Since fragile states contain a large measure of the world's chronically poor, if something is not done to promote more effective forms of administration 'we will have no hope of achieving the Millennium Development Goals. No hope of relieving absolute poverty. No hope of reducing child mortality. No hope of stopping the scourge of HIV/AIDs' (Benn 2004). In the shape of the fragile state – or rather its incumbents – the causes of poverty, and hence global instability, are crystallized into *an enemy*.

In defining the enemy, fragile state discourse contains the post-interventionary injunction that ineffective states have a *responsibility to develop*. As for aid policy, difficult environments are those countries 'where the state is unable *or unwilling* to harness domestic *and international* resources effectively for poverty reduction' (Torres and Anderson 2004: 3, emphasis added). If fragile states are to become good global citizens – that is, 'easy environments' in which international aid organizations can operate – state incumbents must be willing to use international aid effectively for poverty reduction. Since the demand that administrators and practitioners must understand the societies they work in is central to liberal forms of trusteeship, it is periodically rediscovered as the acme of effective policy making (DAC 1997). It forms the basis, for example, of the DFID's (2005a) 'drivers of change' approach, the key elements of which regarding fragile states are the need to understand the history of a country and its people, 'who holds power and how is it brokered and used, the informal "rules of the game" (such as how patronage networks operate in government and business) and the relationship between these and formal institutions (such as appointments to the executive and judiciary)' (ibid.: 14). Whereas Native Administration relied on and encouraged an anthropological understanding, fragile state discourse is premised on political economy. Development in a fragile state is not simply a technical matter; there 'is a growing recognition of the need to understand the political incentives and the institutions that affect the prospects for reform' (DFID 2005a: 14). It involves 'an excellent understanding of the political economy' (PRDE 2004: 9). In relation to fragile states, the DFID's 'drivers for change' approach essentially involves distinguishing between friend and enemy in terms of the willingness to accept external aid and guidance.

> Effective states depend on effective political leadership equipped with the skills to manage conflicting interests, agree effective policies, and see through structural change. Where institutions are weak, personalities often dominate. *In the worst cases, predatory leaders unchecked by institutionalised constraints can steal property, kill people, and ruin the economy.* (DFID 2005a: 15, emphasis added)

Provided that the right type of interlocutor exists, working in difficult environments involves 'being supportive of partner's efforts to create the conditions for political stability, helping build government capacity, encouraging political commitment to stronger policy environments' (PRDE 2004: 6). Once friend and enemy can be distinguished through an understanding of political economy, working in fragile states is a process of alliance building with the former. In governance states, more than a decade of socialization through selective engagement had produced a small but influential pro-reform elite by the mid-1990s. Fragile states often lack this history. While the present reconstruction programmes in Iraq and Afghanistan are also reliant on pro-reform elites occupying key positions in the transitional administration, rather than being formed on the job as in Africa's governance states, they have mainly emerged ready-made from the Iraqi and Afghan diaspora. Prior to return they had already been socialized into neoliberalism in the boardrooms, offices and campuses of Europe and the United States (Herring and Rangwala 2005; Suhrke 2006).

As a guide to understanding the range of difficult (or perhaps 'enemy') environments that are possible, policy documents often give a typology of fragile states based on different combinations of administrative capacity and political will. DFID (2005), for example, lists four broad types of ineffective states: 'good performers' (which would include governance states), 'weak but willing', 'strong but unresponsive/repressive', and 'weak-weak' (ibid.: 7–8; see also Torres and Anderson 2004: 17–18). Despite such attempts to demonstrate policy flexibility and openness to differences between societies, the centrality of pro-reform elites to the development process trumps both detailed social analysis and technically robust prescriptions; without the right type of interlocutor, nothing is going to happen. Like Balibar's observations on the new culturally coded racism discussed in the following chapter, despite being outwardly premised on cultural difference and plurality, it rests on an older division of humanity into two main groups, 'the one assumed to be universalistic and progressive, the other supposed irremediably particularistic and primitive' (Balibar 1991: 25).

The necessity of despotism

Since its emergence as part of modernity, liberalism has been characterized by a recurrent paradox. While embodying a will to govern in the name of people, freedom and rights, it readily accepts despotic rule over others provided that the ultimate outcome is developmental. This paradox informed, for example, nineteenth-century liberal imperialism (Mehta 1999). In addressing the problem of the fragile state, especially the dearth of acceptable interlocutors, the necessity of having to accept despotism is once more at the centre of policy discourse. Torres and Anderson (2004), for example, query as unreliable and contentious any definition of state failure that draws on an inability to generate legitimate support. They argue that legitimacy and effectiveness are ambiguously related. Weak legitimacy does not automatically equate with weak capacity. Legitimacy, moreover, can be strengthened retrospectively by pursuing policies of growth or poverty reduction. At the same time, there is no clear evidence that legitimacy is related to political participation. It is arguable that in many neopatrimonial states, 'it is precisely the pursuit of legitimacy that has made the state a weak partner in poverty reduction' (ibid.: 17). The liberal embrace of despotism is today eloquently evinced in DFID's (2005a) evocative concept of 'good enough governance'. Governance reforms need to be achievable and appropriate to their context. Medium-term realism may need to be exercised if long-term development and stability are to be achieved.

> 'Good enough' governance is about effective states fulfilling certain basic functions, including protecting people from harm and providing an economic framework to enable people to support themselves. *It may involve practices that would not exist in an ideal government* – corruption may be rife, staff may lack necessary skills, and capacity may be chronically weak and under-funded. (Ibid.: 20, emphasis added)

There is no agreed threshold separating 'good enough governance' from 'bad governance'. In its *Responsibility to Protect* (2001) the ICISS, while not defining an actual limit, suggests a very high threshold of systematic abuse and killing before a moral responsibility to intervene can be deemed to have passed to the international community. The report quotes the words of Kofi Annan, the former UN Secretary-General, concerning 'gross and systematic violations of human rights' that affront every precept of a common humanity (ibid.: vii). It speaks in terms of large-scale loss of life or ethnic cleansing carried out, for example through mass murder, rape and starvation, and having societal levels of impact (ibid.: xi). If this is the West's threshold by which it measures its own willingness to intervene, in other words, its own humanity, then good enough governance provides plenty of scope for more generalized misuse that falls short of a 'supreme' emergency: flawed elections, extra-judicial killings and disappearances, pervasive corruption, routinized human rights abuse, ethnic and religious oppression, dereliction of office and so on. Good enough governance is the price the West is willing to pay for building a stable aid relationship along its external sovereign frontier.

Adjusting government to culture

A specifically liberal form of imperialism is continually challenged by the need to adjust the techniques of sound government to the limits set by the social character of the governed (Jahn 2005: 601). Native Administration, for example, was based on devolving appropriate administrative responsibilities, such as public works, tax collection, rural courts, local police and primary education, to indigenous tribal or feudal authorities. In theory, the complexity of the tasks and responsibilities devolved depended on the level of social organization encountered. Decentralized or 'pagan' tribal groups would be given basic tasks (MacMichael 1923), while feudal kingdoms would be entrusted with a wide remit of local government duties. Through devolving more demanding tasks once existing ones were mastered, the aim was to move the peoples concerned progressively towards political maturity and, in the fullness of time, self-determination. To secure this developmental aim, the 'backward races' were not to have an alien model imposed on them. Rather, they were to be empowered 'by their own efforts in their own way, to raise themselves to a higher plane of social organisation' (Lugard [1922]: 215). While the principles of Native Administration were fixed, their application was to vary with levels of social advancement. Moreover, the 'task of the administrative officer is to clothe his principles in the garb of evolution, not revolution' (ibid.: 193–4). In all essentials, Native Administration was a programme of development (Cooke 2003), the aim of which was to initiate a process of controlled social change through incremental self-management while maintaining and strengthening social cohesion. It is this developmental pedigree that links indirect rule with today's fragile state discourse.

Rather than assuming a linear evolution of fragile states into 'good performers' or governance states, there is a recognition of the need for specialist measures and frameworks as a necessary stepping stone (Leader and Colenso 2005: 13–14).

In formulating development tools for fragile states, there are three main issues: first, weak administrative capacity; second, weak or absent political will; and, finally, the anarchy within an aid system composed of multiple agencies, private organizations and 'different perceptions of strategic interest among donors and regional powers' (ibid.: 21). Fragile state policy attempts to address these concerns. The technologies involved have elements of simplification, especially reducing the administrative and accounting demands from those expected of a Poverty Reduction Strategy (PRS) in a governance state. Coherence is improved by building in donor harmonization and alignment from the outset. While often falling short of funding through the budget for accountability reasons, the tools and frameworks nevertheless aim to engage and socialize fragile state incumbents. Many current aid interventions in the Caribbean, Africa, Transcaucasia, south Asia, east Asia, Iraq and Afghanistan, for example, are laboratories for the development of these technologies (PRDE 2004). It should be emphasized, however, that rather than pioneering new technologies as such, fragile state policy is emerging retrospectively through the interpretation and orchestrating of initiatives that have often emerged spontaneously within the space of contingent sovereignty. Given that interventions vary in technical detail, an overview of the main principles behind fragile state policy is given here.

Technologies of post-interventionary governance

Regarding the lack of capacity, a starting point is the emergence of techniques of governance that fall short of the bureaucratic and reporting demands of a formal PRS. A leading example is the Transitional Results Matrix (TRM) pioneered by the World Bank. Typically a TRM is developed in relation to a Joint Assessment Mission (JAM) conducted by donors, UN agencies, NGOs and government representatives. Variants have emerged, for example in East Timor, Liberia, Sudan, Central African Republic and Haiti. They set out 'an agreement between donors and the government about how much support will be given to activities in key areas' (DIFD 2005a: 19). As pre-PRS frameworks they 'aim to provide a government and donor road map for prioritisation, coordination and monitoring' (Leader and Colenso 2005: 19). In attempting to understand and develop further the potential of such technologies and, at the same time, address international concerns over legitimizing unsuitable state incumbents, DFID has introduced the idea of 'shadow alignment' (ibid.: 20). This technology of governmentalization is meant to enable donors to work in such a way as to be compatible with national systems without being subject to government priorities. Possibilities include 'putting aid "on-budget" but not "through budget", working with existing administrative boundaries, and providing information to the recipient in terms that are compatible with their national systems such as the budgetary classifications and cycle' (ibid.).

The essence of shadow alignment is the creation of aid frameworks, for example, a 'shadow budget' or a 'shadow health sector', which can achieve several things to adjust the technologies of aid to existing social conditions. First, it provides a framework against which donors, UN agencies and NGOs can harmonize, align and sequence their activities. Regarding NGOs, for some time they have stood accused of further weakening fragile states by establishing an unconnected and better-resourced parallel system (Ghani et al. 2005: 10). Since shadow alignment seeks to emulate national institutions, harmonization within such a framework can reduce such problems. At the same time, because it is a simulation of a budgetary system, it offers donor governments several points of engagement with state incumbents and opportunities for selective capacity building without necessarily legitimating those incumbents Like the model of progressive evolution contained in Native Administration, these points of engagement range from being kept informed, through joint monitoring arrangements, to eventually taking control of the systems concerned. As an enduring political relationship, shadow alignment is argued to be 'future proof' (Leader and Colenso 2005: 20). It would lead, presumably, to the sort of international regulation of key social and economic functions that exists in the governance state.

There are several existing post-interventionary frameworks of engagement that would lend themselves to techniques of shadow alignment. For example, *trust funds* have emerged as a way of providing budgetary support to countries 'where fiduciary risk is high while simultaneously building capacity of the state to manage and control its own budget' (PRDE 2004: 9). In Afghanistan, for example, the Afghanistan Reconstruction Fund (ARTF) has become the instrument of choice for donors in helping to build trust and capacity. A multi-donor Capacity Building Support Fund (CBSF) has been established in South Sudan to support the recurrent costs of teachers, health workers and administrators in its nascent public administration. In East Timor, a multi-donor Transitional Support Programme (TSP) includes general budget support and a framework for service delivery at an early state of state formation (Leader and Colenso 2005: 23). Sierra Leone and Rwanda have seen more ambitious moves by donors to support government systems. Another existing framework is multi-donor *pooled funding*. It is argued that this increases donor harmonization and allows a more programmatic approach to fragile states. In Burma pooled funding has enabled the donor community to scale up its support of civil society organizations. At the same time, links have been maintained with the state in terms of a joint HIV/AIDS programme, where 'ministry of health officials are part of the coordinating structure' (PRDE 2004: 9). In Afghanistan there are twelve National Priority Programmes (NPPs) that offer donors a way of pooling funds in areas designated by the government as priorities. The National Emergency Employment Programme, for example, is controlled by the Ministry of Rural Rehabilitation and Development, 'both managed by a special programme implementation unit staffed by internationals and Afghans paid considerably more than the normal civil service salaries. It is implemented around the country by

NGOs and private sector engineering firms' (Leader and Colenso 2005: 34).

Another existing post-interventionary framework offering the possibility of shadow alignment is the *social funds*. This aims to bring together communities, donors and government representatives to improve 'social protection, service delivery and livelihoods in fragile states' (PRDE 2004: 9). The Yemen social fund, for example, has attracted £225 million for the period 2004–08 from the World Bank, the EU, Netherlands, United Kingdom, USAID and several Arab donors. Social funds align with government objectives and attempt not to undermine the state. In Afghanistan the National Solidarity Programme (NSP) is based on the social fund principle. Basically, donors pay into the NSP fund and the government, through the management of an oversight consultant, releases directly to community groups project funds which are managed by NGOs. Communities are expected to elect a community development council that is responsible for designing and overseeing the implementation of the project. It is intended to assist communities in rebuilding assets and improving community governance. The programme is managed by an oversight consultant contracted by the Ministry of Rural Rehabilitation and Development. At the community level, work 'is undertaken by facilitating partners under contract to the ministry. Donors contribute to the programme as a whole' (Leader and Colenso 2005: 33). A similar fund also operates in the Ministry of Health, where a private US company contracts out health work to international NGOs. This relationship is interesting, since, basically, it involves a private company emulating a ministry as it channels external donor funding to implementing NGOs. One of the aims of the NSP is to 'provide a new model of the relationship between state and citizen' (ibid.: 33).

Concluding remarks

The above examples of existing privatized, multi-agency technologies of security are indicative of how governance through liberal trusteeship is now an enduring characteristic of the politics of post-interventionary society. In this respect, Afghanistan is currently an important zone of fragile state experimentation. The revival of Taliban resistance, however, and its deliberate targeting of these systems has thrown them into relief as the civilian components of counter-insurgency attempting to create a 'new model of the relationship between state and citizen' alongside ongoing efforts to violently suppress resistance to this project. However, given that Western 'development' means little more than the promise of self-reliance for the majority of the population, Afghanistan's difficult environment is all the more testing. Self-reliance has a dangerous ambiguity in relation to attempts to strengthen state authority. When successfully and innovatively pursued, rather than being a process of governmentalization, self-reliance supports resistance and imparts independence. The 'actually existing development' of informal trade, illegal commodity procurement, transborder smuggling networks and diaspora enterprise can encourage centrifugal forces of autonomy and alternative claims to legitimacy and rights to life. It is ironic that one of the few cases where community self-reliance is possible in Afghanistan – opium poppy cultivation and the manufacture of heroin – is internationally outlawed in favour of legal and thus cheaper substitute crops. Indicative of the contradictions involved, the value of the drug economy is currently estimated to be twice that of the West's combined development assistance and reconstruction efforts in Afghanistan (Whitaker and Huggler 2006).

Native Administration and fragile state discourse are both forms of evolutionary developmental trusteeship exercised with the problem of ungoverned space. Both share a liberal willingness to accept despotism and, at the same time, adjust the mechanisms of government to the limits of culture. They are also different, however. Native Administration problematized an emergent nationalist state. In comparison, acting on fragile states is concerned with supporting an emergent governance state, that is, a zone of contingent sovereignty where the West shapes the basic economic and welfare policies operating at the level of population. Fragile state interventions, together with the technologies of coherence and sustainable development discussed earlier, indicate how the West is attempting to strengthen its external sovereign frontier. This frontier, however, is bracketed together with a metropolitan or internal sovereign zone constructed around identity, entitlements and responsibilities. The following chapter discusses the nature of the international security architecture that bridges the national–international divide and interconnects these two development frontiers.

8 Racism, Circulation and Security

This chapter is concerned with development as a technology of containment associated with the division of the global population into insured and non-insured life at the time of decolonization, and especially the permanent crisis of containment arising from the moral, political and practical impossibility of maintaining this division. The opposite of containment is the unsecured circulation of surplus population that external poverty, instability and associated social breakdown continually threaten. As a supreme technology of containment, the new or culturally coded racism that shapes development discourse is examined. During decolonization an early success of this racism was to place the immigrant within a zone of exception excluded from normal society. At the same time, development became a series of compensatory state-led technologies that divided into interconnected domestic and overseas sites or variants. The former is associated with a state-encouraged race relations industry based on identity, entitlement and integration, while the latter is denoted by the emergence of development as a contemporary inter-state relationship. The policing of global circulation brings together the search for internal harmony and the quest for external homeostasis within an episodic international security architecture. At each crisis of containment, the biopolitical linkages between these sites and technologies multiply and thicken. The governmentalization of the aid industry and the shift to a post-interventionary terrain of contingent sovereignty, for example, interconnects with the abandonment of multiculturalism in favour of more collective forms of national identity and social cohesion. The threat from ungoverned space is now an internal as well as an external problem. In attempting to think across the national–international divide, this chapter begins by examining the blurring of these categories within political imagination.

The collapse of the national–international dichotomy

The end of the Cold War heralded two interconnected revolutions in international affairs. With the weakening of former restrictions, including respect for non-interference, the first was the ability of the UN, donor governments and aid agencies to intervene in ongoing and unresolved internal conflicts. This allowed a step change in all forms of humanitarian, development and peace activism, which, together with its increasing militarization, has contributed to a significant decline in formal civil conflicts within the erstwhile Third World (HSC 2005). While political instability and insecurity are still rife, this process of pacification has produced a new political space of contingent sovereignty; while respect for territorial integrity remains, sovereignty over life within ineffective states is now internationalized, negotiable and conditional. Continent sovereignty, however, is closely associated with another revolution, that is, the collapse of the traditional national–international dichotomy within political imagination. The French sociologist Didier Bigo has commented that many students of crime, conflict and international relations have, for some time, been struck by how the institutions of the police and military, once thought of as belonging to the separate domains of 'national' and 'international' security respectively, 'now appear to be converging regarding border, order and the possible threats to identity, linked to (im)migration' (Bigo 2001: 91). Moreover, this perception of the merging of internal and external security was being driven by practitioners and politicians rather than 'a cross-fertilisation from the literature' (ibid.). As if on cue, in addressing the UK Labour Party's annual conference following the events of 9/11, Tony Blair outlined his now often quoted view of a new and radically interdependent world.

> Today the threat is chaos, because for people with work to do, family life to balance, mortgages to pay, careers to further, pensions to provide, the yearning is for order and stability and if it doesn't exist elsewhere, it is unlikely to exist here. I have long believed this interdependence defines the new world we live in (Blair 2001).

This does not mean that in the past the national and international were somehow unconnected. As suggested by successive epochs of world exploration, trade, conquest and war, the national and the international have for centuries been closely interwoven within the narrative of modernity. Indeed, in all these historic phases of the national/international, one finds 'a temporal bracketing that crucially coincides with fundamental politico-legal changes in the West itself' (Hussain 2003: 23). However, when threats to the territorial nation-state were security's primary concern, the home/foreign distinction played an essential role in the art of government. It helped to mobilize national armies against those of other nations. As the above quote suggests, however, international security is now experienced differently. In a globalized world, international instability menaces society more than it does the state. It undermines the dependability of jobs, careers and livelihoods; it weakens financial stability and savings and pensions; it threatens the ability of people to raise families and secure their futures; and it jeopardizes energy supplies, mass transport systems, centralized food chains, and just-in-time commodity flows. Such threats are biopolitical in nature since they impact upon the collective existence of population. They are, in short, threats to the West's *way of life*. Moreover, these dangers do not emanate from enemy states as such. Apart from the occasional rogue regime, states now figure more frequently as the facilitators, conduits or ineffectual hosts of opposing or *contrary ways of life*. Rather than opposing armies on a battlefield, unending war fields oppose ways of life on the radically interconnected terrain of global society.

The post-Cold War pacification of the global borderland has revealed that ending internal wars within ineffective states is relatively easy. Winning the post-interventionary peace among the world of peoples, however, is more difficult. The danger is no longer the early 1990s fear of uncontrollable local scarcity wars (Kaplan 1994); today the concern is over low-intensity but generalized political instability that threatens mass society's radically interconnected global way of life (Strategy Unit 2005). The interlinkage of homeland and borderland populations through the dynamics of global circulation has moved questions of the integration or non-integration of peoples, regions, religions, cultures, generations and genders into the political foreground (Denham 2001). At the time of writing, the Taliban insurgency in Afghanistan has rekindled and already claimed the lives of a number of British soldiers. Reflecting today's radical interdependence, however, the first British casualties in this long war were not from the British Army. They were five London Muslims killed in October 2001 fighting for the Taliban (Harris et al. 2001).

State-led technologies of development and security now interconnect mass society's internal anthropological frontier built around notions of equality, entitlement and identity, with an external frontier located within the individual psyches, gendered subjectivities, house-holds and self-reliant communities that inhabit zones of crisis. While conditions differ greatly, within both of these frontier zones the key issue is social cohesion and the developmental need to reconcile the necessity of order with the inevitability of progress. The emergent security architecture linking the two is planetary in ambition. Or at least, it predicates the security of the homeland on the stability of a post-interventionary borderland. The national and international have always been interconnected. However, what is happening in, say, the backstreets of Bradford and the alleyways of Islamabad now assumes a new significance. Looking for connections has historically been the task of the police and intelligence services. Today, however, with the collapse of the national–international dichotomy in political imagi-nation they come together as parts of the same developmental chal-lenge. Defending the West's way of life is dependent on promoting social cohesion within the homeland as well as the borderland.

The internal and external frontiers of this security architecture are radically interconnected through the flows and spaces of global circu-lation, which itself creates a need to police its dynamics, that is, allow-ing the 'good' circulation on which globalized markets depend – such as investment, commodity flows, information, patent rights, tech-nology, skilled migration and tourism – while preventing the 'bad' circulation that poses a risk to national and international stability: non-insured migrants, refugees and asylum seekers, together with the shadow economies, money laundering, drugs, international crime, trafficking and terrorism associated with ineffective states and zones of crisis. The development of computers and information technolo-gies, the digitalization of the flows and spaces of circulation, new modes of surveillance and data mining all promise ever more com-prehensive and intimate ways in which movement can be monitored and policed (I-CAMS 2005). It has already been argued that develop-ment offers a liberal alternative to the extermination or eugenic manipulation of surplus population. The scope of the challenge facing development is suggested by claims from political economy that most of the people living on the margins of global society, that is, outside the greater North American, west European and east Asian economic blocs, are now 'structurally irrelevant' to the process of capitalist accumulation (Castells 1998: 75–82). Their only relev-ance is political: an excess freedom to move, flow and circulate, thus potentially destabilizing international society's finely balanced and globally interconnected way of life.

While the differences between the United States' militarized approach to unending war and the more developmental European stance is often flagged (Kagan 2003; Coker 2003), they are united in terms of the need to protect mass consumer society from transborder, non-state asymmetric threats (compare Bush 2002 and Solana 2003). In examining the origins of the NGO movement, chapter 2 outlined the way in which decolonization allowed the re-expansion of international trusteeship based on the non-governmental promotion of community self-reliance. Development as self-reliance, however, exists in relation to a double exception. The expansion of the NGO movement was premised on the condition of permanent emergency in which self-reliance exists. It was this state of exception that called forth the necessity of a developmental trusteeship over non-insured peoples. As well as providing a developmental opportunity, however, permanent emergency also encourages social breakdown, displacement and the circulation of surplus population. In terms of achieving security over life, this double exception constitutes decolonization as both an opportunity and a threat, that is, as an occasion for the consolidating effects of development and, at the same time, as a need for the globalizing reach of security.

Previous chapters have analysed the post-Cold War governmentalization of the aid industry and the emergence of post-interventionary society. This chapter provides a greater appreciation of how this deepening external biopolitical frontier is bracketed together with an internal one. Moreover, within the international architecture of unending war, development as a state-led technology of security now interconnects the two. Since threats to the West's way of life now stem from contrasting and contrary ways of life, it is essential that the place of racism within liberalism and development is considered. Using Foucault's work on state racism as a point of departure, the shift from a biological to a culturally coded racism during the struggle for independence is examined, before the way in which the policing of immigration links to compensating technologies of internal and external development is considered.

From race war to racism

Racism occupies a central, if relatively underappreciated, part of Michel Foucault's work (Foucault [1975–6]).[1] It is intimately connected

[1] For a discussion of Foucault that embraces racism see Stoler (1995); Mendieta (2002); Kelly (2004); Neal (2004).

with his conception of a regulatory biopolitics of life. If disciplinary power, operating through institutions and able to regiment individuals, was an essential prerequisite for the Industrial Revolution and the spread of the factory system, it can be argued that a regulatory biopolitics appears in relation to a new and related mass phenomenon: the emergence of an industrial surplus life that, through dispossession, had lost the resilience of agrarian self-sufficiency (for a related discussion see Arendt [1958]). Rather than focusing on the individual, biopolitics intervenes at the aggregate level of population. It is concerned with supporting and promoting life through, for example, interventions in health, education, employment, housing or pensions, which aim to maintain the equilibrium of a non-self-sustaining population by compensating for differences and ameliorating risk (Foucault [1975–6]: 251). During the nineteenth century, supporting the life of the nation through interventions at the level of population came to define the art of government in mass society. In the twentieth century, in what became the developed world, the solution to the problem of surplus life embraced population-wide welfare regimes having social insurance as their foundation. For societies such as these that celebrate life and whose politicians make huge investments in promoting and protecting it, racism is a means by which the state can allow and author death (Foucault [1976]: 137–8). Racism striates a population, enabling certain categories of life to be excluded – allowing them to die both literally and metaphorically in various and exquisite forms of social death – in order to purify and strengthen society as a whole. For Foucault, it is a manoeuvre that is intimately connected with sovereign power.

In *Society Must be Defended* (Foucault [1975–6]), 'actual racism' (ibid.: 80), that is, the familiar, deterministic and hierarchical categorization of human life according to biological criteria, is understood as a counter-historical means of defending and reasserting sovereign power. It is a normalizing, scientific discourse having the potential to counter and overcome politico-historic challenges to sovereign legitimacy. Actual or state racism emerged in the nineteenth century from a sovereign power whose divine right, and consequent legitimacy, was now sorely threatened. It incorporated, reconfigured and deployed in its own defence an earlier discourse of race war that had previously questioned the divine right of kings and popes. Race war was an originary historical discourse that emerged in the seventeenth century as a challenge to sovereign power. It conceived society as a binary structure; as a permanent war between two races cleft by differences of language and ethnicity, differences of force and violence, differences of savagery and barbarism, and differences created by 'the conquest and subjugation of one race by another' (ibid.: 60). This binary division supported a counter-history that, in the name of the underdog, the vanquished and defeated, challenged sovereign right. The discourse of race war, through narratives of subjection, humiliation and the denial of rights, spoke the language of revolution. During the Reformation and the English civil war, for example, the historicism of race war attempted to reveal what kings would seek to hide, 'that they were born of the contingency and injustices of battles' (ibid.: 72).

The history of race war is contained in the demand for rights by the downtrodden and embattled. It is a discourse that challenged and weakened the natural identification between the people and the monarch. For Foucault, however, actual, biological or state racism is *different*. Rather than challenging the right of kings, it is deployed in its defence. It is a manoeuvre that preserves a sovereign power that, having lost its divinity, can no longer be guaranteed its status. During the nineteenth century the politico-historical discourse of race war was appropriated, changed and redeployed by sovereign power. The resulting state racism 'adopts a bio-medical perspective that crushes the historical dimension that was present in the [race war] discourse' (ibid.: 80). This dimension, with its narratives of past invasion and loss, was replaced by a new vision: a struggle for existence between differentially endowed races in a biological and thus ahistoric sense. Actual racism is a post-evolutionist struggle based on the 'differentiation of the species, natural selection and the survival of the fittest species' (ibid.: 81). Rather than a war between peoples and races with different histories – a war that can be dissipated through treaty, compensation, trade and intermarriage – since its parameters are biological and immutable, actual racism called forth a struggle to the death. At the same time, this sovereign reworking of race war into actual racism significantly changed the role and function of the state.

Within the historic discourse of race war, the state was viewed with suspicion. It was an institution susceptible to capture by foreign usurpers, extremists and oppressors. Consequently, in order to defend themselves, free people had to be ready and prepared to mobilize against it. Like race war, biological racism was also a revolutionary discourse relative to the existing order. However, within actual racism this radicalism presented itself 'in an inverted form' (ibid.). Rather than state sovereignty being a threat to society, it is rehabilitated, turned around and justified *as vital for the defence of society*. Through biologizing and dehistoricizing the discourse of race war, sovereign power reinvented itself as 'imperative to protect the race' (ibid.), that is, as vital for the protection of society from those internal enemies that would otherwise weaken and corrupt its energy and vitality. While having different parameters, this manoeuvre is immediately recognizable, for example, in the role of the state within unending war. Regarding actual or biological racism, this strategization of power achieved its paroxysmal expression within Nazism.

As described by Foucault, racism is a strategization of power that allows a society dedicated to life to author death, both literally and metaphorically. It embodies sovereignty's endless counter-historic will to power. In addressing our present predicament, however, Foucault must serve as a point of departure, rather than a site of arrival. Regarding the underdeveloped world, rather than social insurance, the remedy for surplus population has been a developmental biopolitics of community-based self-reliance. It has been argued in chapter 2 that in bettering surplus life, that is, deciding what life can be supported and what can be disallowed, development embodies a petty or administrative sovereign power. In considering the place of racism within liberalism, we also have to understand the racism within development. Important here is the shift within racial discourse during decolonization from an outwardly biological to a politico-cultural coding.

The biopolitical translation of development and underdevelopment into the differential technologies deemed socially appropriate for supporting developed and underdeveloped life – that is, social insurance and its derivatives as opposed to self-reliance respectively – is itself suggestive of the racism within development. When development became a state-led technology of international security during the process of decolonization, the problem of surplus population became a global one. These shifts, translations and expansions interconnect racism, migration and development within a security architecture of planetary ambitions. At its core is the danger of exposing the fragile identity and welfare systems of mass society to the spontaneous circulation of non-insured global surplus life. Through a consideration of the relationship between liberalism and imperialism, the move to a politico-cultural racial idiom is examined first.

Liberalism, imperialism and culture

Despite its pressing relevance today, the organic connection between nineteenth-century liberalism and empire, that is, the existence of a specifically *liberal* form of imperialism, has been neglected in main-stream international relations theory and development studies (Mehta 1999; Jahn 2005; Cooke 2003; Biccum 2005). This oversight has helped to obscure and hence sustain liberalism's enduring paradox: its ability to speak in the name of people, freedom and rights while at the same time accepting illiberal forms of rule as sufficient or even necessary for backward or underdeveloped societies and peoples. Liberalism's classical authors, together with many innovative practitioners of empire, saw the gradual maturation of representative government in Europe as proof of its unlikely spontaneous occurrence elsewhere. Provided that it was educative and ameliorative in nature, there was a consequent willingness to accept despotic rule abroad (Mehta 1999; Jahn 2005; Pitts 2003). As chapter 1 has indicated, this paradox was also found in the emerging socialist and social democratic move-ments. While the terms used to code the civilized–barbarian dichotomy have changed over time, moving from its nineteenth-century biological variants through the twentieth century's technical concern with development/underdevelopment to today's security worries over effective/ineffective states, the liberal paradox has been continually reproduced.

With the exception of Iraq, it is reflected, for example, in the wide-spread liberal–left support for the upsurge in Western humanitarian and peace interventionism following the end of the Cold War (Douzinas 2003). At the same time, on the back of this interventionism the idea of liberal imperialism, complete with its overtures to voluntarism, part-nership and decentralization, has also been rehabilitated (Cooper 2002; Ferguson 2003; Coker 2003). Regarding the paradox itself, Robert Cooper gives a contemporary gloss when claiming that among European states, 'we keep the law but when operating in the jungle, we need to also use the laws of the jungle' (Cooper 2002: 15). In accepting such laws, we have seen that in relation to fragile states the DFID acknowledges that in some circumstances 'good enough governance' will be all that is possible. As long as basic functions are met, including providing a supportive environment for self-reliance, this may involve accepting 'practices that would not exist in an ideal government – cor-ruption may be rife, staff may lack necessary skills, and capacity may be chronically weak and under-funded' (DFID 2005a: 20). There is a certain irony in the fact that the US neo-con invasion of Iraq dispensed with a liberal imperial framework. It has been much criticized precisely for having no reconstruction or post-war development plan. Instead it adopted the blunt position that if democracy was good enough for the

American people it was good enough for Iraqis, indeed, for all the peoples of the Middle East. Rather than a developmental trusteeship, its hopes were founded on the spontaneous embrace of freedom and democratic values by the liberated masses. With this tragic adventure now drowning in blood, a liberal approach to post-intervention and the governance of others is once again regaining its confidence and composure.

Biological racism, except for an extremist fringe, did not survive the cataclysm of the Second World War. While such actual racism has been discredited and robustly condemned, the possibility of a politico-culturally coded racism existing as the former once did, as part of a normal, acceptable and lived experience of the world, has received less attention. Any division of the human species according to its different potentialities for existence, however – including political existence – is ultimately biological in essence. At the same time, since racism is con-stitutive of its object, a threat to a population need not be couched exclu-sively in biological terms to achieve similar power effects (Kelly 2004: 61). On this premise, this chapter argues that a culturally intoned racism underpins liberalism's acceptance of freedom and democracy for 'us' while tolerating illiberal or 'good enough governance' for 'them'.

There is a close connection between attempts to divide humankind into civilizational or politico-cultural stages and its hierarchical order-ing into biologically determined races. The abolition of slavery raised the possibility of a universal humanity. In response to this emancipa-tory vision, both biological and cultural counter-divisions or redivi-sions of the human species emerged during the first half of the nineteenth century (Hall 2002). Reflecting its Enlightenment her-itage, and still coded within development practice today, liberalism equates culture and government. For J. S. Mill, for example, the history, cultural and moral outlook of a people – its social character – sets the limits and possibilities of its governance (Jahn 2005). From a government-culture perspective, Mill divides human history into four broad evolutionary stages: savagery, slavery, barbarism and civiliza-tion, each having a corresponding and necessary form of government. Civilization, for example, equates with representative government. Similarly, the political expression of barbarism is despotism. Because the social character of a people limits the possibilities of its gover-nance, it follows that one model of government and its associated legal codes, institutions and moral expectations cannot be applied unilater-ally across what is, in practice, a human species striated according to its potential for political existence. For Mill, being able to locate and articulate the politico-cultural discontinuities between nations and peoples, that is, how culture divides humankind politically, represented a major advance over the ideas of many Enlightenment theorists, especially those believing in the universality of European laws and institutions.[2]

Because of the limiting effect of social character, the emergence of civilization cannot be taken for granted; it is something that has to be consciously maintained and pursued. In exceptional circumstances, progress in government can occur through the local or internal actions of highly gifted and determined indigenous actors . As a rule, however, change is the result of the external intervention of culturally superior powers, 'carrying the people rapidly through several stages of progress, clearing away obstacles to improvement which might have lasted indefinitely if the subject population had been left unassisted to its native tendencies and chances' (Mill quoted by Jahn 2005: 603). A specifically liberal form of imperial trusteeship is continually challenged by the need to make government appropriate to social character. Because of its limiting effects on political existence, the mechanics of government 'must be adjusted to the capacities and qualities of such men as are available' (Mill quoted by Jahn 2005: 601). In other words, representational arrangements, economic architecture, criminal and judicial systems, manufacturing methods or agricultural techniques must be made appropriate to the social level they serve and improvement they hope to effect. At the same time, to render such trusteeship legitimate and effective, it must be based on principles of education and guidance that actively involve the governed in their own improvement; as a relation of external tutelage liberal imperialism is, essentially, developmental (Mehta 1999: 198–211).

Although he was writing in the mid-nineteenth century, there are powerful resonances between Mill's liberal imperialism and the renewed surge in Western interventionism since the end of the Cold War. While the institutions are radically different, moving from chartered companies and European states to international coalitions, multilateral bodies and integrated aid missions, the experience of the problems of pacification and government, together with their generic

---

[2] There is an important non-imperial trend in Enlightenment thinking. Unlike development, Kant's understanding of perpetual peace, for example, was not based on others having to change their behaviour or forms of social organization (Kant [1795]). At the same time, Pitts (2003) and Mehta (1999) have re-evaluated the work of Bentham and Burke respectively in a similar light.

solutions, remain immediately recognizable. One is struck by how the 'clearing away of obstacles to improvement', for example, chimes with the growing trend in recent years to embark on transforming societies as a whole (Stiglitz 1998), the shift to greater coercion in securing the transition from war to peace (Eide et al. 2005) and, not least, the move to pre-emptive regime change (Ignatieff 2003). At the same time, 'adjusting the means of government to existing capacities' is an apt summary not only of sustainable development (Schumacher 1974) but, as we have seen, of current thinking on how to improve the capacity of fragile states (Leader and Colenso 2005). Constantly making these connections, however, would soon become tedious and distracting, since they are, quite literally, too numerous to mention; they pervade the whole enterprise.

The challenge is to make visible the largely concealed or commonsense politico-cultural racism that development embodies. This involves specifying the function and relationship of a culturally coded racism to its biological foundations. Although cultural and biological approaches to the striation of humankind are outwardly different, they are both concerned with dividing, ranking and ordering population according to its capacities and worthiness of life. While capable of forming contrary and often opposed conclusions, both agree that peoples are inherently different, either culturally or biologically. On the basis of this ultimately biological agreement, they constitute the opposing terms of a shared racist logic. Although J. S. Mill, for example, held that the politico-cultural differences between peoples and nations were mutable and open to change through external education and guidance (he thus opposed a rigid biological determinism), he still found it necessary to describe these differences through such dichotomies as civilized/barbarian, advanced/backward, active/passive or industrious/ sensuous, while assigning the former terms to 'all the English and Germans and the latter terms to the Irish, French, Southern Europeans, and the "Orientals" (more and more so as one moved south and east)' (Pitts 2003: 222).

Where a cultural coding informs a liberal practice of developmental trusteeship, a biological one is linked to an exterminatory impulse. Since its inception in the abolition of slavery and the Industrial Revolution, as a liberal solution to the problem of surplus population, development has always existed in the shadow of modernity's other answer: extermination or eugenics. Just as US forces destroyed villages in the Vietnam war so that their inhabitants could be saved, Afghanis are today being killed by NATO in order to make the country safe for development. Similarly, as already argued, NGO-led sustainable development is premised on the permanent humanitarian emergency of self-reliance. While biological racism finds surplus life an abomination, its culturally coded conscience offers betterment as a way of redemption. However, while different and opposed, since they share the same biological foundation they interconnect; they are unalike but symbiotic and mutually conditioning, conflicting but capable of collapsing one into the other in times of emergency (Duffield 1984). One example of this organic connection can be seen in the late-nineteenth-century liberal critique of the rampant New Imperialism then existing. Speaking for the betterment of humanity, the authors of the New Imperialism swallowed wholesale those largely tropical and subtropical regions of the planet still unclaimed by external powers. Often associated with the Scramble for Africa, this act of fraud, seizure and violence that resulted in the rapid closure of the 'global commons' was accompanied by a justifying biological racism (Arendt [1951]; Hochschild 2002). A will to govern these newly conquered territories and peoples in a liberal manner, that is, in the name of rights and freedom, emerged out of a genuine horror and disgust with the nature of their acquisition. Edmund Morel, a tireless campaigner against imperial excess, left a record of a meeting with Roger Casement in which, talking far into the night, Casement recounted his experience of the Congo Free State.

> I was mostly a silent listener, clutching hard upon the arms of my chair. As the monologue of horror proceeded . . . I verily believe I *saw* those hunted women clutching their children and flying panic stricken to the bush: the blood flowing from those quivering black bodies as the hippopotamus hide whip struck again and again; the savage soldiery rushing hither and thither amid burning villages; the ghastly tally of severed hands. . . (quoted in Hochschild: 205).

The violence and exterminatory impulse of the time combined to form what Hobson called 'insane imperialism' (Hobson [1902]: 246; also Morel 1920). However, at issue was not so much the *legitimacy* of conquest; of greater importance was the feeling that if the territories and peoples now acquired were to be more effectively and efficiently run, they had to be more *humanely* governed. The connection between Fabian socialism and the liberal colonial practice of indirect rule has already been mentioned, as has the way in which this practice, involving empowerment through the decentralization of administrative tasks according to existing levels of social organization, is reproduced in current fragile state discourse. When Sidney and Beatrice Webb visited India in 1912, their willingness to criticize the hidebound nature of the British Raj and concern to promote effective administration, especially through the incorporation of gifted and intelligent Indians, is clearly evident (Webb 1990). So too, however, is their sense of superiority and racist comportment towards the peoples of Empire (Winter 1974).

Liberalism does not challenge the fundamental principles of imperial rule; neither does it seriously question the necessity of conquest or the inevitability of external trusteeship. Similarly, as discussed in chapter 2, during the process of decolonization it failed to comprehend fully or learn from the struggle for freedom by others. Regardless of circumstances, liberalism sets itself up as a more inclusive, effective and humane will to power. It is a timeless urge to govern in a liberal manner, that is, in the name of people, rights and freedom. The following section begins an exploration of how, in seeking social cohesion at home while pursuing development abroad, liberalism is again presenting itself as the most effective and humane means of governing the world of peoples. First, however, it examines how a culturally coded racism entered the public realm during decolonization.

Decolonization and the new racism

With the movement of biological racism into the background, the foregrounding of its cultural alter ego took place during the struggle for independence. The decades spanning the 1950s to the 1970s saw the fantastic birth of a *world of states*; for the first time in history not only was the world populated with territorial nation-states, each enjoyed legal equality on the international stage (Elden 2006). It was a heroic age of independence movements, liberation struggles and geopolitical drama (Derlugian 1996). The world of independent states, however, also called forth a related phenomenon: millions of new citizens living for the first time within their own national borders. As Hannah Arendt ([1951]: 230–1) has cautioned, however, each new state with its fresh batch of citizens increases the number of potential non-citizens, stateless persons and refugees. Besides a world of states, decolonization also gave rise to an emergent and potentially threatening *world of peoples*. Almost from birth, many of the newly independent states began to move into a deepening crisis of capacity and legitimacy. As the ability of states to contain and police the movement of population weakened, growing numbers of people, either looking for a better life or fleeing trouble, began for the first time to move legally or illegally across international borders; in other words, they began to circulate.

As part of the expansion of European empires and spheres of influence, excluding the slave trade, for several centuries prior to decolonization the broad pattern of migration had been north to south, especially outwards to the non-European world (Held et al. 1999: 284–302). Such migration was associated with sentiments of escape, fortune and freedom. Decolonization, however, reversed the overall direction of this circulatory movement so that it now flowed from south to north. At the same time, it added a new dimension to the perception of migration itself, a change reflecting

> a new model of articulation between states, peoples and cultures on a world scale. . . . The new racism is a racism of 'decolonisation', the reversal of population movements between old colonies and the old metropolises. (Balibar 1991: 21)

Instead of representing fortune or escape, by the 1950s immigration from the colonies and former colonies was already a subject of growing unease in Europe (Duffield 1988: 35). During the nineteenth century, liberalism usually experienced culturally unfamiliar life as being incomplete or somehow lacking a vital trait or disposition. In the name of completion through education and guidance, this experience of absence was sufficient in itself to justify liberal tutelage. Consequently, arguments for intervention based on a right to conquer or an imminent external threat 'are almost entirely absent or, when invoked, are of a secondary status' (Mehta 1999: 191). Today, given the change in circulatory flow, the situation is very different. External threats, for example spontaneous migration, the dangers of fragile states or terrorist networks, are constantly invoked within liberal fears as able to penetrate the porous borders of mass society and hence destabilize it. Politico-cultural categories provide the means of striation necessary to classify and manage a threatening and potentially dangerous world of peoples. It marks a shift in racial discourse from a colonial preoccupation with 'biological types in location' to a contemporary concern with 'cultural types in circulation'. The immigrant – the embodiment of cultural difference in motion – became its first iconic figure.

What Martin Barker called the 'new racism' (Barker 1981) first came into view in Britain during the immigration debate of the 1950s and 1960s (see also Duffield 1988: 34–8, 98–108; Balibar 1991). According to Barker, this racism is new because it dispenses with a need to rely on what, even at this time, were increasingly contested and outmoded notions of innate biological difference and hierarchy. The new racism modernizes racism by once again making it an acceptable tool of state intervention. Its key manoeuvre is to highlight cultural difference as natural, that is, both something that people understandably wish to cultivate and maintain and consequently something that a sensible government has to take into account. The danger, however, is that cultural difference is a largely unreasoned condition: most people do not choose their culture, religion or belief system; they are born with them. The fear that drives new racism is that when such unreasoned differences find themselves in close proximity, the risk of inter-ethnic violence and social breakdown is increased (Barker 1981: 13–29, 38–53). A responsible government has therefore little choice but to undertake measures to contain or ameliorate the threat posed by cultural difference. Barker distilled this cultural racism from the political and media discourse of the early post-war decades. Written as world history, however, one finds similar views, for example, in Samuel Huntington's more recent *Clash of Civilisations* thesis (Huntington 1993). Whether internally or externally, the new racism seeks to provide an explanation for the West's existential unease by pointing out the security implications of cultural difference; not only do contrary ways of life challenge internal social cohesion, they also threaten the West's international security. Since the mid-1960s in Britain, there has been an all-party consensus on the need to restrict spontaneous immigration which has subsequently spread to other parts of Europe. This consensus, moreover, has defined an increasingly restrictive debate around refugees and asylum seekers (Schuster 2003). It also informs the architecture of unending war which similarly interconnects circulation, cultural difference and security. It is important, therefore, to understand the nature of new racism and what makes it acceptable, indeed, what makes it appear as common sense (ibid.; Kundnani 2001).

For cultural discourse it is human nature to form groups based on notions of similarity which then set themselves apart from other groups perceived as different. The resulting shared way of life, or culture, is what binds people together. Culture in this sense is seen as synonymous with ethnic identity. A shared identity provides individuals with a sense of belonging and solidarity. Without this there would be no wider form of social organization. The nation, for example, is nothing if not an expression of a people's traditions and way of life (Huntington 1993). What people feel about their culture and identity is paramount. According to the new or cultural racism, if people sense that their way of life is threatened it will arouse deep-seated fear and hostility. Migrants, for example, because they have a different way of life, can elicit this response. Importantly, it does not matter whether these fears are real or imaginary. The recurrent logic of this new racism, indeed, all that it requires, is for *ordinary people* to hold *genuine fears* that their sense of identity, security or welfare is threatened for social order to be at risk (Balibar 1991). This racial discourse is acceptable because you do not need to think of yourself as superior, 'you do not even need to dislike or blame those who are so different from you – in order to say that the presence of these aliens constitutes a threat to our way of life' (Barker 1981: 18).

Today, it is both unacceptable and *unnecessary* to rank races or cultures hierarchically. All human beings are sufficiently biologically alike to form closed cultural communities; in this respect, we are *all the same*. As Balibar has argued, it is a 'racism without races' (1991: 21) in which immigration, especially the spontaneous or unsecured circulation of surplus population, substitutes for the notion of race. When faced with such movement, either real or potential, the new racism holds that it is natural to rise to the defence of one's community if it is genuinely felt to be threatened. It is a reaction which cultural racism holds to be innate and rooted in a people's common sense. Since it is instinctive, the defence of a way of life or identity is largely non-rational and unreasoned. This inherent irrationality, however, is not necessarily a bad thing, especially when it provides a wellspring for the defence of society. The determining principle of contemporary cultural racism is that the innate and unreasoned nature of cultural difference inevitably leads to societal conflict. Since the 1960s it has enabled states first to halt spontaneous immigration and then systematically to exclude certain groups from the welfare state, the criminal justice system and the remit of anti-discrimination legislation – indeed, to place them in a state of exception – in order to detain, disperse or deport as part of the state's role in defending society (Bloch and Schuster 2005). While not biologically coded, 'the insurmountability of cultural differences' (Balibar 1991: 21) is racist in that it provides states with an argument 'that the human species is composed of discrete groups in order to legitimate inequality between those groups of people' (Robert Miles, quoted by Schuster 2003: 244).

Racism and anti-racism

The politico-cultural categories that inform a specifically liberal racial discourse interconnect the policing of international migration, the promotion of internal social cohesion and the external development of global surplus life. This discourse has propelled the emergence of the security architecture of planetary ambitions, the foundations of which were laid during decolonization. Because this structure is episodic in nature, each new circulatory threat to the integrity of mass society's way of life creates fresh possibilities for the counter-historic reassertion of sovereign power through the search for stability and coherence across its internal and external frontiers. While recognizable in the present contours of unending war, the origins of this architecture can be traced, for example, in the emergence in Britain of a cross-party political consensus supporting immigration control in the mid-1960s. Until the Conservative Party's 1962 Commonwealth Immigration Act, British subjects were those people born within the territories of the Crown, having 'the right to enter, work and settle with their families in Britain' (Bloch and Schuster 2005: 495). The act, which attempted to regulate immigration according to economic demand, was the first weakening of that right, and, once a cross-party consensus had been reached, was quickly followed by other exclusionary measures.

During the 1950s and early 1960s, while divided on the issue, the Labour movement officially opposed immigration control. Importantly, the way in which immigration was discussed at this time is well reflected in present concerns over immigration and asylum policy. Then, as now, the focus was on expounding the genuine public fears over the impact on employment, housing, school places, hospital beds and so on, together with concerns about the negative effects on social cohesion of cultural difference. Within the terms of this debate, Asian migrants have always been categorized as having an 'excess' of culture. Where religion now intervenes, initially this often took the form of allegations of social conservatism resulting from a narrow rural upbringing. During the 1950s, before a political consensus to ban immigration had appeared, an ongoing debate on immigration did exist. An important characteristic of this debate, however, was that both sides, those for and against immigration, accepted that the crux of the matter – the terrain on which the outcome would be decided – was indeed public concern over social resources and cultural difference. This gave the views of the pro-immigration camp a certain predictability (Duffield 1988: 36–7). If immigrants threatened scarce public resources, *then more should be made available*; rather than poverty and backwardness being a natural condition, *this was the result of colonial mismanagement*; instead of undermining living standards, *immigrants were potentially productive members of society*, and so on. This debate cut across the political spectrum, dividing trade union and Labour Party members at the same time as supporting a number of cross-parliamentary alliances.

While the Labour Party formally contested the 1962 Act, between 1961 and 1964 it came full circle 'from unconditionally opposing immigration control to unconditionally accepting its need' (ibid.: 99). This change came when Asian immigration to Britain was at its peak. In the debates surrounding the introduction of 1962 Act, the party's position had already begun to weaken, with several senior figures indicating that they would change their views if evidence was forthcoming that control was necessary. When Harold Wilson became party leader in 1963, it was clear that he favoured control in principle. Like the TUC, however, he preferred control at source, that is, in the country of origin, rather than the point of entry. Although it won the 1964 general election, Labour's experience of losing a safe West Midlands seat over its opposition to immigration control acted as a catalyst for a rapid change of heart. In power Labour would outbid the Conservative opposition in showing which party was the toughest on immigration. The subsequent 1965 White Paper on Immigration from the Commonwealth 'officially marked the emergence of an all-party consensus on the need to control immigration at the point of entry' (ibid.: 100). A number of increasingly restrictive measures were introduced. The 1968 Commonwealth Immigration Act, for example, was passed within a week in order to limit the number of Kenyan Asians holding British passports able to enter Britain. Other restrictions and amendments enacted were eventually rationalized in the Conservatives' 1971 Immigration Act. The cumulative effect of these measures was to reduce primary immigration to Britain to a trickle by the early 1970s. In a world where self-reliance exists in a permanent state of emergency, however, crises of circulation are episodic. Following the joint agreement to control, in facing this constant threat the main issue is which party is the toughest and most restrictive. Ever since 1964, in one form or another – immigrants, refugees, asylum seekers, and so on – the 'race card' has been a regular feature of British general elections. Decolonization moved the goalposts and set in train the political foregrounding of the need to defend the West's way of life against circulatory non-state threats. The state now addresses the interplay between the spontaneous movement of non-insured peoples, fears over cultural difference, the fragility of identity, finite welfare resources and the dangers posed to national and international security. It does so by responding to the genuine fears of ordinary citizens through pre-emptive actions to defend society.

Just as the Labour Party never reconciled itself with colonialism (see chapter 2), it never offered an official explanation for its embrace of immigration control (Foot 1965: 186–7). In a sense, however, none was needed. Since both sides of the debate accepted that the basic issues were resources and cultural difference, the problem for the pro-immigration camp – or rather the room for manoeuvre it enjoyed – was that 'in sharing key assumptions with its opponents, its own arguments already had theirs inscribed within them' (Duffield 1988: 99). It only required evidence to come to light, as it did on the doorsteps in the 1964 election campaign, that ordinary people did in fact have genuine fears over the impact of immigration on social cohesion for senior party figures to begin openly admitting that they had simply changed their minds. As Balibar has argued, the new racism conceals itself in the claim that it is anti-racist (Balibar 1991); by restricting and controlling the sources of genuine fear, that is, the unchecked circulation of cultural difference, the state presents itself as acting to curb the spread of racism and xenophobia. In an extraordinary reversal of the expected, control and exceptionalism become part of the project 'to *explain racism* (and ward it off)' (ibid.: 22 (emphasis in original)). This turnaround helps to explain why new racism remains curiously submerged. In Britain, the 1960s was a period in which, to paraphrase Balibar, a new model of articulation between states, peoples and cultures on a world scale was initiated. The collapse of an older left–liberal discourse on citizenship and belonging, however, also 'saw the simultaneous reappearance of liberalism in a new form' (Duffield 1988: 99). The restriction of immigration on the grounds that it threatened to overwhelm the welfare state was itself the beginning of the 'the death of social' (Rose 2000), that is, the vision of a universal and inclusive welfarism. For the purposes of this chapter, however, what is more important are the elements of this neoliberalism that begin to configure and interconnect the 'national' and the 'international' in a new world of independent states.

Conjoining the internal and external frontiers

The Labour Party's 1964 election manifesto, *The New Britain*, contains in embryonic form the planetary security architecture that currently connects the policing of global circulation with the search for social cohesion within homeland and borderland populations. Although the manifesto would now be regarded as 'old' Labour, New Labour has significantly built on the rearticulation of the national and international it initiated. While restriction is today normal and routinized, four decades ago it was controversial. For some socialists and liberals it represented the abandonment of debts to former colonial subjects and the end of inclusive welfarism. To ease the move towards restriction, two compensatory measures were brought together in *The New Britain*. Epitomized as impoverished and culturally backward in the press, the first measure was a pledge to help integrate into British society existing immigrants and their communities. In the words of the then Labour MP, Roy Hattersley, without integration 'limitation is inexcusable; without limitation, integration is impossible' (quoted by Bourne 1980: 335). The second measure was contained in the announcement of the intention to centralize and strengthen Britain's overseas development efforts the better to tackle poverty abroad.

The idea that improving living conditions in the colonies and former colonies would reduce migratory pressures had existed in the labour movement since the 1950s. As a reaction to genuine fears over the asymmetric demands of non-insured migrants on the scarce resources of the welfare state, *The New Britain* promised to 'give special help to local authorities where immigrants had settled' (Labour Party 1964). Rather than attempting to improve welfare provision for all, the approach was to channel special developmental funds to areas of settlement in the form of extra measures to compensate local authorities and communities for the effects of cultural difference. Section 11 of the 1966 Local Government Act, for example, gave local authorities additional funding to take on specialist staff. This was followed by special funding to affected schools trying to cope with an influx of non-English-speaking pupils. Under the new urban renewal programme, in 1969 a dozen Community Development Projects were initiated. This directed small grants to voluntary organizations (or internal NGOs) working in immigrant communities (Duffield 1988: 101). Through such measures, pre-dating the governmentalization of external aid by several decades, the state soon established itself as a source of funding for legal advice centres, self-help groups, adventure playgrounds, youth clubs and hostels. In support of these measures of internal development to promote integration, *The New Britain* also announced an intention to legislate against racial discrimination. Since the 1950s such legislation had been a Labour aim, and, within months of its election victory, the 1964 Race Relations Act outlawing discrimination and incitement in places of public resort came into effect. The act also established the Race Relations Board (now the Commission for Racial Equality) and the National Council for Commonwealth Immigrants (now the Community Relations Commission). The main function of the latter was to promote voluntary liaison committees operating between the wider society and immigrant communities. Between 1964 and 1968, the number of such committees grew from fifteen to more than sixty (ibid.: 101–2). The 1968 Race Relations Act subsequently extended anti-discrimination law into the field of housing and employment.

In addition to initiating an internal development regime centred on a 'race relations industry' geared to integrating existing immigrant communities, *The New Britain* also laid the foundations of a state-led 'aid industry' fitted to a new external world of independent states. With poverty facing more than half of the world's population, Labour's manifesto argued that 'there is a growing danger that the increasing tensions caused over gross inequalities of circumstances between rich and poor nations will be sharply accentuated by differences of race and colour' (Labour Party 1964). Although earlier development initiatives had existed, these were essentially ad hoc colonial measures that, at best, sought to secure a continuing if attenuated special relationship with Britain. The manifesto proposed something different, that is, the creation of a new Ministry of Overseas Development which eventually became the Overseas Development Administration (ODA), the forerunner of the DFID. Not only did it centralize earlier initiatives, but for the first time development was framed in relation to a world of independent states and its future. Apart from promising to increase government aid spending and support for the UN, in an innovative move it would also encourage the work of NGOs. Harold Wilson, the Labour leader, had been involved in the 1953 founding of the campaigning NGO War on Want. The proven enterprise of NGOs, it was argued, must be matched 'with Government action to give new hope in the current United Nations Development Decade' (ibid.).

The emergence of a political consensus on the need to restrict immigration was tantamount to taking immigration, and therefore the immigrant, out of politics. As a means of compensating or offsetting this state of exception, a national race relations industry was called forth to integrate existing settlers by acting to reduce their poverty and social isolation and, at the same time, sensitizing the host population to the irreducibility of cultural difference. It also demanded the creation of a forward-looking international aid industry to tackle poverty and backwardness abroad. In response to genuine fears over the integrity and sustainability of Britain's way of life, controlling immigration, strengthening internal social cohesion and reducing external poverty came together in a security architecture of planetary ambitions, indeed, a new post-colonial 'model of articulation between states, peoples and cultures on a world scale'. Previous chapters have examined decolonization as providing an opportunity for the expansion of development as an international technology of security. The growth of NGOs and sustainable development, for example, has been discussed; so too, has the governmentalization of these institutions and relations through technologies of coherence and the growing state interventionism of the post-Cold War period. The issue under consideration here is the bracketing together of this external regime of development with an internal one through the circulatory effects of the episodic crises of borderland self-reliance and homeostasis. Before examining the changing regime of internal development, the wider implications of the sovereign ban on spontaneous migration will first be examined.

Migration and the European state of exception

At times of political emergency, when culture and biology draw together, racism and anti-racism are capable of blurring the one into the other. Now sensitized to the permanence of cultural difference and its potentially destabilizing effects, public opinion has been able to accept the restrictive migration and asylum regime that has been intensifying not only in Britain but in the EU as well. The restrictions on immigration enacted by member states vectored into the beginning of an EU immigration policy during the 1970s (Huysmans 2000: 755). While often contradictory and disjointed at the level of its operation (Baldin-Edwards 2005), the overall trend of EU immigration policy embodies a collective political will to control and restrict. During the 1980s, measures to create the European single market, involving the easing of internal border controls, the free movement of goods and peoples and the harmonization of welfare entitlements, were accompanied by a strengthening of the EU's external border controls, including the alignment of member states' visa policies (Huysmans 2000: 759). Arising from the growing search for coherence, by the end of the decade commentators were warning of a Fortress Europe in the making. This included decisions on immigration moving away from traditional humanitarian and human rights fora to those dealing with terrorism, drugs, policing and economic immigration (ibid.: 756). At the same time, the number of deportations for violating British immigration legislation, for example, began to rise (Bloch and Schuster 2005: 496).

With the Treaty on European Union (1992) the restriction of immigration began its move into the constitutional architecture of the EU. In Europe generally, the number of failed asylum seekers began to represent an increasing proportion of deportees and, at the same time, the detention of undocumented migrants and asylum seekers began to grow (ibid.: 496, 500). In 1995, the Schengen Information System laid the foundations for an EU-wide change in the policing of immigration based on security and efficiency rather than the law. It made possible detention on administrative rather that judicial grounds (Hörnqvist 2004: 44). From the mid-1990s, the EU also began to 'externalize' its attempts to control immigration in various ways. Against a backdrop of a hardening asylum regime, humanitarian intervention in the former Yugoslavia, for example, saw the pioneering of methods for supporting civilians in war zones, thus deterring international displacement (Duffield 1994). In 1999 the EU High Level Working Group on Asylum and Immigration began a discussion on methods to prevent immigration from designated countries such as Afghanistan, Albania, Kosovo, Morocco, Somalia, Sri Lanka and Iraq. Policies have also been initiated relating to the use of aid and trade as a means of controlling immigration. In 2000, for example, the Lomé Convention was redrawn to make £8.5 billion in aid conditional on repatriation and expulsion agreements (Fekete 2001: 27–8). Within this process of externalization one can also include the new technologies of intervention and reconstruction already discussed in relation to fragile states.

As Lisa Schuster has argued, since the 1980s the European states have developed immigration regimes and practices 'that once would have been only possible in wartime, but are today considered "normal", part of the everyday experience of hundreds of thousands of people across Europe' (Schuster 2003: 246). The political consensus that emerged in Britain in the mid-1960s on the need to control immigration took immigration and the immigrant out of politics. This position of ambivalence has since developed into a manifest state of exception (Agamben 2005). Although unskilled migrants and asylum seekers are not criminals in seeking to enter Europe, their freedom to do so is experienced as a threat. As a way of countering this excess freedom, such wartime countermeasures as dispersal, detention and deportation have reappeared. In the name of burden sharing, dispersal to areas of little or no previous settlement removes asylum seekers from the protection and support of others with a similar history. Reducing the level of welfare support below statutory minimum levels, or payment through vouchers, removes them from the welfare state. Housing asylum seekers in hostels or reception centres separates them from local communities. Detaining them while their cases are examined excludes them from the checks and balances of the criminal law system. As a final indication of the opening of a state of exception in the midst of mass consumer society, Britain's 2000 Race Relations Amendment Act also excludes migration and nationality from the provisions of existing anti-discrimination legislation (Schuster 2003: 254). In response to our genuine fears, the liberal state has reduced undocumented migrants and asylum seekers, as a surplus population with excess freedom to circulate, to a condition of bare life stripped of all legal and political rights. Administered and controlled by an army of private security companies, they now find themselves in a zone of indistinction beyond society, morality and the law.

As Agamben has warned, the state of exception 'tends to increasingly appear as the dominant paradigm of contemporary politics' (Agamben 2005: 3). In relation to immigration and asylum, such a paradigm of government begins to appear with restrictive and exclusionary policies that no longer have any connection with actual trends, that is, the number of wars, levels of spontaneous migration or existing demands for asylum. All that is necessary is a sufficient *threat* of undocumented migration or *risk* of asylum seeking, either now or in the future, real or imagined, for genuine fears to be aroused and preemptive action to ensue (Hörnqvist 2004). In Britain, for example, reflecting the downward trend in internal conflict, the overall number of asylum seekers has been declining since their early 1990s peak. The number of deportations, however, and the sense of political urgency surrounding them has been rising (Bloch and Schuster 2005). In March 2003 the British government announced a two-stage plan for processing asylum claims outside the United Kingdom. This involved regional processing areas in or near theatres of conflict or natural disasters, where asylum requests could be processed on the spot, so to speak. It also included proposals for transit processing zones to be run in cooperation with UNHCR, situated in countries neighbouring the EU, for example Albania, Croatia, Romania or Ukraine. These would also be used to process asylum claims without people having to travel to their preferred country destination.

Moreover, it was suggested that any future spontaneous asylum seekers arriving through other means would also be removed to these zones for processing. Only those passing through such external centres and approved by the UNHCR would be classed as 'genuine' (Schuster 2003: 234).

Since its announcement, variants of this initiative have had a rolling history, attracting some member states only to be rejected at EU level for other states to press again for their trialling and adoption. The point to be emphasized here is not so much the practicalities of the project; what is important is the will to power that it embodies. As Gregor Noll has argued, 'the UK proposal could represent a serious challenge to the institution of asylum as we know it' (Noll 2003: 304). The proposal changes the historic relationship between the state and migration. Although there is no actual crisis of immigration in Europe – if anything, figures are down and there are labour shortages in areas of the economy – the proposal represents a proactive measure to establish a zone of exception, in the form of a series of camps that can be used to contain any future risk of spontaneous migration. Already effectively removed from society and the law within Europe, such camps would be even further removed from public scrutiny and judicial control. They would constitute a 'Guantánamo Bay'-type archipelago for asylum seekers. The reason for the European states' creation of such a state of exception *ex nihilo* 'has to be sought in their political will alone' (ibid.: 340). While not usually placed together, such an exceptional urge to govern is interconnected with the step change in Western humanitarian, development and peace interventionism following the end of the Cold War. The attempts to police spontaneous migration are intimately bound up with the wider technologies of humanitarian intervention, sustainable development, human security and fragile state support that seek to contain global surplus population *in situ*. Viewed together, one begins to glimpse in them the depth of the West's sovereign frontier and its ability to blur the established boundaries between time and space.

The changing regime of internal development

By the close of the 1960s the integrationist and legislative measures to compensate for the control of immigration and the potentially negative effects of cultural difference had encouraged the emergence within Britain of an ameliorative and developmental race relations industry. This comprises a range of state-sanctioned professional, community and voluntary bodies and interventions through which cultural racism is concealed and reproduced as liberal anti-racism, that is, as a means of banishing racism and its causes while upholding the sanctity of the divisions on which racism is said to rest. Until recently the philosophical basis of this anti-racism was *multiculturalism*. This was presented as a shift away from an earlier idea of assimilation – that is, the cultural absorption of immigrants into Western society – to that of integration based on respect for cultural difference. In 1966, Roy Jenkins, then a Labour MP, gave a succinct definition of multiculturalism in Britain 'as not a flattening process of assimilation, but as equal opportunity, accompanied by cultural diversity, in an atmosphere of mutual tolerance' (Jenkins 1966). As already discussed, those for and against immigration control in the 1950s agreed that the debate was about resources and identity. This consensus enabled the latter to accept the case for restriction once it was clear that the public had genuine fears over immigration. A reading of multiculturalism's early anti-racist texts similarly reveals a number of basic assumptions shared with new racism (Duffield 1984). For both, society is synonymous with culture – that is, shared ways of life or ethnic identities. These identities are of an enduring nature and reproduce themselves in time and space, even in the changed circumstances of migration and resettlement in different countries. Culture and cultural difference endure because they are what people themselves both want and need. Full assimilation is not only impossible, it is also undesirable. Ethnic identity is an unreasoned process; what people feel about themselves is as important as what they know. Importantly for both cultural racism and cultural anti-racism, it is not a question of one culture being superior or better than another; cultures are just different. Given this range of shared assumptions connecting new racism and multiculturalism, what separates them is narrower and more restricted. Indeed, there is only one fundamental difference: the approach to the issue of *breakdown and violence*.

For new racism, cultural difference inevitably leads to antagonism and hostility. Excessive pluralism is a threat against which society must be defended. For multiculturalism, however, violence is not inevitable. As a liberal alternative to exclusion and repression, through developmental technologies of targeted support and, especially, individual, group and community education, breakdown can be avoided. Indeed, society can be strengthened through the acceptance of difference and plurality. Reflecting the will of liberal imperialism to govern the colonies more harmoniously, liberal anti-racism embodies a similar will to govern a domestic population striated by the insurmountability of cultural difference more *humanely* and hence effectively. Apart from addressing the special needs of immigrants themselves, during the 1970s the race relations industry expanded into explaining to non-immigrants the importance of accepting the intercultural, personal and psychological underpinnings of cultural difference as a way of overcoming or compensating for prejudice and intolerance. Advice centres, community projects, support groups and racism awareness training in employment and the professions blossomed (ibid.). Much of this training was geared to making recipients aware of the insurmountability of cultural difference and testing their acceptance and sensitivity to it. Indeed, such training reinforces the cultural divide through its central premise that all whites are inevitably racist.[3] Through the shared assumptions linking new racism and anti-racism, multiculturalism has racism coded within it. As part of the process of making cultural difference visible and amenable to surveillance, vetting and acting on it in the name of social cohesion, an internal development regime emerged, concerned with changing behaviour and encouraging new forms of social organization. It was the domestic equivalent of a deepening external regime centred on community-based technologies of self-reliance and sustainable development.

During the 1990s, through growing concerns over terrorism and Islamic fundamentalism, multiculturalism came under increasing pressure (Fekete 2004). In Britain the violence in the northern towns of Oldham, Bradford and Burnley between white and Asian youths during summer 2001, however, (several months before 9/11) visibly signalled the shift to a new mode of internal development. While these disturbances have usually been presented as marking the death of multiculturalism (Young 2001), they are better understood as indicating the new or desired form of integration – the developmental fitness test as it were – corresponding to the changed political interpretation of what constitutes the *genuine fears* of *ordinary people*. Unlike the circumstances surrounding the founding of multiculturalism, this new mode of integration is better suited to a radically interconnected world

---

[3] In 1984/5 the author was project leader for an equal opportunities programme based in Birmingham Social Services Department. While it was located in Birmingham, the project was region-wide and concerned with encouraging the employment of more black and Asian social workers. Among other things, it involved reviewing the anti-racist measures being developed and applied within the public sector.

of insurgent non-state threats. Moreover, it has to coexist with the zone of exception surrounding migrants and asylum seekers and a step change in Western international interventionism.

During the 1960s and 1970s concerns over Asian 'self-segregation' related to the Asian tendency to concentrate within specific parts of the economy and labour process, for example the technologically advanced metal and foundry industries linked to car manufacturing, where Asian workers developed a reputation for shop-floor militancy and collective 'wild cat' strikes independent of the trade union movement (Duffield 1988). At a time of just-in-time volume manufacturing, Asian inter-factory solidarity exerted an asymmetric pressure on employers. Indeed, the 'racial balance' clause within the 1968 Race Relations Act, allowing employers in the interests of racial harmony to disperse ethnic concentrations within the workplace, was included as a way of tackling this problem (Duffield 1988: 137). In the case of the west Midlands, some of the company disinvestment from the region during the 1980s was prompted by this history of Asian militancy. Following the general contraction of manufacturing, however, initial concerns over Asian self-segregation have moved out of the labour process and are now reproduced in the fields of housing, education, community and, especially, religion and culture.

The new racism holds that cultural difference inevitably leads to violence. As anti-racism, multiculturalism argues that this need not happen given education, understanding and assistance to integrate. Building on existing tensions, the summer disturbances of 2001 in northern England quickly altered the terms of this 'bad cop good cop' double act. Reflecting the genuine fears of ordinary people, Muslims in particular are now regarded as having a non-integrating core. Indeed, unless proven otherwise, Muslims are potential enemies within (Fekete 2004). In a radically interconnected world they are the internal equivalents of the non-integrators in the 'arc of extremism now stretching across the Middle East and touching, with increasing definition, countries far outside that region' (Blair 2006). Reproducing the recurrent cultural binaries such as progressive/conservative, open/closed, receptive/non-receptive and modern/traditional, British Muslims have been redivided in terms of the 'segregation of a "faith" group and the exclusion of a generation of young Asians within that' (Burnett 2004: 6). Whereas the whites involved in the disturbances were identified as extremists and not representative of 'ordinary people', the Asian youth 'were seen as "normal" examples of a generation of discontent and representative of an audacious criminal community as a whole' (ibid.: 6–7). Community cohesion was identified as the main component in formulating a response to the social malaise underlying the troubles – that is, the exposure of Muslims as an ungoverned space buttressed by inner cultural tendencies towards segregation and isolation.

Having accepted the existence of genuine fears over Asian segregation, the internal development regime shifted away from a multicultural framework based on focusing resources on deprived areas and special groups. It has prioritized more collective and inclusive technologies of development that emphasize shared citizenship, nationality and belonging (Cantle 2001; Denham 2001). Based on the assumed existence of common values within society, especially liberal values of tolerance, the aim now is to disburse aid in ways that either address joint concerns or encourage communities to work to achieve a shared aim. In the form of projects that encourage patterns of cooperative integration between different ethnic groups, many of these developmental technologies have been pioneered externally as means of conflict resolution within crisis states, for example, in the Balkans (Duffield 1996; CMI 1997). The intention is to use aid to create joint goals and objectives. In Bosnia and Herzegovina, for example, this approach was used to disburse materials for the rebuilding of damaged housing. In the hope of building confidence and familiarity, NGOs would only provide this assistance on condition that interethnic work parties were formed. In Britain it is envisaged that urban aid used in similar ways, together with such measures as the twinning of schools, will promote a greater collective sense of Britishness while preserving the right to be culturally different. Rather than encouraging cultural pluralism for its own sake, technologies of social cohesion are being deployed 'to control non-white communities designated a risk to "Britishness" because of their resistance to even more intrusive control' (Burnett 2004: 8).

Concluding remarks

The shift to a new regime of internal development is based on the threat of ungoverned space within Britain's cultural landscape. It is bracketed together with technologies of security facing similar bids for autonomy beyond the ramparts of Fortress Europe. State-led development originated in the 1960s during the UN's first Development Decade and at a time when decolonization was at its height. During the 1990s, state-led and independent NGO development underwent a process of governmentalization in which the petty sovereignty of the NGOs was reorchestrated within an interventionary web of mutual and overlapping interests. Within the political space of contingent sovereignty, new technologies of fragile state reconstruction and the governmental recapture of autonomous populations are being pioneered. Post-interventionary society, in which the international community exerts trusteeship over the basic biopolitical economic and welfare functions of the state, is now an enduring political relationship. Islamic fundamentalism and the threat of terrorism have the strategic ability to interconnect and mobilize all aspects of the international security architecture linking immigration, internal social cohesion and external social reconstruction. While terrorism challenges democratic states, the hidden complicities and mutual conditioning existing between them has allowed the latter to embark on an unprecedented interconnection and extension of the West's internal and external sovereign frontiers. As a technology of security dedicated to reconciling progress with order by changing attitudes, behaviour and forms of social organization, development bridges the two.

9 Conclusion: From Containment to Solidarity

At the time of writing, the recent deployment of British troops under NATO auspices in southern Afghanistan has, contrary to expectations, generated considerable resistance from a resurgent Taliban. Indeed, it has been necessary to adopt a more aggressive, war-fighting posture than was originally intended. Reminiscent of having to destroy villages in Vietnam in order to save them, we are told that military suppression is necessary so that development can 'follow behind' and take root (Norton-Taylor 2006). That development can be used to further political aims; indeed, that it is a form of politics by other means is a possibility that is often overlooked in mainstream international relations and development studies. Development is usually taken at face value as embodying a benign set of techniques and international interventions to improve the lot of those less fortunate than ourselves. Where problems do exist, they usually concern immediate technical considerations relating to effectiveness, appropriateness or best practice. Critical literature and its implications, including the path-breaking work by Ferguson (1990), Escobar (1995), Crush (1995), Cowen and Shenton (1996), Mitchell (2002) and Harrison (2004), remain largely unexplored in mainstream policy discourse. While appearing to learn from the past, development has a marked ability to absorb criticism by constantly repackaging its basic tenets as an outwardly 'new and improved' formula for sharing the world with others (Easterly 2002). With the advent of unending war and the political foregrounding of development as a civilian technology of counter-insurgency, the need to break out of this enclosure is more pressing than ever. This conclusion outlines the book's main themes before addressing the issue of alternatives to development.

The biopolitics of insured and non-insured life

As a design of power, liberalism is concerned with the security of people, their well-being, freedom and rights (Dean 1999). While different from liberalism, development is intimately connected with it. Development emerges with the advent of the modern world as a practical technology for the protection and betterment of life through harnessing its powers of becoming. The abolition of slavery, the rise of industrial capitalism and imperial expansion called forth development's referent object, that is, modernity's predilection constantly to produce life that is either politically or economically surplus to requirements. As a way of redeeming and making safe surplus population, development constitutes a liberal problematic of security. Surplus life is a potentially dangerous life in need of constant rescue and reintegration as a necessary part of constituting liberal political order itself (Agamben 1998). Embracing freed slaves, Europe's industrial reserve army and the indigenous peoples of Empire, development appears as a technology of security that brackets together and works across national and international boundaries. Cowen and Shenton (1996) have argued that development emerges during the nineteenth century as a means of reconciling the need for order with the necessity of progress. Its key institution is the exercise of an educative and empowering trusteeship over the surplus life that modernity constantly creates. It is thus a liberal alternative to extermination or eugenics, modernity's other answers to the problem of surplus population. Development shares with liberalism an experience of life that is culturally different as always being somehow incomplete or lacking. As Mehta (1999) has argued, this impoverished experience of life, and its accompanying will to exercise moral tutelage, is an enduring feature of liberal imperialism. It characterizes nineteenth-century British attitudes towards India, for example, just as it shapes today's post-interventionary terrain in Iraq, Afghanistan and beyond.

Since the nineteenth century liberal notions of development have been based on securing or redeeming surplus life through strengthening its powers of self-reliance and self-management. A recurrent theme of development, well reflected in contemporary notions of sustainable development, is a concern to maintain the authenticity of local organization and community in the face of the disruptive and anarchic effects of progress. Then, as now, the foundation of an authentic community-based political voice is the small-scale ownership of land or property. Apart from experiments involving former slaves, development as community-based self-reliance emerged in nineteenth-century Europe in response to the underdevelopment of capitalism (Cowen and Shenton 1996). Underpinned by radical and liberal demands to break up large estates and redistribute land, self-reliance offered a future for the dangerous masses of unemployed and destitute that were a feature of the new industrial towns and cities. Until the end of the nineteenth century development was an important part of domestic welfare discourse. By this time, however, a different and more effective liberal approach to the problem of surplus population began to emerge in Europe – that is, social insurance based on the principle of members making regular payments into a centrally managed fund that can be drawn on at times of need. Extended and deepened by the societal effects of two world wars, this principle would eventually expand to shape the European welfare state, where social protection became a right of citizenship (Rose 2000).

In presenting development as a technology of security, development and underdevelopment are distinguished biopolitically, that is, as connected but separate assemblages of institutions, techniques and interventions by which life is supported and distinguished internationally. In this respect biopolitics is not a single strategization of power in the sense of a globalizing or universal disposition for acting on and promoting life at the level of world population. Reflecting its organic ties with racism, development embodies the biopolitical division and separation of the human species into developed and under-developed species-life. With the advent of social insurance, earlier developmental approaches to the problem of surplus population based on community self-reliance were eclipsed in Europe. While not disappearing completely, by the beginning of the twentieth century development as a liberal technology of security based on self-reliance migrated and consolidated its association with the protectorates and colonies.

Drawing on Enlightenment views on the self-sufficient nature of natural man, development as decentralized self-management emerged, for example, in the liberal colonial practice of indirect rule or Native Administration (Cooke 2003). Following the inability of indirect rule to curb the growth of nationalism, however, by the 1940s it had vectored into the colonial practice of community development and the encouragement of producer cooperatives (Kelemen 2006). During the contested process of decolonization, development became an interstate means of differentiating and governing the new world of peoples that nationalism had called forth. The struggle for independence, however, did not expose the connection between liberalism and imperialism thus subjecting it to critique. Decolonization was experienced as revealing a threatening world of poverty that, once again, demanded Western tutelage and trusteeship. In these momentous events, the global bio-political divide between a developed or 'insured' life versus an under-developed or 'non-insured' life expected to be self-reliant life was sealed. The effect of development as a technology of security has been to deepen this divide until today it forms the basis of unending war.

Development and emergency

Viewing development biopolitically throws underdevelopment into a new perspective. Conventional wisdom sees underdevelopment in economic, institutional and social terms, that is, as an absence of growth, investment, capacity, skills or appropriate attitudes. Development is about acting on these economic, institutional and social disadvantages in order to reduce poverty. In the last analysis, however, for the majority of those defined by underdevelopment any reduction in their poverty, in other words any 'development' they may experience, is to be achieved through improving self-reliance. Faith in self-reliance is the obscured heart of development – habituated to the senses, never problematized in theory but instrumental in practice. This non-material notion of betterment is not concerned with extend-ing levels of social protection similar to those enjoyed in Europe to, say, the peoples of Africa. On the contrary, essential needs are seen as being met naturally from self-reliance. Social protection is experi-enced as residing in the reciprocal relations that constitute house-holds, families and communities. Improving economic opportunity through, for example, increased market integration is understood as augmenting the natural welfare role that communities play. Such a natural welfare economy is regarded by international development institutions as obviating the need for centralized or extensive social support or pension provision (Deacon et al. 1997). Arguably, however, since the end of the nineteenth century self-reliance in a globalizing world has been increasingly impossible (Davis 2001). Indeed, capital-ist accumulation tirelessly seeks to break down and absorb areas of autonomy and self-reliance, continually creating and recreating surplus population in the process (Harvey 2003).

As a technology for securing life, social insurance is designed to compensate for the risks and contingencies of existence. In this role, insurance and its related institutions has become a powerful instrument of governance within mass consumer society (Rose 2000). In comparison, underdeveloped life is governed differently. Communities that are expected to be self-reliant live under the permanent threat of humanitarian emergency. Given the impossibility of self-reliance, humanitarian assistance functions as a regime of international indemnity of last resort that comes complete with its own dedicated small print, inconsistencies and moral contradictions (Edkins 2000; Marriage 2006). As a liberal alternative to extermination, development has always existed in relation to a state of exception or, rather, two interconnected states of exception. As self-reliance moves into crisis it calls forth a globalizing and intrusive humanitarian urge to protect. The breakdown of self-reliance, however, is also synonymous with anomie, political extremism and the unchecked international circulation of surplus population. These threats simultaneously invoke a complementary will to consolidate and contain such life through the efforts of development to reconstitute a better mode of self-reliance. As a technology of international security, development bridges this double exception. While providing an alternative to extermination, development does not draw into the open or critique the state of exception on which it rests. Regardless of the situation, it simply embodies a timeless urge to govern more humanely and, consequently, more effectively and efficiently.

Indicative of the relationship between development and emergency is the expansion of the international NGO movement since the Second World War. Central to the growing numbers of organizations and their increasing influence has been the permanence of humanitarian emergency among the world of peoples. Emergency, with its easing of norms and expectations, the weakening grip of states and the ability to engage the public, was – and continues to be – an essential engine of NGO expansion. Humanitarian emergency enables NGOs to fulfil a globalizing liberal urge to protect and, at the same time, to use this entry to consolidate the exposed surplus life through technologies of betterment. Rather than questioning the viability of self-reliance, development works on the principle that the emergencies exist because the communities concerned are not self-reliant enough. Consequently, its various interventions and projects endlessly attempt to re-establish and improve community-based self-reliance. In the form of sustainable development, NGOs became the heirs of a nineteenth-century technology of development that had already vectored through the liberal colonial practices of Native

Administration and community development. At a time when independent nationalist elites were pursuing state-based, 'top-down' strategies of modernization that attempted to reduce the wealth gap, NGOs provided a 'bottom-up' liberal critique of the state.

The recurrent shift from protecting to bettering life involves NGOs making a fundamental biopolitical choice. This is often expressed as a persistent moral dilemma typically presented as the choice between saving a starving child who will die unless urgent help is given and helping the many poor children who otherwise face lives of chronic destitution. Since this dilemma involves deciding the point of exception, it is a sovereign choice (Agamben 1998); in this case, separating the life to be supported from that which can be ignored or allowed to die (Foucault 2003). On the basis of this recurrent challenge, routinely enacted in everyday programme and project decisions, NGOs expanded among the world of peoples as an administrative, non-state or petty sovereign power (see Butler 2004: 56). During the Cold War the NGO movement grew within an international political architecture in which respect for territorial integrity was matched by non-interference in domestic affairs. NGOs expanded as petty sovereigns in the liminal space between corrupt and inefficient Third World states on the one hand and complicit and bureaucratic Western governments on the other. Within this space the NGO movement positioned itself as efficient, flexible, supportive of sustainable solutions and, importantly, expressing the wishes and needs of ordinary people. During the 1980s international NGOs reached the zenith of their independent 'non-governmental' expansion. While the movement has continued to grow significantly during the post-Cold War period, it has done so within the political architecture of post-interventionary society.

Governmentalizing petty sovereignty

Decolonization was a world-historic event. The geopolitical world of states that emerged called forth a corresponding world of peoples and, in the process, reconstituted the biopolitics of population as a global phenomenon. The world of peoples had a major impact on the dynamics and potentialities of global migration. From an earlier north to south trajectory, with growing independence migratory pressures and flows swung south to north (Balibar 1991). The world of states would henceforth increasingly be judged on its members' ability to police population and contain the spontaneous circulation of non-insured peoples; the opposite of this ability is located in the failed state. Soon reflected in the rest of Europe, by the mid-1960s a political consensus emerged in Britain to ban primary migration from the former colonies; by the early 1970s, it had been reduced to a trickle. This consensus placed immigration, and therefore the immigrant, within a deepening zone of exception beyond morality and the law. As part of an evolving Fortress Europe, spontaneous migration and asylum seeking would effectively be criminalized, with migrants being removed from society, for example through dispersal, the denial of benefit rights, the growth of administrative detention, reduced rights of appeal and summary deportation (Schuster 2003).

The banning of immigration emerged as a consequence of decolonization and, among other things, the fear of uncontrolled, asymmetric demands on the welfare state being made by culturally distinct migrants. The zone of exception that opened around international immigration had important implications for development as a technology of security. It encouraged the emergence of compensatory *state-led* internal and external development initiatives (Labour Party 1964). The former established the field of race relations, concerned with multiculturalism and social cohesion. It was initially based on a raft of anti-discrimination legislation and associated urban renewal, capacity building and community projects among Britain's black and Asian populations. The external frontier involved the creation of a modern, state-led development programme. While formal development initiatives had existed previously, these were primarily concerned with maintaining a special relationship with Britain's colonies and former colonies. It was not until the formation of the Ministry of Overseas Development (the forerunner of the DFID) in 1964 that Britain had a forward-looking and increasingly centralized development programme geared to a world of independent states.

The control and management of migration established an international security architecture that connects the search for homeland social cohesion with the need to reterritorialize borderland populations. This risk-based architecture is planetary in ambition and episodic in nature. With each crisis of global circulation, the interconnections between its internal and external development frontiers deepen and thicken. The end of the Cold War was one such crisis. Internal conflict, state failure and its associated circulatory effects, including transborder criminality and increased numbers of refugees and asylum seekers, entered the political foreground as an historic challenge to international security (Jackson 1990; Kaplan 1994; Castells 1998). The response was a growing interventionism, initially humanitarian in nature, on the part of Western states (Boutros-Ghali [1995]). Reflecting its earlier function for NGOs, during the 1990s humanitarian emergency was the portal through which Western states, speaking on behalf of people, rights and freedom, increased their influence in erstwhile independent countries (Douzinas 2003). Overturning Cold War conventions, the growing ease of state-led humanitarian intervention has effected a major change in the status of the world of states. Whereas states had previously interacted on the basis of a *de jure* equality, growing Western interventionism confirmed what many had long suspected; the world of states is a system of *de facto* inequality (Tamás 2000). At the same time, the humanitarian justification for intervention redefined the basis of this inequality in biopolitical terms. That is, rather than its power to defend territory or militarily suppress opposition movements, the measure of an effective versus an infective state now lies in its ability to promote, support and protect human security (ICISS 2001). Effective states have relegated the sovereignty of ineffective ones in the name of securing life itself.

The international political architecture of the Cold War was based on respect for territorial integrity and sovereign competence or non-interference in domestic affairs. While territorial integrity remains central, sovereignty over life in ineffective states is now internationalized, negotiable and contingent (Elden 2006). On the basis of humanitarian emergency and peace activism, Western influence has increased in the biopolitical space of contingent sovereignty. It has expanded, however, on a terrain already staked out by the petty sovereigns of the NGO movement. Humanitarian emergency cleared away Cold War restrictions, allowing UN agencies and NGOs to work legitimately on all sides in unresolved internal wars. Fuelled by a marked increase in Western emergency funding, the end of the Cold War saw the emergence of system-wide relief operations drawing together donor governments, UN agencies, NGOs, private companies and defence establishments into new forms of interaction, cooperation and competition (Duffield 2001). During the Cold War the recurrent move from relief to development had primarily functioned to establish the NGO movement's sovereignty among the world of peoples; this time it was synonymous with the governmentalization of the movement itself. Through such measures as the growth of donor funding, the creation of new working practices and more comprehensive contractual arrangements and auditing tools, the petty sovereignty of the NGO movement was reorchestrated within a thickening web of overlapping aims and mutual interests connecting donor states, recipient governments, UN agencies and militaries.

The governmentalization of the aid industry is an essential aspect of contingent sovereignty and the advent of a post-interventionary political terrain. While presented as a relation of mutual self-interest, this increased penetration is experienced as essential for the West's own security. Although territorial integrity is respected, populations within ineffective states are nonetheless being reterritorialized through multi-agency programmes aimed at reconstructing weak and fragile states. Effective states attempt to govern through these anarchic strategic complexes using technologies of coherence, that is, the search for methodologies, dispositions and administrative arrangements allowing aid and politics to work together in the interests of peace and stability. While the search for coherence invokes the centralization of power, it also provokes new sites of resistance on the part of the independent administrative sovereigns on which aid as governance depends.

The biopolitics of unending war

The rising tide of Western post-Cold War interventionism, and its accompanying governmentalization of aid, has contributed to a significant drop in the number of open civil wars since their peak in 1992 (HSC 2005). The global incidence of such wars, which for decades formed the majority of all armed conflicts, has more than halved. Even in Africa the overall trend is downwards (Marshall 2005). Despite being a major achievement of Western humanitarian, development and peace activism, this decline remains curiously under-researched or even widely acknowledged. When comment has been made, it has been argued that while ongoing wars have declined, levels of generalized instability and human insecurity have increased (Strategy Unit 2005). The decline in open conflict can be reinterpreted as a new political phenomenon: the pacification of civil war has given way to an enlarging zone of Western occupation and contingent sovereignty. Rather than a temporary measure based on the exigencies of emergency, we are witnessing the emergence of an enduring post-interventionary political relationship. All liberal empires, it would seem, are acquired in 'a fit of absence of mind'. The single most important lesson of this process, however, is that ending wars in ineffective states is relatively easy; far more difficult is winning the peace among the people living there. The direction of change is indicated in the contrast between UN 'negotiated access' humanitarian operations of the early 1990s and today's 'integrated missions' concerned with supporting the transition from war to peace (Eide et al. 2005). Whereas the former involved the UN seeking agreement between *all* warring parties, including non-state actors which were thereby indirectly legitimated, the latter now usually mandate the UN to take on militarily any spoilers to internationally brokered peace agreements. While this shift can be interpreted as a rational response to changing conditions, there has been a narrowing of scope for political negotiation and compromise, which is well captured in unending war's axiomatic demand – either you are with us, or you are with the terrorists.

Pacification, occupation and contingent sovereignty are ideas that engage the under-theorized political space of the post-interventionary global borderland. The largely civilianized occupation of formally independent societies has been synonymous with an expanding governmentalization of the aid industry, enabling Western governments to include or exclude ineffective states in the name of securing life itself. The policy adage that 'security without development is unlikely, while development without security is impossible' reflects the counterinsurgency turn within development discourse, even when, as in most cases, aid agencies operate outside military operations (Anderson 1996; OECD 1998; Solana 2003). This connection also has to be seen in relation to the episodic security architecture that bridges the homeland–borderland dichotomy and aligns insured and non-insured populations. Called forth by the banning of spontaneous international migration, the interconnection between internal and external sovereign frontiers has deepened with each crisis of circulation. As every politician would now agree, we live in a radically interconnected world. The current search for domestic social cohesion, for example, with its concern over self-segregation among Muslim communities (Burnett 2004), is bracketed with anxieties over ungoverned space abroad and the measures necessary to secure the humans living there (DFID 2005b). One aspect of this concern is reflected in attempts to transform fragile states into post-interventionary governance states, that is, stable funding regimes in aid-dependent societies where the basic economic and welfare functions, that is, core biopolitical functions, are shaped and controlled by the international community. In so far as the technologies involved are adjusted to match existing administrative capacity and, by design, provide stepping stones to increased competence and political maturity, they reflect the current reworking of the liberal colonial practice of indirect rule or Native Administration.

Domestic ethnic and religious antagonisms, together with difficulties in Iraq and Afghanistan, however, are but a few indications that attempts to govern the internal and external sovereign frontiers in a liberal manner, that is, through an educative trusteeship, are constantly questioned and resisted. The liberal preference to govern surplus life through the prudent exercise of its own freedom is prone to reversal and disillusionment. If development is a liberal alternative to a state of exception, resistance is the terrain on which liberalism (regrettably but necessarily) shades into its opposite. The zone of exception surrounding immigration that connects the internal and external development frontiers has been widening since the moment of its appearance. The ending of the Cold War and the war on terrorism have been important episodic events. The immigrant, in all his or her circulatory guises, has been progressively criminalized and placed beyond normal society and the law. The association of migration with crime and terrorism during the 1990s has been instrumental in this respect (Fekete 2004). At the same time, just as poverty, underdevelopment and ignorance used to be a breeding ground for communism, it now provides an opportunity for 'fundamentalist indoctrination, filling the void created by our failure to act' (Brown 2007).

Liberalism rests on an originary paradox – while speaking in the name of people, freedom and rights at home, liberals have been willing to accept illiberal forms of rule abroad (Mehta 1999). In response to resistance, a new international relationship between democracy and despotism had begun to take shape. Regarding fragile states, for example, donor governments are prepared to accept 'good enough governance' as the price of security (DFID 2005a). However, apart from interventions to support and reconstruct ineffective, fragile or 'pre-modern' states, new forms of interaction and alliance have emerged with what Robert Cooper describes as the world's remaining 'modern' states. Unlike the European transnational project of increasing national integration, these are states that continue to behave as states always have done, 'following Machiavellian principles and *raison d'état*' (Cooper 2002: 12). The necessity of defending society against terrorism has required politicians to establish a new relationship with effective but illiberal states. Building on its lack of clear definition, combating terrorism has made possible the discovery of new mutual interests: 'the truth is Russia has as much interest in defeating terrorism as we have. In a different way, but compatibly, we can develop relations with China and India' (Tony Blair, quoted by Elden 2005: 2094).

In relation to immigrant and refugee flows, a reworking of the relationship between democracy and despotism has been evident since the mid-1990s. In order to discourage movement from such places as Afghanistan, Kosovo, Somalia and Sri Lanka, for example, through the lever of EU trade and development assistance, refugee sending and transit countries have been encouraged to play a policing role (Waever et al. 1993). At the same time, many political groups struggling for self-determination or cultural autonomy – some of which would have been regarded as liberation movements during the Cold War – have been redefined as terrorist organizations and consequently criminalized. In Britain, the Terrorist Act 2000, enacted before the events of 9/11, brought together a series of pre-existing ad hoc juridical measures that now effectively outlaw refugee solidarity work. The naming within the act of organizations allegedly connected with terrorism and their proscribing has not criminalized these groups only; by extension a similar fate has befallen any supporter protesting against human rights abuse or seeking self-determination in places such as Egypt, Algeria, Saudi Arabia, India, Pakistan, Sri Lanka, Palestine and Turkey. Even before the events of 9/11, the effect of the 2000 Act was to regularize the growing jurisdiction of British courts over acts committed or planned abroad. In what the human rights lawyer Gareth Peirce has described as a gift to authoritarian states, 'countries like Russia are applauding the New Labour government for introducing legislation which, as they see it, will stifle criticism of their regimes' (quoted by Fekete 2001: 99).

If the outlawing of exiled groups calling for political change has been a gift to despotic regimes, these regimes are reciprocating by providing democratic states with covert security services such as detention without trial, torture and extrajudicial murder that are otherwise illegal under their own laws. Due to the growing opposition by the US Supreme Court to the rendering facility at Guantánamo Bay, Cuba, for example, places such as Afghanistan are allegedly emerging as hubs of a much wider shadow network of detention centres created through commandeering foreign jails, building cell blocks at US military bases or the establishment of covert CIA facilities located anywhere 'from an apartment block to a shipping container. This network has no visible infrastructure – no prison rolls, visitor rosters, staff lists or complaints procedures' (Levy and Scott-Clark 2005: 20). Linked by covert air transport, terrorist suspects are being processed in facilities strung across such places as Afghanistan, Pakistan, Uzbekistan, Jordan, Egypt, Thailand, Malaysia and Indonesia (Grey 2006). Agamben (1998) has warned that the architecture of the camp – the zone of exception beyond morality and the law where anything becomes possible – has once again entered the political foreground. In addition to the familiar barbed wire enclosures, within a planetary technology of security the camp also takes the form of a covert transborder network of detention and rendition centres, interconnected by air transport and hidden within the folds of strategically allied despotic states.

Extraordinary rendition lies in the shadows of a zone of exception that connects internal and external sovereign frontiers with the policing of international circulation. Also located within this zone are the banning and detention without trial of terrorist suspects in democratic countries, together with a willingness to accept high levels of civilian casualties in overseas interventionary operations as the necessary price of freedom. A culturally coded racism striates the world of peoples, separating good from bad, useful from useless in terms of their contribution to international security. Based on the political interpretation of the genuine fears of ordinary people, this racism decides the sovereign boundary between the included and the excluded, between those exempted from the zone of exception and those destined to disappear within it. As a liberal alternative to emergency, development exists in constant thrall to it.

Is there an alternative development?

Development embodies an urge to protect and better others less fortunate than ourselves. As such, it indicates a noble and emancipatory aspiration. Development, however, transforms this urge into a liberal will to govern through the assertion of an educative trusteeship over life that is always experienced as somehow incomplete and consequently surplus or in excess of prevailing requirements. Can the urge to protect and emancipate be rescued from development's organic association with security and emergency? At the outset, it can be argued that release does not lie in the search for an 'alternative' development with its perennial promise of freedom through the delineation of ever more genuine forms of community and, consequently, ever more authentic visions of partnership and empowerment (Chambers 1983; Korten 1990). While development studies and postcolonialism sit uncomfortably together, the one belonging to the immediate world of practice and the other to cultural analysis and reflection, when attempts have been made to bring the two together, it is often to argue that the insights of the latter can somehow help or enhance the former (Simon 2006). As Cowen and Shenton have pointed out, however, calls for greater 'authenticity' invariably reduce to advocating, yet again, the need for more 'appropriate' or 'sensitive' forms of trusteeship (Cowen and Shenton 1996: 452–71; also Cooke and Kothari 2001). Liberal colonial administrators, for example, also believed that indirect rule 'put the last first' and directly challenged those who held that 'it was no concern of theirs to know or care how the black man looked at life, what they thought, or why they thought it' (MacMichael 1923: 18).

In attempting to rescue the emancipatory impulse locked within development, the biopolitical distinction between 'insured' and 'non-insured' life is also worth considering. This metaphor highlights how life in the mass consumer society is supported by technologies of welfare associated with social and private insurance, and contrasts it with the situation beyond its borders, where human populations are expected to be self-reliant. It signals two broad or generic ways of acting at the aggregate level of population both to support life and globally to divide it. Rather than lessening this generic divide, development is a technology of security to contain its circulatory effects. Given the impossibility of universal self-reliance – hence the permanence of humanitarian emergency – it could be argued that another avenue of alternative development could involve the abandonment of self-reliance in favour of 'insuring' the world's surplus population – that is, of drawing it within collective, insurance-based forms of social protection.

In some respects, this endeavour is already under way. However, rather than challenging self-reliance, the trend has been to adapt insurance technologies to reconfirm homeostatic and small-scale conceptions of sustainability. The World Bank and the ILO, for example, recognize the differences and impediments preventing the emergence of large-scale, contributory-financed social insurance programmes in underdeveloped countries, notably that traditional state-led social insurance is largely concerned with ameliorating labour-market defined risks through various forms of income replacement, while in recent decades employment expansion in the developing world has mainly been informal and unregulated. In addressing such obstacles the World Bank has argued for an adaptive approach involving the need to redefine social protection in terms of individual needs rather than labour-market requirements. From this perspective, similar to pronouncements on human security, social protection has to 'encompass all public interventions that help individuals, households, and communities to manage risk and that provide support to the critically poor' (World Bank quoted by McKinnon 2004: 10). Rather than taking us somewhere new, however, we are back in the world of self-reliance, this time repackaged as a system of risk management that requires greater understanding and external support.

Similarly, where actual NGO or government programmes have been initiated, one encounters social insurance adapted to the require-ments of sustainable development. For example, there is a growing interest in small-scale, non-statutory but contributory micro-insur-ance projects that cover specific groups or sub-communities (ibid.). Compared with universal social insurance, such schemes are limited in both scope and entitlements. Under government sponsorship, a number of non-contributory tax-based schemes have also emerged. Rather than being based on the labour market, these programmes embody a shift from risk compensation to enhancing individual and collective rights in relation to citizenship. South Africa, together with the governments of Mauritius, Namibia and Botswana, has, for example, pioneered non-contributory old-age pensions for citizens. Apart from foregrounding the sovereign issue of where citizenship ends and non-citizenship begins, such measures do not seek to extend the levels of social protection existing, for example, in Europe to the developing world. In fact, they have been interpreted as signalling that this outcome is unlikely if not impossible. Such an eventual con-vergence had, for example, been a founding assumption of the International Social Security Association when it was established in Geneva in 1927. In recent years such ideas have come 'under serious review' (ibid.: 9). There has been a downgrading of any ambitions of universal social insurance in favour, at best, of segregated or pluralist systems which, apart from the measures above, include ad hoc NGO- and UN-established interventions and projects to improve human security and self-reliance. In such circumstances, realism is held to dictate that ideas of inclusive social protection 'must start small-scale and work up from the local or workplace level' (ibid.: 17).

There is, however, another factor in relation to convergence and social insurance that, irrespective of the material conditions in the developing world, questions the underlying assumptions and aims of such an endeavour. Of relevance here is that the return of the state to the centre of development discourse conceals a curious inversion. During the anti-colonial and revolutionary wars of the past, national-ist and left-wing groups often sought to capture states in order to remake them in the name and desires of the people. During the Cold War, Western aid usually included military assistance to such states to help them defeat these challenges. It is amidst the debris of these past struggles that the West now finds itself intervening and taking on the radical task of directly reordering states to satisfy better the needs of the people. While humanitarian emergency and the urge to protect has often provided the spur for such activism, by altering one's viewpoint, it is possible to see a dimension that is usually hidden.

Humanitarian emergencies are, in some respects, not the result of the breakdown of self-reliance but of its *essential success*; that is, its ability to allow non-insured people, groups and communities to forge livelihoods and survival strategies beyond and outside the state (Keen 1994 and 1998; Duffield 2001: 136–60). The increase in Western interventionism is occurring at a time when people are actively deserting the state. The vast literature on 'war economies', for example, is illustrative of an innovative and radical self-reliance. Transborder and shadow economies have expanded at the same time as a medley of actors – ranging from ethnic associations, clan leaders and religious groups to warlords, Mafiosi and terrorist organizations – have all learned the biopolitical art of enfranchising the dispossessed through alternative forms of protection, legitimacy and welfare as a necessary adjunct of their own political survival (Tishkov 1997; Goldenburg 2001; Kent et al. 2004). Such 'actually existing development' beyond and outside the state deepens the crisis of containment and gives urgency, for example, to Western efforts to reconstruct fragile states and reterritorialize the people living within them. Apart from highlighting the fact that such states have no established or centralized welfare function, the difficulty is that even if successfully reconfigured as governance states, they can only promise the non-material salvation of sustainable development through social reorganization around basic needs and self-reliance.

The success of surplus life in forging patterns of actually existing development beyond states defines an important area of contestation and recapture within the framework of unending war. In one of the few attempts to examine global development from a comparative welfare regime perspective, Wood and Gough (2006) identify three generic types: the welfare state, the informal security regime and the insecurity regime. The last two are systems where self-reliance, in terms of the family and community forms of reciprocity, provides the bulk of public welfare. The insecurity regime, however, corresponds to zones of crisis and state fragility where these reciprocities have broken down. Whereas welfare states are characterized by the de-commodification of life, for example, through protection from employment risks, within informal security regimes patron–client relations predominate. Reflecting the absence of a mass labour market rather than de-commodification, especially within insecure societies, generalizing welfare is argued to require a process of 'de-clientization' – that is, the practice 'of de-linking client dependants from their personalized, arbitrary and discretionary entrapment to persons with intimate power over them' (ibid.: 1708). In framing this argument, the authors have unwittingly rearticulated the global 'hearts and minds' role into which unending war has channelled development assistance (DAC 2003). When nationalists and liberation movements sought to remake the state during the Cold War, such events were labelled as radical or even revolutionary. Today, as the West takes on this role directly, it finds itself embroiled in expansive and totalizing forms of counter-insurgency.

The idea that an alternative development lies in the 'insuring' of the non-insured raises many difficulties. Given the widespread desertion of the borderland state by the dispossessed, such endeavours easily become means of recapturing and bolstering the West's own security; in other words, it would have to contend with the governance function of insurance-based technologies of biopower. This includes the importance of welfare rights as a means of excluding migrants and encoding racial identity and conflict in mass consumer society. At the same time, through the digitalization of life processes, insurance technologies are providing increasingly finely textured mechanisms for the monitoring and modulation of conduct more generally (Ericson and Doyle 2003). These difficulties suggest that, in attempting to rescue the emancipatory urge embedded in development, we should consider following the lead of the dispossessed and global justice movements and also desert the state (Patel and McMichael 2004). Or at least, in the process, the power of an already monstrously powerful state should not be further extended or deepened. Freeing the impulse to protect and better should avoid measures that further privilege the state or, like human security, invoke the state as central to its own existence. This concern underlines the tragedy of the NGO movement and its hopeless enmeshment. That a distancing is required is also suggested from a different but related quarter.

During the course of the twentieth century, invoking a state of emergency has become a normal and accepted paradigm of government (Agamben 2005). Following Foucault, Agamben has argued that security can be distinguished from disciplinary power in that the latter seeks to isolate and close territories in the pursuit of order, while security 'wants to regulate disorder' (Agamben 2001: 1). A dangerous contemporary development is the thought of security itself (Hörnqvist 2004). As security becomes the basic task of the state, politics is progressively neutralized. The thought of security 'bears with it an essential risk. A state which has security as its sole task and source of legitimacy is a fragile organism; it can always be provoked by terrorism to become itself terroristic' (Agamben 2001). Between terrorism and counter-terrorism a curious complicity exists in which each needs the other for its own existence, whether as a legitimation of its own violence or a justification for the draconian methods it requires in defending society. Both share a common ground in the acceptance of a design of war that privileges the state. During the Cold War the geopolitical stand-off between nuclear-armed superpowers was underpinned by the threat of 'mutually assured destruction' or MAD. Today we have acquired a sort of biopolitical MADness that interconnects the survival and various fundamentalisms of insurgents and counter-insurgents alike in the fateful and mutually conditioning embrace of unending war. In this encounter the inevitable victor is the state and the unavoidable victim is politics itself. Like actually existing development, the pursuit of emancipation involves working beyond and outside the state, ignoring rather than confronting it, as part of the rediscovery of politics in the practical solidarity of the governed.

The solidarity of the governed

In June 1984 Michel Foucault released a statement on behalf of several NGOs to mark the formation of the International Commission Against Piracy and to protest against the interdiction at sea and summary return of Vietnamese boat people. In his statement Foucault stressed that all were present as private individuals, with no grounds for speaking other than 'a certain shared difficulty in enduring what is taking place' (Foucault [1984]: 474). In setting out the aims of the group he listed several principles, including the existence of an 'international citizenship' with rights, duties and obligations to speak out against the abuse of power, whoever the author. After all, 'we are all of the community of the governed, and thereby obliged to show mutual solidarity' (ibid.). The sentiment that 'we are all governed and therefore in solidarity' is present in different ways and degrees in today's anti-globalization campaigns, such as global justice movements, the World Social Forum, the Zapatistas in Mexico or the international peasant farmers' movement Via Campesina. It disturbs and questions earlier forms of Third World solidarity coalescing around politics, rights and aid (Olesen 2004). Rights and aid solidarity in particular, including humanitarian and development assistance, imply a one-way process between the provider and beneficiary of solidarity. It is a process that emphasizes differences in power and distance, with providers in places of safety and beneficiaries in zones of crisis. It is also apolitical and does 'not fundamentally challenge the underlying causes of grievances that inspire the solidarity effort' (ibid.: 258).

In contrast, global solidarity emphasizes mutuality and reciprocity between provider and beneficiary while blurring the differences between them. It involves a 'more extensive global consciousness that constructs the grievances of physically, socially and culturally distant people as deeply intertwined' (ibid.: 259). While difference is acknowledged, *it is the similarities that are important*. Global solidarity is also political: distant struggles are common points of departure that collectively problematize the overarching, anti-democratic and marginalizing effects of global neoliberalism, whether as struggles against hospital closures in mass consumer society or the ruination of pastoralist livelihoods beyond its borders. In this respect, it minimizes attempts to divide and striate humankind either according to measures of development and underdevelopment or those of culture. Today the fear of radical interconnection, with its ability to threaten the stability of mass consumer society, dominates Western political imagination. For an international citizenship, however, it offers possibilities for new encounters, mutual recognition, reciprocity and hope: it represents the magic of life itself.

The principles of mutuality and interconnectedness provide a chance to rediscover politics as a practical interrogation of power. If biopolitics and its technologies of security have absorbed the political, the task is not so much to reinvent it as to reclaim it. It involves questioning the assumptions and practices that support life while at the same time disallowing it to the point of death. Called into question are those acts of administrative or petty sovereignty that, acting through the lens of race, class and gender, order the way we live and dictate how we develop the rest of the world in our own interests. We are all governed by these practices – providers and beneficiaries alike – which themselves are directly or indirectly the result of states. Through interconnectedness, mutuality and conversations among the governed, they can be compared, reconnected and interrogated. Such mutuality, however, demands a change of comportment. In a reversal of the Schumachian paradigm of knowledge, instead of educating the poor and marginalized, it is more a question of learning from their struggles for existence, identity and dignity and together challenging the world we live in. As a precondition, the liberal inclination to prejudge those who are culturally different as somehow incomplete and requiring external betterment has to be abandoned. It requires a willingness to engage in unscripted conversations and accept the risks involved, including the inability to predict or control outcomes – a situation that a security mentality continually tries to avoid. Through a practical politics based on the solidarity of the governed we can aspire to opening ourselves to the spontaneity of unpredictable encounters. It also entails a willingness to help without expecting anything in return, that is, abandoning the security prescription which argues that in helping others we should also help ourselves. While mandatory for donor and NGO assistance, offers of support from and between international citizens would not insist that beneficiaries change their beliefs, attitudes or forms of social organization.

If development encloses an emancipatory urge, it does not lie in the formulation of endless 'new and improved' technologies of betterment nor the search for more authentic forms of community – it is found in the solidarity of the governed made possible by a radically interconnected world and the insatiable will to life that flows and circulates through it.

References

'Abd al-Rahim, Muddathir. 1969. *Imperialism and Nationalism in Sudan: A Study in Constitutional and Political Development, 1899–1956.* Oxford: Oxford University Press.

Abiri, Elisabeth. 2001. Risky business: the securitisation of migration and its consquences. Paper presented at RC40/EGDI Research Workshop on New Regionalisms and New/Old Security Issues. Göteborg University, Sweden: Department of Peace and Development Research (Pagrigu).

Abrahamson, Rita. 2004. The Power of Partnerships in Global Governance. *Third World Quarterly*, 25, 1453–67.

—— 2005. Blair's Africa: the politics of securitization and fear. *Alternatives*, 30, 55–80.

Abrahamsson, Hans and Nilsson, Anders. 1995. *Mozambique: The Troubled Transition – From Socialist Construction to Free Market Capitalism.* London: Zed Books.

Adams, Bill. 1993. Sustainable development and the greening of development theory. In Frans J. Schuurman (ed.), *Beyond the Impasse: New Directions in Development Theory.* London: Zed Books, 207–22.

Adams, Nassau A. 1993. *Worlds Apart: The North–South Divide and the International System.* London: Zed Books.

Agamben, Giorgio. 1998. *Homo Sacer: Sovereign Power and Bare Life.* Stanford: Stanford University Press.

—— 20 September 2001. On security and terror. *Allgemeine Zeitung*, available at http://www.egs.edu/faculty/agamben/agamben-on-security-and-terror.html (accessed 9 June 2004).

—— 2005. *State of Exception.* Chicago and London: University of Chicargo Press.

Aicken, Gareth. 5 April 1995. Memo to Mr Coverdale: Mozambique – A Sharper Strategy and Closer Coordination?

Anderson, Mary B. 1996. *Do No Harm: Supporting Local Capacities for Peace Through Aid*, Local Capacities for Peace Project, The Collaborative for Development Action, Inc, Cambridge, MA.

Anderson, M. B. and Woodrow, P. J. 1989. *Rising From the Ashes: Disaster Response Toward Development*. Boulder: Westview.

Arendt, Hannah. [1951] 1994. *The Origins of Totalitarianism*. New York: Harcourt.

—— [1958] 1998. *The Human Condition*. Chicago: University of Chicago Press.

Baitenmann, Helga. 1990. NGOs and the Afghan war: the politicisation of humanitarian aid. *Third World Quarterly*, 12 (1), 62–86.

Baldin-Edwards, Martin. 21–23 September 2005. Migration into southern Europe: non-legality and labour markets in the region. Paper presented at 11th General Conference of EADI. Bonn: EADI.

Balibar, Etienne. 1991. Is there a 'neo-racism'? In Etienne Balibar and Immanuel Wallerstein, *Race, Nation, Class: Ambiguous Identities*. London: Verso, 17–28.

Barker, Martin. 1981. *The New Racism: Conservatives and the Ideology of the Tribe*. London: Junction Books.

Barrett, Tom, Cadwallader, Robin, Hall, Andrew, Hansell, John, Gorie, Helen and Zeitlyn, Sushila. 1995. *Mozambique Zambezia Strategy Review: 22 October–3 November 1995*. British Development Division in Central Africa, Harare.

Batten, T. R. 1957. *Communities and Their Development*. London: Oxford University Press.

Bauman, Zygmunt. 2001. Sociology after the Holocaust [1989]. In *The Bauman Reader*, ed. Peter Beilharz. Oxford: Blackwell Publishers, 230–58.

—— 2004. *Wasted Lives: Modernity and its Outcasts*. Cambridge: Polity.

BDDCA. 1994a. *Mozambique: Country Strategy Paper 1994/95*. British Development Division in Central Africa, Harare.

—— 1994b. *Mozambique: Feeder Roads Project*. British Development Division in Central Africa, Harare.

—— 1995. *Project Memorandum for the Participatory Extension and Improved Household Food Security Project – EPSAM*. British Development Division in Central Africa, Harare.

—— 1996a. *Mozambique Review of Agricultural Projects in Zambezia: Participatory Extension and Improved Household Food Security Project (EPSAM) – Annual Review*. 19–20 February, British Development Division in Central Africa, Harare.

—— 1996b. *Emergency Assistance Strategy Paper for Mozambique*. British Development Division for Central Africa, Harare.

—— 1997. *Project Concept Note: Zambezia Agricultural Development Project (ZADP) Phase II.* British Development Division for Central Africa, Harare.

Beck, Ulrich. 1992. *Risk Society: Towards a New Modernity.* London: Sage Publications.

Benn, Hilary. 2004. The development challenge in crisis states. Speech, London School of Economics.

Biccum, April R. 2005. Development and the 'New' Imperialism: a reinvention of colonial discourse in DFID promotional literature. *Third World Quarterly,* 26, 1005–20.

Bigo, Didier. 2001. The Möbius ribbon of internal and external security(ies). In Albert Mathias, David Jacobson and Yosef Lapid (eds), *Identities, Borders, Orders: Rethinking International Relations Theory.* Minneapolis: University of Minneapolis Press.

Black, Maggie. 1992. *A Cause for Our Time: Oxfam – The First 50 Years.* Oxford: Oxfam and Oxford University Press.

Blair, Tony. 3 October 2001. This is the battle with only one outcome: our victory. *Guardian,* 4–5.

—— 12 March 2005. I believe this is Africa's best chance for a generation. *Guardian,* 22.

—— 1 August 2006. Speech on world politics, World Affairs Council, Los Angeles, available at http://newsvote.bbc.co.uk (accessed 20 December 2006).

Bloch, Alice and Schuster Liza. 2005. At the extremes of exclusion: deportation, detention and dispersal. *Ethnic and Racial Studies* 28, 491–512.

Blumenthal, Sidney. 1 June 2006. A state of emergency. *Guardian,* 31.

BOND. 2003. Global Security and Development. BOND Discussion Paper, British Overseas NGOs for Development (BOND), London.

Bookstein, Amelia. 2004. Interview, Oxfam Humanitarian Department, Oxford.

Booth, David. 1993. Development research: from impasse to a new agenda. In Frans J. Schurman (ed.), *Beyond the Impasse: New Directions in Development Theory.* London: Zed Books, 49–76.

Borton, J. 1993. Recent trends in the international relief system. *Disasters* 17 (3), 187–201.

—— 16 February 1994. Personal communication.

Bourne, Jenny. 1980. Cheerleaders and ombudsmen: the sociology of race relations in Britain. *Race and Class,* 21, 331–52.

Boutros-Ghali, Boutros. [1992] 1995. An agenda for peace: preventive diplomacy, peacemaking and peace-keeping (17 June 1992). In Boutros Boutros-Ghali (ed.), *An Agenda for Peace: 1995.* New York: United Nations, 39–72.

Brahimi, Lakhdar. 2000. *Report of the Panel on United Nations Peace Operations*. New York: United Nations General Assembly and Security Council.

Brigg, Morgan. 2002. Post-development, Foucault and the colonial metaphor. *Third World Quarterly* 23, 421–36.

Brown, Gordon. 4 January 2007. Our 2p pledge to all children. *Guardian*, 26.

Bryant, Raymond L. 2002. Non-governmental organizations and governmentality: 'consuming' biodiversity and indigenous people in the Philippines. *Political Studies* 50, 268–92.

Buchanan-Smith, Margaret and Maxwell, Simon. 1994. Linking relief and development: an introduction and overview. *Institute of Development Studies Bulletin: Special Issue on Linking Relief and Development* 25 (4), 2–16.

Burnett, Jonathan. 2004. Community, cohesion and the state. *Race and Class* 45 (3), 1–18.

Bush, George W. 2002. *The National Security Strategy of the United States of America*. Washington, DC: White House.

Butler, Judith. 2004. *Precarious Life: The Powers of Mourning and Violence*. London and New York: Verso.

Buzan, Barry, Waever, Ole and de Wilde, Jaap. 1997. *Security: A New Framework for Analysis*. Boulder, CO: Lynne Rienner.

Campbell, David, Clark, D. J. and Manzo, Kate. 2005. *Imaging Famine*. An exhibition at the Newsroom. London: Guardian and Observer Archive and Advisor Centre. Available at www.imaging-famine.org.

Cantle, Ted. 2001. *Community Cohesion: A Report of the Independent Review Team*. London: Home Office.

Carnegie Commission. 1997. *Preventing Deadly Conflict: Executive Summary of the Final Report*. Washington, DC: Carnegie Commission on Preventing Deadly Conflict.

Castells, Manuel. 1996. *The Rise of the Network Society*. Oxford: Blackwell.

—— 1998. *End of Millennium*. Oxford: Blackwell.

Chambers, Robert. 1983. *Rural Development: Putting the Last First*. Harlow: Longman.

Chen, Lincoln, Fukuda-Parr, Sakiko and Seidensticker, Ellen (eds). 2003. *Human Insecurity in a Global World*. Cambridge, MA: Harvard University Press.

Chesterman, Simon. 2001. *Just War or Just Peace? Humanitarian Intervention and International Law*. Oxford: Oxford University Press.

Chingono, Mark F. 1996. *The State, Development and Violence*. Brookfield: Avebury.

Christian Aid. 2004. *The Politics of Poverty: Aid in the New Cold War*. London: Christian Aid,

CHS. 2003. *Human Security Now*. New York: Commission for Human Security.

Clay, Edward, Borton, John et al. 1995. *Evaluation of ODA's Response to the 1991–1992 Southern Africa Drought: Vol. II*. London: Evaluation Department, Overseas Development Administration.

Clough, M. 1992. *Free at Last? US Policy Toward Africa and the End of the Cold War*. New York: Council on Foreign Relations.

CMI. 1997. *Humanitarian Assistance and Conflict: Report Prepared for the Norwegian Ministry of Foreign Affairs*. Bergen: Chr. Michelsen Institute, Development Studies and Human Rights.

—— 2005. *Humanitarian and Reconstruction Assistance to Afghanistan 2001 – 05 (From Denmark, Ireland, the Netherlands, Sweden and the United Kingdom): A Joint Evaluation*. Bergen: Chr. Michelsen Institute (lead agency), Copenhagen Development Consultancy and German Association of Development Consultants on behalf of Danida, Ministry of Foreign Affairs, Copenhagen.

Coker, Christopher. 2003. *Empires in Conflict: The Growing Rift Between Europe and the United States*. Whitehall Paper 58. London: Royal United Services Institute.

Collier, Paul. 2000. Doing well out of war: an economic perspective. In Mats Berdal and David M. Malone (eds), *Greed and Grievance: Economic Agendas in Civil Wars*. Boulder and London: Lynne Rienner, 91–112.

Collier, Paul, Elliot, Lani, Hegre, Harvard, Hoeffler, Anke, Reynal-Querol, Marta and Sambanis, Nicholas. 2003. *Breaking the Conflict Trap: Civil War and Development Policy*. Washington, DC and Oxford: World Bank and Oxford University Press.

Cooke, Bill. 2003. A new continuity with colonial administration: participation in development management. *Third World Quarterly* 24 (1), 47–61.

Cooke, Bill and Kothari, Uma (eds). 2001. *Participation: The New Tyranny?* London: Zed Books.

Cooper, Robert. 2002. The post-modern state. In Mark Leonard (ed.), *Re-ordering the World: The Long-Term Implications of 11 September*. London: The Foreign Policy Centre, 11–20.

Cornia, Giovanni Andrea. 1987. Economic decline and human welfare in the first half of the 1980s. In G. A. Cornia, R. Jolly and F. Stewart (eds), *Adjustment With a Human Face: Volume I*. Oxford: Clarendon Press, 11–47.

Cosgrave, John. 2004. *The Impact of the War on Terror on Aid Flows*. London: Action Aid.

Costy, Alexander. 2004. The dilemma of humanitarianism in the post-Taliban transition. In Antonio Donini, Norah Niland and Karin Wermester (eds),

Nation-Building Unravelled? Aid, Peace and Justice in Afghanistan. Bloomfield: Kumarian Press, 143–65.

Cowen, M. P. and Shenton, R. W. 1996. *Doctrines of Development.* London and New York: Routledge.

CPRC. 2005. *The Chronic Poverty Report 2004–5,* Manchester: Chronic Poverty Research Centre, University of Manchester, Institute for Development and Policy Management.

Cramer, Christopher and Pontara, Nicola. 1997. *Rural Poverty and Poverty Alleviation in Mozambique: What's Missing From the Debate?* Department of Economics, Working Paper Series No 68. London: University of London, School of Oriental and African Studies, 1–44.

Crombe, Xavier. 2005. *Humanitarian Action in Situations of Occupation: The View from MSF.* London: Overseas Development Institute, Humanitarian Policy Group. Available at http://www.odihpn.org/reports.asp?ID=2794 (accessed 26 May 2006).

Crush, Jonathan (ed.). 1995. *Power of Development.* London: Routledge.

Cuppens, Yvonne. 1998. *Research into Food Security in Maganja da Costa, Zambezia, Mozambique.* Action Aid Mozambique, Maputo.

DAC. 1997. *DAC Guidelines on Conflict, Peace and Development Co-operation.* Paris: Development Assistance Committee (DAC), Organisation for Economic Co-operation and Development (OECD).

—— 2003. *A Development Co-operation Lens on Terrorism Prevention: Key Entry Points for Action.* Paris: DAC, OECD.

Darby, Phillip. 1987. *Three Faces of Imperialism: British and American Approaches to Asia and Africa 1870–1970.* New Haven and London: Yale University Press.

Davies, Ioan. 1963. The labour commonwealth. *New Left Review* 1 (22), 75–94.

Davis, Mike. 2001. *Late Victorian Holocausts: El Nino Famines and the Making of the Third World.* London: Verso.

DCD. 2004. Harmonisation and Alignment in Fragile States: Draft report by Overseas Development Institute (ODI), United Kingdom, Senior Level Forum on Development Effectiveness in Fragile States, Meeting in London, 13–14 January 2005. Paris: Development Co-operation Directorate (DCD), OECD.

Deacon, Bob et al. 1997. *Global Social Policy: International Organisations and the Future of Welfare.* London: Sage Publications.

Dean, Mitchell. 1999. *Governmentality: Power and Rule in Modern Society.* London: Sage.

Demirovic, Alex. 1996. NGOs: social movements in global order? Paper presented at American Sociological Association Conference, New York.

Denham, John. 2001. *Building Cohesive Communities: A Report of the Ministerial Group on Public Order and Community Cohesion*. London: Home Office.

Derlugian, Georgi M. 1996. The social cohesion of the states. In Terence K. Hopkins and Immanuel Wallerstein (eds). *The Age of Transition: Trajectory of the World-System, 1945–2025*. London: Zed Books, 148–77.

Development Initiatives. 2003. *Global Humanitarian Assistance 2003*. Evercreech: Development Initiatives.

—— 2005. *Global Humanitarian Assistance Update: 2004–2005*, Evercreech: Development Initiatives.

DFID. 1997. *Eliminating World Poverty: A Challenge for the 21st Century*. White Paper on International Development. London: The Stationery Office for the Department of International Development (DFID).

—— 1998. PEC *Submission 98 (6): Mozambique – Zambezia Agricultural Development Project (ZADP Phase 2)*. London: DFID.

—— 2005a. *Why We Need to Work More Effectively in Fragile States*. London: DFID.

—— 2005b. *Fighting Poverty to Build a Safer World: A Strategy for Security and Development*. London: DFID.

DFID, FCO and MoD. 2003. *The Global Conflict Prevention Pool: A Joint UK Approach to Reducing Conflict*. London: DFID, Foreign and Commonwealth Office and Ministry of Defence.

Dillon, Michael. 2004. The security of governance. In Wendy Larner and William Walters (eds), *Global Governmentality: Governing International Spaces*. New York: Routledge, 76–94.

Dillon, Michael and Reid, Julian. 2000. Global governance, liberal peace and complex emergency. *Alternatives* 25 (1), 117–43.

Donini, Antonio. 1996. *The Policies of Mercy: UN Coordination in Afghanistan, Mozambique, and Rwanda*. Occasional Paper No. 2. Providence, RI: Thomas J. Watson Jr. Institute for International Studies.

—— 2001. *Engagement with the Authorities: Principles and Pragmatism*. Islamabad: UN Office for the Coordination of Humanitarian Assistance to Afghanistan.

Donini, Antonio, Niland, Norah and Wermester, Karin (eds). 2004. *Nation-Building Unravelled? Aid, Peace and Justice in Afghanistan*. Bloomfield CT: Kumarian Press.

Douzinas, Costas. 2003. Humanity, military humanism and the new moral order. *Economy and Society* 32 (2), 159–83.

Duffield, Mark. 1984. New racism . . . new realism: two sides of the same coin. *Radical Philosophy*, 37, 29–34.

—— 1988. *Black Radicalism and De-Industrialisation: The Hidden History of Indian Foundry Workers*. Aldershot: Gower.

Duffield, Mark. 1991. *Oxfam's Emergency Response to the Gulf War: August 1990–August 1991*. Oxford: Oxfam.

—— 1994. *Complex Political Emergencies: An Exploratory Report for UNICEF With Reference to Angola and Bosnia*. Birmingham: School of Public Policy.

—— 1996. *Social Reconstruction in Bosnia and Croatia: An Exploratory Report for SIDA*. Birmingham: Centre for Urban and Regional Studies, University of Birmingham.

—— 2001. *Global Governance and the New Wars: The Merger of Development and Security*. London: Zed Books.

—— 2006. Racism, migration and development: the will to planetary order. *Progress in Development Studies* 6 (1), 68–79.

Duffield, Mark, Gossman, Patricia and Leader, Nicholas. 2002. *Review of the Strategic Framework for Afghanistan*. Kabul and Islamabad: Afghanistan Research and Evaluation Unit (AREU).

Duffield, Mark and Prendergast, John. 1994. *Without Troops and Tanks: Humanitarian Intervention in Eritrea and Ethiopia*. Trenton, NJ: Red Sea Press/Africa World Press Inc.

Duffield, Mark and Waddell, Nicholas. 2006. Securing humans in a dangerous world. *International Politics*, 43, 1–23.

Duffield, Mark, Young, Helen, Ryle, John and Henderson, Ian. 1995. *Sudan Emergency Operations Consortium (SEOC): A Review*. Birmingham: School of Public Policy.

Easterly, William. 2002. The cartel of good intentions: the problem of bureaucracy in foreign aid. *Journal of Policy Reform* 5 (4), 223–50.

EC. 1996. *Linking, Relief, Rehabilitation and Development (LRRD)*, Brussels: Commission of the European Communities.

Edis, R. J. S. 9 December 1994. An assessment of the performance of UNOHAC. Letter to Jim Drummond.

Edkins, Jenny. 2000. *Whose Hunger? Concepts of Famine, Practices of Aid*. Minneapolis: University of Minnesota Press.

Eide, Espen Barth, Kaspersen, Anja Therese, Kent, Randolph and von Hippel, Karen. 2005. *Report on Integrated Missions: Practical Perspectives and Recommendations*. Independent study for the expanded UN ECHA Core Group.

Elden, Stuart. 2005. Territorial integrity and the war on terror. *Environment and Planning A*, 37, 2083–104.

—— 2006. Contingent sovereignty, territorial integrity and the sanctity of borders. *SAIS Review of International Affairs*, 29, 11–24.

Ericson, Richard V. and Doyle, Aaron. 2003. *Insurance as Governance*. Toronto: Toronto University Press.

Eriksson, John. 1996. *The International Response to Conflict and Genocide: Lessons from the Rwanda Experience – Synthesis Report.* Copenhagen: Joint Evaluation of Emergency Assistance to Rwanda.

Escobar, Arturo. 1995. *Encountering Development: The Making and Unmaking of the Third World.* New Jersey: Princetown University Press.

Fekete, Liz. 2001. The emergence of xeno-racism. *Race and Class* 43 (2), 23–40.

—— 2004. Anti-Muslim racism and the European security state. *Race and Class* 46 (1), 3–29.

Ferguson, James. 1990. *The Anti-politics Machine: 'Development', Depoliticisation, and Bureaucratic Power in Lesotho.* Cambridge: Cambridge University Press.

Ferguson, Niall. 2003. *Empire: How Britain Made the Modern World.* London: Allen Lane/Penguin.

Fielden, Matthew and Azerbaijani-Moghadam, Sippi. 2001. *Female Employment in Afghanistan: A Study of Decree # 8.* Islamabad: Inter-Agency Task Force.

Fielden, Matthew and Goodhand, Jonathan. 2001. *Peace-Making in the New World Disorder: A Study of the Afghan Conflict and Attempts to Resolve It.* Peace Building and Complex Political Emergencies Working Paper Series, Paper No. 7 Manchester: IDPM, and Oxford: INTRAC.

FIFC. 2004. *The Future of Humanitarian Action: Implications of Iraq and Other Recent Crises,* Boston, MA: Feinstein International Famine Centre (FIFC)/Friedman School of Nutritional Science Policy, Tufts University.

Firebrace, J. 1982. Statement to the European Parliament re tins of EEC butteroil observed at Sheraro, Tigray Province, Ethiopia 12/4/82, War on Want, London.

—— 1984. Food as military aid. *New Statesman,* 108 (2,803), 5–6.

Fleming, Sue and Barnes, Colin. 1992. Poverty Options in Mozambique: Strategy Options for Future Aid, Manchester.

Foley, Conor. 25 August 2004. The terrible cost of saving lives. *Guardian,* 15.

Foot, Paul. 1965. *Immigration and Race in British Politics.* Harmondsworth: Penguin Books.

Forman, Shepard and Steward, Patrick (eds). 2000. *Good Intentions: Pledges of Aid for Postconflict Recovery.* Boulder and London: Lynne Rienner.

Foucault, Michel. [1975] 1991. *Discipline and Punish: The Birth of the Prison.* Harmondsworth: Penguin.

—— [1975–6] 2003. *Society Must be Defended: Lectures at the College de France, 1975–76.* London: Allan Lane, The Penguin Press.

—— [1976] 1998. *The Will to Knowledge: The History of Sexuality Volume 1.* Harmondsworth: Penguin.

Foucault, Michel. [1978] 1991. Governmentality. In Graham Burchell, Colin Gordon and Peter Miller (eds), *The Foucault Effect: Studies in Governmentality*. London: Harvester Wheatsheaf, 87–104.

—— [1984] 2000. Confronting governments: human rights. In *Essential Works of Foucault 1954–1984: Volume 3, Power*, ed. James D. Faubian, 474–5. Harmondsworth: Penguin.

Furedi, Frank. 1994. *The New Ideology of Imperialism*. London: Junius Publications Ltd.

Galloway, G. 1984. The Mengistu famine. *Spectator*, 6–7.

Gantzel, K. J. 1997. War in the post-World-War-II-world: empirical trends, theoretical approaches and problems on the concept of 'ethnic war'. In David Turton (ed.), *War and Ethnicity: Global Connections and Local Violence*. Rochester NY: University of Rochester Press, 115–30.

Ghani, Ashraf, Lockhart, Clare and Carnahan, Michael. 2005. *Closing the Sovereignty Gap: An Approach to State-Building*. Working Paper 253. London: Overseas Development Institute.

Goldenburg, Suzanne. 6 December 2001. Islamists fill vacuum left by Arafat's waning star. *Guardian*, 15.

Gordon, Stuart. 2006. The changing role of the military in assistance strategies. In Victoria Wheeler and Adele Harmer (eds), *Resetting the Rules of Engagement: Trends and Issues in Military–Humanitarian Relations*. HPG Report 21. London: Humanitarian Policy Group, Overseas Development Institute, 39–52.

Goulding, M. 1993. The evolution of United Nations peacekeeping. *International Affairs*, 69 (3), 451–64.

Grey, Stephen. 2006. Ghost plane: the inside story of the CIA's secret rendition programme. London: Hurst.

Gursony, R. 1988. *Summary of Mozambican Refugee Accounts of Experience in Mozambique*. New York: Bureau for Refugee Programmes, Department of State.

Hall, Catherine. 2002. *Civilising Subjects: Metropole and Colony in the English Imagination 1830–1867*. Cambridge: Polity.

Hall, M. n.d. The Mozambican national assistance movement (RENAMO): a study in the destruction of a country. Mimeo.

Hanlon, Joseph. 1991. *Mozambique: Who Calls the Shots?* Oxford: James Currey.

Hansell, John, Zeitlyn, Sushila, Potter, Harry, Smart, Malcolm and Scott, Michael. 1996. *Mozambique: Final Review of the Zambezia Agricultural Development Programme, 16–20 November 1996*. Harare: British Development Division for Central Africa.

Harding, Luke and Wray, Richard. 28 December 2004. Counting the cost of devastation. *Guardian*, 6.

Harris, Paul, Bright, Martin and Wazir, Burham. 28 October 2001. Five Britons killed in 'Jihad Brigade'. *Observer*, 2.

Harrison, Graham. 2001. Post-conditionality politics and administrative reform: reflections on the case of Uganda and Tanzania. *Development and Change*, 32, 657–79.

—— 2004. *The World Bank and Africa: The Construction of Governance States.* London: Routledge.

Harvey, David. 2003. *The New Imperialism.* Oxford: Oxford University Press.

HDC. 2003. *Politics and Humanitarianism: Coherence in Crisis?* Geneva: Henry Dunant Centre for Humanitarian Dialogue.

Held, D., McGrew, A., Goldblast, D. and Perraton, J. 1999. *Global Transformations: Politics, Economics and Culture.* Cambridge: Polity Press.

Herring, Eric and Rangwala, Glen. 2005. Iraq, imperialism and global governance. *Third World Quarterly*, 26, 667–83.

Hewitt, Vernon. 2006. A cautionary tale: colonial and post-colonial conceptions of good government and democratisation in Africa. *Commonwealth and Comparative Politics*, 44, 41–66.

Hirst, Paul. 2005. *Space and Power: Politics, War and Architecture.* Cambridge: Polity.

Hobsbawm, Eric. 1994. *The Age of Extremes: The Short Twentieth Century.* London: Michael Joseph.

Hobson, J. A. [1902] 1938. *Imperialism: A Study.* London: George Allen & Unwin.

Hochschild, Adam. 2002. *King Leopold's Ghost: A Story of Greed, Terror, and Heroism in Colonial Africa.* London: Pan.

—— 2006. *Bury the Chains: Prophets and Rebels in the Fight to Free an Empire's Slaves.* Boston and New York: Houghton & Mifflin.

Holden, Pat. 7 September 1993. Letter to Jim Drummond, ODA, London.

Hörnqvist, Magnus. 2004. The birth of public order policy. *Race and Class* 46 (1), 30–52.

Howe, Stephen. 1993. *Anticolonialism in British Politics: The Left and the End of Empire.* Oxford: Clarendon Press.

HRW. 2001. *Crisis of Impunity: The Role of Pakistan, Russia and Iran in Fuelling the Civil War in Afghanistan.* New York: Human Rights Watch.

HSC. 2005. *The Human Security Report 2005: War and Peace in the 21st Century.* Vancouver: Human Security Centre, University of British Colombia.

Huntington, Samuel P. 1993. The clash of civilisations. *Foreign Affairs*, 72 (3), 22–50.

Hussain, Nasser. 2003. *The Jurisprudence of Emergency: Colonialism and the Rule of Law.* Michigan: University of Michigan.

Huysmans, Jef. 2000. The European Union and the securitization of migration. *Journal of Common Market Studies*, 38 (5), 751–77.

I-CAMS. 2005. The emergence of a global infrastructure for mass registration and surveillance. Report, International Campaign Against Mass Surveillance.

ICISS. 2001. *The Responsibility to Protect: Report of the International Commission on Intervention and State Sovereignty*. Ottawa: International Development Research Centre.

IDC. 1999. *Conflict Prevention and Post-Conflict Reconstruction. Volume I, Report and Proceeding to the Committee*. London: The Stationery Office, for the International Development Committee.

Ignatieff, Michael. 2003. *Empire Lite: Nation-Building in Bosnia, Kosovo and Afghanistan*. London: Vintage.

International Alert. 1999. Memorandum from International Alert: 6 March 1998. In *Conflict Prevention and Post-Conflict Reconstruction, Vol II, Minutes of Evidence and Appendices*. Sixth Report of the International Development Committee. London: The Stationery Office, 73–9.

IRC. 2003. *Mortality in the Democratic Republic of the Congo: Results from a Nationwide Survey, September – November 2002*. New York: International Rescue Committee.

Jackson, I. C. 1956. *Advance in Africa: A Study of Community Development in Eastern Nigeria*. London: Oxford University Press.

Jackson, Robert H. 1990. *Quasi-States: Sovereignty, International Relations and the Third World*. Cambridge: Cambridge University Press.

Jahn, Beate. 2005. Barbarian thoughts: imperialism in the philosophy of John Stuart Mill. *Review of International Studies*, (31), 599–618.

Jenkins, Roy. 1966. Speech to the National Committee of Commonwealth Immigrants.

Jockel, Joe and Sokolsky, Joel. 2000–2001. Lloyd Axworthy's legacy: human security and the rescue of Canadian defence policy. *International Journal*, 56 (1), 1–18.

Jones, Beverley. 2003. Interview, CAFOD, London.

Jones, Bruce D. 2001. *The Challenges of Strategic Coordination: Containing Opposition and Sustaining Implementation of Peace Agreements in Civil Wars*. IPA Policy Paper. New York: International Peace Academy.

Jones, Mervyn. 1965. *Two Ears of Corn: Oxfam in Action*. London: Hodder & Stoughton.

Kagan, Robert. 2003. *Paradise and Power: America and Europe in the New World Order*. London: Atlantic Books.

Kaldor, Mary. 1999. *New and Old Wars: Organised Violence in a Global Era*. Cambridge: Polity.

Kant, Immanuel. [1795] 1983. *Perpetual Peace and Other Essays*, trans. Ted Humphrey. Indianapolis: Hackett.

Kaplan, Robert D. 1994. The coming anarchy: how scarcity, crime, overpopulation, and disease are rapidly destroying the social fabric of our planet. *Atlantic Monthly*, 273 (2), 44–76.

Karim, Ataul, Duffield, Mark, Jaspars, Susan, Benini, Aldo, Macrae, Joanna, Bradbury, Mark, Johnson, Douglas and Larbi, George. 1996. *Operation Lifeline Sudan (OLS): A Review*. Geneva: UN Department of Humanitarian Affairs.

Keen, David. 1994. *The Benefits of Famine: A Political Economy of Famine and Relief in Southwestern Sudan, 1983–1989*. Princeton, NJ: Princeton University Press.

—— 1998. *The Economic Functions of Violence in Civil Wars*. Adelphi Paper 320. London: International Institute of Strategic Studies.

Kelemen, Paul. 2006. Modernising colonialism: the British labour movement and Africa. *Journal of Imperial and Commonwealth History* 34 (2), 223–44.

Kelly, Mark. 2004. Racism, nationalism and biopolitics: Foucault's *Society Must be Defended*, 2003. *Contretemps*, 4, 58–70.

Kent, R. C. 1987. *Anatomy of Disaster Relief: The International Network in Action*. London: Pinter.

Kent, Randolph, von Hippel, Karin and Bradbury, Mark. 2004. *Social Facilitation, Development and the Diaspora: Support for Sustainable Health Services in Somalia*. London: International Policy Institute, King's College.

King, Gary and Murray, Christopher J. L. 2001. Rethinking human security. *Political Science Quarterly*, 116, 585–610.

Kloeck-Jenson, Scott. 1998. Land tenure, rural livelihoods, and democracy in rural Mozambique: options for a harmonized Oxfam strategy. Consultant report, Land Tenure Centre, Mozambique.

Korten, D. C. 1990. *Getting to the 21st Century: Volutary Action and the Global Agenda*. Bloomfield, CT: Kumarian Press.

Kundnani, Arun. 2001. In a foreign land: the new popular racism. *Race and Class*, 43 (2), 41–60.

Labour Party. 1964. *The New Britain*. 1964 Labour Party election manifesto. London: Labour Party.

Leader, Nicholas and Colenso, Peter. 2005. *Aid Instruments in Fragile States*. PRDE Working Paper 5. London: Poverty Reduction in Difficult Environments Team, DFID.

Levy, Adrian and Scott-Clark, Cathy. 19 March 2005. One huge US jail. *Guardian Weekend*, 16–25.

Lockhardt, Clare. 2005. From aid effectiveness to development effectiveness: strategy and policy coherence in fragile states. Background paper prepared for the Senior Level Forum on Development Effectiveness in Fragile States. London: Overseas Development Institute.

Luetchford, Mark and Burns, Peter. 2003. *Waging the War on Want: 50 Years of Campaigning Against World Poverty*. London: War on Want.

Lugard, Lord. [1922] 1965. *The Dual Mandate in Tropical Africa*. London: Frank Cass.

Luxemburg, Rosa. [1913] 1971. *The Accumulation of Capital*. London: Routledge & Kegan Paul.

Maass, Gero and Mepham, David. 2004. *Promoting Effective States: A progressive policy response to failed and failing states*. Institute for Public Policy Research and Friedrich-Ebert-Stiftung, London Office, London.

McGillivray, Mark. 2005. Aid allocation and fragile states. Background paper for the Senior Level Forum on Development Effectiveness in Fragile States, Lancaster House, London.

Mack, Andrew. 2002. *The Human Security Report Project: Background Paper*. Vancouver: Human Security Centre, Liu Institute for Global Issues, University of British Columbia.

McKinnon, Roddy. 2004. Promoting social security worldwide: the role of the ISSA. *International Social Security Review*, 57 (3), 3–23.

MacMichael, H. A. *c*.1923. *Indirect Rule for Pagan Communities*. Sudan Archive, Durham (586/1/1–55).

—— 10 May 1928. Arabic and the Southern Sudan. Memorandum issued by the Civil Secretary's Office, Khartoum. Sudan Archive Durham (586/1/1–55).

—— 1934. *The Anglo-Egyptian Sudan*. London: Faber & Faber.

McNerney, Michael J. 2005. Stabilization and reconstruction in Afghanistan: are PRTs a model or a muddle? *Parameters*, 32–46.

Macrae, Joanna. 1998. The death of humanitarianism? An anatomy of the attack. *Disasters*, 22 (4), 309–17.

Macrae, Joanna and Leader, Nicholas. 2000. *Shifting Sands: The Search for 'Coherence' Between Political and Humanitarian Responses to Complex Emergencies*. Humanitarian Policy Group (HPG) Report 8. London: Overseas Development Institute.

Macrae, Joanna, Collinson, Sarah, Buchanan-Smith, Margie, Reindorp, Nicola, Schmidt, Anna, Mowjee, Tasneem and Harmer, Adele. 2002. *Uncertain Power: The Changing Role of Official Donors in Humanitarian Action*. HPG Report 12. London: Humanitarian Policy Group, Overseas Development Institute.

MAF. 1998. *PROAGRI – Sectoral Programme Investment: Land Component*. Maputo: Ministry of Agriculture and Fisheries, Republic of Mozambique.

Mamdani, Mahmood. 1996. *Citizen and Subject: Contemporary Africa and the Legacy of Late Colonialism*. Princeton: Princeton University Press.

Marriage, Zoë. 2006. *Not Breaking the Rules Not Playing the Game: International Assistance to Countries at War*. London: Hurst.

Marshall, Monty G. 2005. *Conflict Trends in Africa, 1956–2004: A Macro-Comparative Perspective*. Report Prepared for the Africa Conflict Prevention Pool (ACPP), Government of the United Kingdom, Centre for Global Policy, George Mason University, Arlington, VA.

Mehta, Uday Singh. 1999. *Liberalism and Empire*. Chicago: University of Chicago Press.

Mendieta, Eduardo. 2002. 'To make live and let die' – Foucault on racism. Meeting of the Foucault Circle, APA Central Division Meeting, Chicago.

MFA. 1997. *Preventing Violent Conflict: A Study – Executive Summary and Recommendations*. Stockholm: Ministry for Foreign Affairs.

Mitchell, Timothy. 2002. *Rule of Experts: Egypt, Techno-Politics, Modernity*. Berkeley: University of California Press.

Morel, E. D. 1920. *The Black Man's Burden*. Manchester and London: The National Labour Press Ltd.

MPPA. 1996. Mozambique Participatory Poverty Assessment: Phase 1 Rural Summary.

Myers, Gregory W. and Eliseu, Julieta. 1997. Land tenure security in Zambezia Province: a report to the Zambezia Agricultural Development Project (ZADP). World Vision International Mozambique, Zambezia, Mozambique.

Myrdal, G. 1957. *Economic Theory and Underdeveloped Regions*. London: Gerald Duckworth.

Neal, Andrew W. 2004. Cutting off the king's head: Foucault's *Society Must be Defended* and the problem of sovereignty. *Alternatives*, 29, 373–98.

Nelson, Valerie. 1996. Draft report on a visit to the Feeder Roads Project: Zambesia Province Monitoring Mission (4–13 September 1996).

—— 1997. Feeder Roads Project – Zambezia Province, Mozambique: 3–21 November 1997.

Newburg, Paula R. 1999. *Politics at the Heart: The Architecture of Humanitarian Assistance to Afghanistan*. Global Policy Program, Working Paper Number 2. Washington, DC: Carnegie Endowment for International Peace.

Noll, Gregor. 2003. Visions of the exceptional: legal and theoretical issues raised by transit processing centres and protection zones. *European Journal of Migration and Law*, 5, 303–41.

Nordstrom, Carolyn. 2001. Out of the shadows. In Thomas Callaghy, Ronald Kassimir and Robert Letham (eds), *Intervention and Transnationalism in Africa: Global–Local Networks of Power*. Cambridge: Cambridge University Press, 216–39.

Norton-Taylor, Richard. 22 July 2006. Afghanistan close to anarchy, warns general. *Guardian*, 19.

ODA. 1996. *Conflict Reduction Through the Aid Programme: A briefing for agencies seeking support for conflict reduction activities.* London: Overseas Development Administration.

OECD. 1998. *Conflict, Peace and Development Co-operation on the Threshold of the 21st Century.* Development Co-operation Guideline Series. Paris: Organisation for Economic Co-operation and Development.

Olesen, Thomas. 2004. Globalising the Zapatistas: from Third World solidarity to global solidarity? *Third World Quarterly*, 25, 255–67.

OSAGI. 1997. *Report of the United Nations Interagency Gender Mission to Afghanistan: 12–24 November 1997.* New York: UN Office of the Special Adviser on Gender Issues and Advancement of Women.

Ostby, Knut. 2000. *Community Development in Afghanistan: Empowerment, Self-Help and Local Governance.* Islamabad: UNDP Afghanistan.

Owen, Margaret. 1996. *Widowhood, Inheritance, Land Rights and Food Security in Zambezia.* London: Empowering Women in Development.

Pandolfi, Mariella. 2002. 'Moral Entrepreneurs', souverainetés mouvantes et barbelé: le bio-politique dans les Balkans post-communistes. *Anthropologie et Sociétés*, 26 (1),1–24.

Paris, Roland. 2001. Human security: paradigm shift or hot air? *International Security*, 26 (2), 87–102.

Patel, Rajeev and McMichael, Philip. 2004. Third Worldism and the lineage of global fascism: the regrouping of the global South in the neoliberal era. *Third World Quarterly*, 25 (1), 231–54.

Pender, John. 1–2 December 2005. Less interests, more influence: the paradox of poverty reduction and the redefinition of development. Paper presented at SAID International Conference, 'Sovereignty in the 21st Century', Colombia University, New York.

Picciotto, Robert, Alao, Charles, Ikpe, Eka, Kimani, Martin and Slade, Rodger. 2004. *Striking a New Balance: Donor Policy Coherence and Development Cooperation in Difficult Environments.* Background paper commissioned by the Learning and Advisory Process on Difficult Partnerships of the Development Assistance Committee of the OECD, Global Policy Project, King's College London.

Pitts, Jennifer. 2003. Legislator of the world? A rereading of Bentham on colonies. *Political Theory*, 31 (2), 200–34.

Pratt, Brian. 2003. Interview, INTRAC, Oxford.

PRDE. 2004. *Improving the Development Response in Difficult Environments: Lessons from DFID Experience.* PRDE Working Paper 4. London: Poverty Reduction in Difficult Environments Team, DFID.

Pronk, Jan P. 2001. Aid as a catalyst. *Development and Change*, 32, 611–30.

Pupavac, Vanessa. 2001. Therapeutic governance: pyscho-social intervention and trauma risk management. *Disasters*, 25, 358–72.

—— 2005. Human security and the rise of global therapeutic governance. *Conflict, Development and Security*, 5 (2), 161–82.

Reno, William. 1998. *Warlord Politics and African States*. Boulder: Lynne Rienner.

Richards, Paul. 1996. *Fighting for the Rain Forest: War, Youth and Resources in Sierra Leone*. Oxford: James Currey.

Roitman, Janet. 2001. New sovereigns? The frontiers of wealth creation and regulatory authority in the Chad basin. In Thomas Callaghy, Ronald Kassimir and Robert Letham (eds), *Intervention and Transnationalism in Africa: Global–Local Networks of Power*. Cambridge: Cambridge University Press, 190–215.

Rose, Nikolas. 2000. *Powers of Freedom: Reframing Political Thought*. Cambridge: Cambridge University Press.

Rostow, W. W. 1960. *The Stages of Economic Growth: A Non-Communist Manifesto*. Cambridge: Cambridge University Press.

Rubin, Barnett R. 2000. The political economy of war and peace in Afghanistan. *World Development*, 28, 1789–803.

Rubin, Barnett R, Ghani, Ashraf, Maley, William, Rashid, Ahmed and Roy, Oliver. 2001. *Afghanistan: Reconstruction and Peacebuilding in a Regional Framework*. KOFF Peacebuilding Reports 1/2001. Bern: Centre for Peacebuilding (KOFF)/Swiss Peace Foundation (SPF).

Saferworld. 1999. Memorandum from Saferworld: February 1998. In *Conflict Prevention and Post-Conflict Reconstruction, Vol. II, Minutes of Evidence and Appendices*. Sixth Report of the International Development Committee. London: The Stationery Office, 68–73.

Said, Edward W. 1995. *Orientalism*. Harmondsworth: Penguin.

SCF. 2006. *About us/History*. Save the Children Fund, available at http://www.savethechildren.org.uk/scuk/jsp/aboutus (accessed 2 March 2006).

Schierup, Carl-Ulrik. 1992. Quasi-proletarians and a patriarchal bureaucracy: aspects of Yugoslavia's re-peripheralisation. *Soviet Studies*, 44 (1), 79–99.

Schmitt, Carl. [1963] 2004. *The Theory of the Partisan: A Commentary/Remark on the Concept of the Political*. East Lansing: Michigan State University.

Schumacher, E. F. 1974. *Small is Beautiful: A Study of Economics as if People Mattered*. London: Abacus.

Schuster, Liza. 2003. Common sense or racism? The treatment of asylum-seekers in Europe. *Patterns of Prejudice*, 37 (3), 233–55.

Seshadri-Crooks, Kalpana. 2002. 'I am a master': terrorism, masculinity, and political violence in Franz Fanon. *Parallax*, 8 (2), 84–98.

Sida, Lewis. 2005. *Challenges to Humanitarian Space: A review of humanitarian issues related to the UN integrated mission in Liberia and to the relationship between humanitarian and military actors in Liberia.* Monrovia: Monitoring and Steering Group (MSG) Liberia.

Simkin, Peter. 10 April 1992. Letter to Joaquim Chissano, President of the Republic of Mozambique. UK High Commission, Maputo.

Simon, David. 2006. Separated by common ground? Bringing (post) development and (post) colonialism together. *Geographical Journal*, 172 (1), 10–21.

Slim, Hugo. 1997. *Doing the Right Thing: Relief Agencies, Moral Dilemmas and Moral Responsibility in Political Emergencies and War.* Studies on Emergencies and Disaster Relief, Report No. 6. Uppsala: Nordic Africa Institute.

—— 2004a. *A Call to Alms: Humanitarian Action and the Art of War.* Geneva: hd Opinion, Centre for Humanitarian Dialogue.

—— 2004b. *With or Against? Humanitarian Agencies and Coalition Counter-Insurgency.* Geneva: hd Opinion, Centre for Humanitarian Dialogue.

Smith, Rupert. 2006. *The Utility of Force: The Art of War in the Modern World.* Harmondsworth: Penguin.

Solana, Javier. 2003. *A Secure Europe in a Better World: European Security Strategy.* Paris: European Union Institute for Security Studies.

Stiglitz, Joseph E. 1998. *Towards a New Paradigm for Development: Strategies, Policies, and Processes.* 9th Raúl Prebisch Lecture. Geneva: UNCTAD.

Stockton, Nicholas. 2002. *Strategic Coordination in Afghanistan.* Kabul: Afghanistan Research and Evaluation Unit.

Stoler, Ann Laura. 1995. *Race the Education of Desire: Foucault's History of Sexuality and the Colonial Order of Things.* Durham, NC, and London: Duke University Press.

Strategy Unit. 2005. *Investing in Prevention: An International Strategy to Manage Risks of Instability and Improve Crisis Response.* A Strategy Unit Report to the Government. London: Prime Minister's Strategy Unit, Cabinet Office.

Suhrke, Astri. 1993. A crisis diminished: refugees in the developing world. *International Journal*, 48, 215–39.

—— 1994. Towards a comprehensive refugee policy: conflict and refugees in the post-Cold War world. In W. R. Bohning and M. L. Schloeter-Paredes (eds), *Aid in Place of Migration?* Geneva: International Labour Office, 13–38.

—— 2006. The limits of statebuilding: the role of international assistance in Afghanistan. Paper presented at International Studies Association Annual Meeting, San Diego.

SW. 1997. DNEP/ODA Feeder Roads Project Zambezia Province – Quarterly Report: April–June 1997, Scott-Wilson.

Tamás, Gaspar Miklos. 2000. On post-facism. *Boston Review*, 1–20.

Thane, P. 1989. The British welfare state: its origins and character. In Anne Digby and Charles Feinstein (eds), *New Directions in Economic and Social History*. Basingstoke and London: Macmillan, 143–56.

Thomas, Caroline. 2001. Global governance, development and human security: exploring the links. *Third World Quarterly*, 22 (2), 159–79.

Thompson, Robert. 1966. *Defeating Communist Insurgency: Experiences from Malaya and Vietnam*. New York: Frederick A. Praeger.

Tinbergen, J. 1954. *International Economic Integration*. Amsterdam: Elsevier.

Tishkov, Valery. 1997. *Ethnicity, Nationalism and Conflict in and after the Soviet Union: The Mind Aflame*. London: Sage.

Torres, Magüi Moreno and Anderson, Michael. 2004. *Fragile States: Defining Difficult Environments for Poverty Reduction*. PRDE Working Paper 1. London: Poverty Reduction in Difficult Environments (PRDE) Team, DFID.

Twigg, John. 2004. *Disaster Risk Reduction: Mitigation and Preparedness in Development and Emergency Programming*. Good Practice Review No. 9. London: Humanitarian Practice Network, Overseas Development Institute.

UKHC. 1993. *Mozambique: Emergency (Part I of II)*, UK High Commission, Maputo.

UN. 1998. *Strategic Framework for Afghanistan: Towards a Principled Approach to Peace and Reconstruction*. New York: United Nations.

UNCO. 2000. *The Three Pillars: Strengthening the Foundations*. Islamabad: UN Co-ordinator's Office.

UNDP. 1994a. *Human Development Report, 1994*. New York and Oxford: United Nations Development Programme/Oxford University Press.

—— 1994b. *Position Paper of the Working Group on Operational Aspects of the Relief to Development Continuum*. New York: UNDP.

—— 1996. *Human Development Report 1996*. New York: Oxford University Press for UNDP.

—— 1997. *Formulation of Strategic Framework*, United Nations Development Programme: Afghanistan Programme.

UNICEF. 1993. *UNICEF Response to Emergencies*. New York: UNICEF.

UNOCHA. 1998. *Next Steps for the United Nations in Afghanistan*, New York: UN Office for the Coordination of Humanitarian Affairs (UNOCHA).

UNOCHAA. 1999. *Next Steps in Afghanistan: March to June 1999*. Islamabad: UN Office for the Coordination of Humanitarian Assistance to Afghanistan.

—— 2000. *Principles and Pragmatism in Afghanistan*. Discussion paper prepared by the UN Coordinator of Afghanistan, ECHA Meeting, 7 November

2000, UN Office for the Coordination of Humanitarian Assistance to Afghanistan, Islamabad.

UNSMA. 2000. *Report on Administrative and Judicial Structures of Afghanistan: A First Inquiry*. Islamabad: UN Special Mission to Afghanistan, Civil Affairs Unit.

Uvin, Peter. 1999. *The Influence of Aid in Situations of Violent Conflict*. Paris: Development Assistance Committee, Informal Task Force on Conflict, Peace and Development Co-operation, OECD.

van Creveld, Martin. 1991. *The Transformation of War*. New York: Free Press.

van der Pijl, Kees. 11 December 2002. The aesthetics of empire and the defeat of the left. Paper presented at Exploring Imperium, Department of International Relations and Politics, University of Sussex.

Vaux, Tony. 2004. Humanitarian trends – a strategic view for CAFOD, Phase I. Report, Humanitarian Initiatives.

Vines, Alex. 1991. *Renamo: Terrorism in Mozambique*. Oxford: James Currey.

Waever, Ole. 1995. Securitization and desecuritization. In Ronnie D. Lipschutz (ed.), *On Security*. New York: Colombia University Press, 47–86.

Waever, O., Buzan, B., Kelstrup, M. and Lemaitre, P. (eds). 1993. *Identity, Migration and the New Security Agenda in Europe*. London: Pinter.

Wallerstein, Immanuel. 1996. The global picture, 1945–90. In Terence K. Hopkins and Immanuel Wallerste (eds), *The Age of Transition: Trajectory of the World-System, 1945–2025*. London: Zed Books, 209–25.

Warner, Daniel. 2003. The responsibility to protect and irresponsible, cynical engagement. *Millennium: Journal of International Studies*, 32 (1), 109–21.

Webb, Sidney and Beatrice. 1990. *Indian Diary*, ed. Niraja Gopal Jayal. Oxford and New York: Oxford University Press.

Weiss, Thomas G. 1999. *Military–Civilian Interactions: Intervening in Humanitarian Crises*. Lanham, MD: Rowman & Littlefield.

Wheeler, Nicholas J. 2000. *Saving Strangers: Humanitarian Intervention in International Society*. Oxford: Oxford University Press.

Wheeler, Victoria and Harmer, Adele. 2006. *Resetting the Rules of Engagement: Trends and Issues in Military–Humanitarian Relations*, London: Humanitarian Policy Group, Overseas Development Institute.

Whitaker, Ben. 1983. *A Bridge of People: A Personal View of Oxfam's First Forty Years*. London: Heinemann.

Whitaker, Raymond and Huggler, Justin. 29 January 2006. Mission impossible? *Independent on Sunday*, 43.

Wilder, Andrew. 30 October 1997. Letter to Alfredo Witschi-Cestari, UN Coordinator Islamabad.

Williams, Michael C. 1998. *Civil–Military Relations in Peacekeeping*. Adelphi Paper (International Institute for Strategic Studies) no. 321, 1–93.

Wilson, Harold. 1953. *The War on World Poverty*. London: Victor Gollancz.

Winter, J M. 1974. The Webbs and the non-white world: a case of socialist racism. *Journal of Contemporary History*, 9 (1), 181–92.

Witschi-Cestari, Alfredo, Newburg, Paula and Keating, Michael. 1998. Coping with complexity: reforming international assistance to Afghanistan 1996–1998. Consultants' report, Islamabad.

Wolpe, Harold. 1972. Capitalism and cheap labour power in South Africa: from segregation to apartheid. *Economy and Society*, 1, 425–56.

Wood, Geof and Gough, Ian. 2006. A comparative welfare regime approach to global social policy. *World Development*, 34 (10), 1696–712.

Woods, Ngaire. 2004. Reconciling effective aid and global security: implications for the emerging international development architecture. Global Economic Governance Programme, University College, Oxford.

Woollacott, Martin. 2 April 2004. Humanitarians must avoid becoming tools of power. *Guardian*, 15.

World Bank. 1990. *World Development Report 1990: Poverty*. Oxford: Oxford University Press.

—— 1995. The Participatory Poverty Assessment in Mozambique. Maputo: World Bank.

World Vision. 1996. *Evaluation of the Impact of the Zambezia Agricultural Development Project*. Quelimane: World Vision.

—— 1997. *Zambezia Agricultural Development Project: A Participatory Rural Appraisal of Seven Communities in Namacurra and Gurue Districts of Zambezia Province*. Quelimane: World Vision.

Young, Helen and Jaspars, Susanne. 2006. *The Meaning and Measurement of Acute Malnutrition in Emergencies: A Primer for Decision-Makers*. Network Paper 56. London: Humanitarian Policy Group, Overseas Development Institute.

Young, Hugo. 6 November 2001. A corrosive national danger in our multicultural model. *Guardian*, 18.

Index